Translations of Christian Literature
Series I—Greek Texts

SELECTIONS FROM THE COMMENTARIES
AND HOMILIES OF ORIGEN

Also by Dr. Tollinton :
> *Clement of Alexandria, A Study in Christian Liberalism.* 2 vols. 21s. 1914.
> Publishers : Messrs. Williams and Norgate.

Pyrrho, A Historical Novel. 4s. 6d. 1926.
The Sheldon Press.

SELECTIONS FROM THE COMMENTARIES AND HOMILIES OF ORIGEN

TRANSLATED BY

R. B. TOLLINTON, D.D.

Rector of Tendring and Canon of Chelmsford.

WIPF & STOCK · Eugene, Oregon

Wipf and Stock Publishers
199 W 8th Ave, Suite 3
Eugene, OR 97401

Selections from the Commentaries and Homilies of Origen
By Tollinton, R. B.
Softcover ISBN-13: 979-8-3852-0932-3
Hardcover ISBN-13: 979-8-3852-0933-0
eBook ISBN-13: 979-8-3852-0934-7
Publication date 12/6/2023
Previously published by SPCK, 1929

This edition is a scanned facsimile of the original edition published in 1929.

CONTENTS

			PAGE
PREFACE	... ...		vii
ORIGEN AS EXEGETE	... ...		ix
BIBLIOGRAPHY	... ...		xlviii
ABBREVIATIONS	... ...		l
LIST OF PASSAGES TRANSLATED	... ...		li
PART	I.	The Being and Nature of God ...	1
,,	II.	The Work and Office of the Divine Word	25
,,	III.	The Holy Scriptures—Principles and Examples of Exegesis ...	47
,,	IV.	The Holy Scriptures—Problems and Criticism	94
,,	V.	The Christian Church ...	128
,,	VI.	The Teacher and His Task ...	156
,,	VII.	Speculations and Enquiries ...	194
,,	VIII.	The Christian Life ...	249
INDEX	... ...		269

PREFACE

THE present series of translated extracts from the Commentaries and Homilies of Origen has occupied such time as I have been able to devote to it since I was invited three years ago to undertake its preparation. In the selection of passages for translation I have in part been guided by the principle, recognized in these *Translations of Christian Literature*, that preference is given to works which deal with subjects of living interest. In accordance with this I have endeavoured to provide a modern reader, who has not time for a fuller study of the original, with an English version of such portions of Origen's extant expositions of Scripture as may enable him to understand Origen's point of view in regard to subjects which retain their interest for us in spite of changed conditions and the lapse of many years.

I have translated, with rare deviations, from the text of the Berlin edition, where that is available; otherwise from that of Lommatzsch. In translating I have endeavoured to give Origen's meaning without being too literal, sometimes breaking up long sentences, and occasionally using two terms in English for one in the original. It is frequently a tedious matter to identify a reference in Origen's exegetical writings, for a single section often covers several pages and in the case of certain books different divisions of the text are adopted in different editions. In these books I have therefore for the reader's convenience given, both in the notes and at the head of the various translated passages, references to the pages of the Berlin edition, of Lommatzsch's text and of Brooke's text of the Commentary on St. John. The references to passages in the *De Principiis* are according to the chapters and sections of the Berlin edition. The reader will recognize that I have adhered somewhat strictly in the Introduction to the subject of Origen's Exegesis. The other points of interest suggested are so numerous that the only safe course was to leave them alone, or at most to make a passing reference in the notes.

English theology already owes not a little to Origen. It will be in accordance with the central purpose of his life, it will be in keeping with some of the best traditions of the Church of England, it will possibly be also of assistance towards the solution of some of our latter day problems, if this honourable indebtedness is increased in the present century. In much Origen was the man of his own time, but it is also true that in much his teaching is of abiding value.

R. B. TOLLINTON.

TENDRING RECTORY,
   ESSEX,
    Easter, 1922.

Circumstances have delayed the publication of this book. At the date of its appearance seven years will probably have elapsed since it was written.

The references have been brought up to date, so as to include vols. vii and viii of the Berlin edition. Otherwise I have made few changes. I regret that the recent works of Harnack and De Faye were not available while this volume was in preparation.

R. B. T.

Christmas, 1928.

ORIGEN AS EXEGETE

[The importance attached by Origen to the Scriptures —Four periods in his life—(1) Childhood and education, A.D. 185–202 —(2) Head of the Catechetical School, the teacher but not yet the author, A.D. 202.–c. 220—(3) His work as a writer in Alexandria, A.D. 220–231—(4) Afterwards in Cæsarea. The close of his life, A.D. 231–254—His Exegesis—Scripture a unity—This maintained against the denials (1) of Jews and (2) of Heretics—By reason of this unity Scripture cannot contradict itself—And any passage may be used to explain any other—The Inspiration of Scripture—The Word and the Spirit—Scripture and Nature—Difficulties involved by these principles—Certain statements not literally true—Some injunctions impossible—Inconsistencies—Unreasonable Legislation—To these Allegory provides the solution—The three senses of Scripture—The contrast between the literal and the spiritual sense—Examples of allegorical interpretation—It may be urged in defence of Allegory that (1) it was a matter of degree, (2) there were important precedents, (3) it had been used by philosophy, (4) it had the sanction of Paul—We must admit (1) that Origen failed to grasp the primary meaning of his texts, (2) and that he misconceived the method of inspiration—But we may claim that (1) Allegory saved the Scriptures for the Church, (2) and that it secured freedom—Among other characteristics we notice Origen's interest in critical questions—The influence of the LXX —His concern with details—His mystical view of Names and Numbers—His limitations admitted—But unquestionable are his humility and his high ideal of the office of the Teacher.]

Of the extant writings of Origen more than three quarters are devoted to the exposition of Scripture. Among his other works the *De Principiis* and the *Contra Celsum*, better known and commonly regarded as of greater value, depend in large measure upon the authority of Scripture. The Christian religion, as Origen understood it, rested upon a divine revelation, of which the accepted books of the Old and New Testaments were the assured guarantee. To whatever extent his standpoint was determined by other influences, by philosophy, by tradition, by the established practice of the Church, by the controversies of his day, the Scriptures remained for him the centre of interest and the main source of truth. Through many years of arduous labour, beginning in boyhood and only closing with his death at the age of sixty-nine, his recognized task was that of the student and teacher in one, and alike in study and in teaching the Scriptures were his primary concern.

His life,[1] so far as its outward circumstances need detain us in this connection, falls into four periods.

Origen was born in Alexandria, probably in A.D. 185,[2] in a home which was certainly Christian, though whether his parents were of Greek or of Egyptian nationality is uncertain. His father, Leonidas, secured for him a good

---

[1] The main authorities for his life are Eusebius, *H. E.* vi; Jerome, *De Viris Illust*, liv; Epiphanius, *Adv. Haeres*, lxiv; among modern writers especially Redepenning, *Origenes ;* De Faye, *Origène sa Vie, Son Oeuvre, sa Pensée*, vol. i; and Westcott, article in *D.C.B.*

[2] His father died in the persecution of Severus in A. D. 202, at which date Origen was seventeen years of age.

education in the recognized subjects of the schools, himself supplementing this by teaching him the Scriptures with especial care. Even before his school days the boy had begun to learn and recite to his father daily passages from the sacred books. He sang the psalms with his mother in later life and possibly did so also while he was still a child. The quickness of his mind, Eusebius says, was remarkable, and the conviction that there was a deeper meaning, underlying the letter of Scripture, possessed him so early that his father, thinking his enquiries on such matters premature, though secretly delighted at this grace and promise in his son, would bid the boy look no further than the evident meaning of the passage. For Origen, even then, this was probably a difficult restriction. All these early tendencies were further developed when he became a student at the famous Catechetical School of Alexandria. There is some evidence that Pantaenus was still teaching there when Origen entered, though chronological difficulties are involved.[1] Clement in any case was his master. From both, supposing both to have been his teachers, Origen would hear Christianity philosophically interpreted. Lectures, nominally based on Scripture, would wander far from the sacred text, and with apt pupils the restraint of the letter was frankly abandoned. So he learned and developed and acquired mental characteristics which were never lost. His student days closed suddenly with the persecution of Severus in A.D. 202, which was especially severe in Alexandria. Leonidas was a martyr. His son would gladly have suffered with him. Clement saved his own life by justifiable retirement, and the Catechetical School was left without a head.

[1] These are most fully discussed in Zahn, *Supplementum Clementinum*, pp. 156–76.

In the second period of his career, roughly from his eighteenth to his thirty-fifth year, Origen established his fame and position as a teacher, though as yet he did not publish any books. After the martyrdom of Leonidas and the confiscation of his property the finances of the home—Origen was the eldest of seven sons—were difficult. A rich and generous lady came however to his aid, and Origen also turned his education to good account, earning an income large for his years by teaching literature. This may have continued for some months. Then came a significant and probably unexpected request. With the Catechetical School in abeyance Alexandria was bereft of regular Christian instruction, which for the thirty preceding years had never failed and had been always in demand. It was to Origen, the youth of eighteen, that certain enquirers, among whom were Heraclas and his brother Plutarch, came with the request that he would conduct a class in religious knowledge. In this informal fashion Origen's life work began. An audience quickly gathered round him, of which the bishop, Demetrius, soon heard, and before long Origen was officially appointed by the bishop to the place Clement had left. We hear nothing of any suggestion that Clement should return. There is some evidence to support the conjecture that a certain coolness afterwards existed between the former master and this pupil who so early succeeded to his chair. But Demetrius had made no mistake. Origen devoted himself wholeheartedly to his task. He sold his pagan library for a daily pension of four obols.[1] He taught by day and studied the Scriptures by night. The severity indeed of his labours was such as to affect his health. Men and

---

[1] About sixpence ; possibly equal in purchasing power to four shillings of our money, as in 1921.

women alike were among his pupils, not a few of them subsequently suffering martyrdom. Especially was he successful in winning the educated for Christianity. With some interruptions, notably a journey to Rome, a retirement to Palestine, a visit to Antioch where he had an interview with Julia Mammaea, none of them very easy to date with precision, this was his manner of life for perhaps seventeen years after his appointment to the School. They were important years for developing Christianity and not less so for Origen himself. But as yet he had written nothing, and it will be important to bear this in mind when we come to speak of Origen as an exegete.[1] His habits of mind, largely formed in these particular years, are those of the teacher. Primarily he is not the literary theologian but the lecturer before his audience, quick to see points, ever ready to anticipate objections, or to criticize the other view, or to notice parallels, and never failing to make use of gathered resources and of a memory that rarely played him false. His convictions, method, point of view were all acquired under the stress of daily teaching and in the intercourse with men and women of diverse capacity and of very varied estimates of the Christian religion.

A third period now commences, lasting for some eleven years, till A.D. 231. As before he still taught in the School, but from this date onwards he is author as well as lecturer. Origen had a wealthy friend, Ambrosius, whom he had converted from the Valentinian heresy. It was at the instigation of Ambrosius that Origen began his Commentaries. It was also at his expense, for the rich

---

[1] E.g. the fact that in its main principles Origen's teaching, as evidenced by what he wrote, shows so little change or development, becomes quite natural and accountable when we recollect that he was thirty-five when he wrote his earliest books.

patron provided amanuenses, copyists and girls skilled in calligraphy. His predecessors had been authors as well as teachers, though Pantaenus left nothing that has survived[1] and Clement only published after hesitation.[2] And Origen also took to writing with reluctance. Ambrosius, whom he calls his 'taskmaster', had to use much persuasion. Before the fifth book of his *Commentaries* on John's Gospel was finished,[3] Origen seriously contemplated the abandonment of the whole scheme. Not till he was sixty years old would he allow his Homilies to be published. So keenly did he feel the responsibilities of the author. Yet before he died he had achieved a total of six thousand books. So at least Epiphanius asserted, though Jerome's estimate was under one-third of this number.[4] Even two thousand 'books' in an authorship lasting for thirty years is hardly credible. Dictation of course is more rapid than writing, and Origen is no master of the considered style. In any case his work received now a more permanent form, and before he left Alexandria he had completed five books of the *Commentaries* on John, eight on Genesis, an exposition of the first five and twenty Psalms and at least five books on the Lamentations. Less definitely

---

[1] Note the phrase ζώση φωνῇ καὶ διὰ συγγραμμάτων in *H. E.* v. 10.
[2] See *Strom.* i. 1.
[3] Fragmenta xvi (Br. ii. 227 *sqq.*; B. iv. 100 *sqq.*)
[4] Epiph *Adv. Haer.* lxiv. 63; Jerome, *Ep.* lxxxii. 7; *Adv. Rufinum* ii. 13, 22. Epiphanius credits Origen with 6,000 books— βίβλοι—not 'works' (as *D. C. B.*). No doubt by a 'book' he means a single roll of papyrus, which is also the meaning of τόμος. The length of the rolls was fairly constant. A book of the *Com. in Joann.* is just about as long as a book of Thucydides. The Homilies were numbered separately but must have been collected in rolls. Jerome says, *loc. cit.* '*non dicam sex millia, sed tertiam partem non reperies* '.

connected with Scripture were works on the Resurrection, ten volumes of *Stromateis*, after Clement's example, and, most important of all, the *De Principiis*. How much preparatory work he had done for the *Hexapla* we cannot say. Some certainly. Textual subjects were already in his mind.[1]

Into the merits of the differences which arose between Origen and his bishop, Demetrius, it lies beyond our purpose to enter. They resulted in his enforced departure from Alexandria in A.D. 231. He had good friends in Palestine. Alexander, bishop of Jerusalem, and Theoctistus, bishop of Cæsarea, had already with some irregularity admitted him to orders at Cæsarea. To this city not unnaturally he made his way on leaving Alexandria, and in Cæsarea he retained his home until the persecution of Decius broke out in A.D. 249. His life there was much what it had been in Alexandria. Here also he had his school and his pupils;[2] here also he dictated his books; here again were the occasional interruptions, a visit to Firmilian, his friend, bishop in the northern Cæsarea ; the short sharp persecution of Maximinus; journeys to Nicomedia and to Arabia. When the attack of Decius fell upon the church many good men met their death in martyrdom. But Origen survived torture in prison and lived on till A.D. 254, when in his seventieth year he breathed his last in Tyre.[3] In the years which preceded the Decian persecution his activities as a writer seem to have been at their highest.

---

[1] See the reference to his critical methods in the *Epistola ad Africanum*, 4, 5 ; Lomm. xvii. 25. The mention of Gen. i. 8 connects the passage with his years in Alexandria.

[2] See especially the *Address to Origen* of his pupil, Gregory (Thaumaturgus).

[3] Jer. *De Vir. Illust.* liv, '*mortuus est Tyri, in qua urbe et sepultus est*'. There is no reason to doubt this statement.

Three important books, the *Commentaries* on the Romans and on Matthew and the *Contra Celsum*, all belong to this time. Then there are the *Homilies* and the *Hexapla*, to say nothing of the many works of which only fragments have survived. Few careers have been more laborious, yet his mental alertness remained to the last unimpaired. The daily contact in church or lecture room with other minds contributed to preserve even his latest books from all touch and trace of senility. Such in outline were the conditions under which the works of Origen, so far as we possess them, were achieved.

For the rest we must concern ourselves with the characteristics of his Exegesis.

Of primary importance among these is his belief in the unity of Scripture. Differences among the several elements which formed this unity he recognized quite clearly. Nor does he draw the boundary lines of canonical inspiration with entire precision; there might be two Epistles of Peter, and people might accept the *Shepherd* and the *Acts of Paul* as authoritative if they chose. But for practical purposes Law, Prophets, Gospels and Apostolic writings formed a whole, an instrument whose various chords contributed to the harmony,[1] a Passover lamb which must not be divided but dealt with as a whole.[2] Origen's insistence on this point is the stronger from his constant intercourse with two classes of people who denied it. The Jews maintained that the church had no title to the Old Testament; the heretics asserted that the church had no use for it. It was with Origen a constant task to combat both these views. The Jews were the less dangerous. With their city lost, their temple destroyed, their ritual an impossi-

---

[1] § xxii.
[2] *In Joann* x. 18; Lomm. i. 306; Br. i. 203; B. iv. 188–89.

bility, the plight of this ancient people of God moved him to pity rather than to antagonism. Still, they were numerous and insistent, willing neither in Alexandria nor in Cæsarea to surrender Moses to the Christian lecturer. ' Our prophecies,' they urged, ' are not fulfilled in your Jesus.'[1] ' The law was given to Jews and has no reference to you Christians.'[2] The church's appropriation of the older Scriptures was in their view as unjustifiable as Isaac's wells had appeared to the Philistines who claimed the land in which they were dug.[3] Origen had a Hebrew teacher before he wrote his earliest books.[4] He had listened frequently to Jewish exegetes expounding prophecy. And sometimes a convert from Judaism would discuss with him the interpretations which were most favoured in Rabbinical circles.[5] Origen knew the whole field well and is never at a loss for arguments or replies which from his standpoint were sufficiently convincing. Occasionally indeed there is something forced and strained in his contentions, as when he urges that four hundred years may really mean the same thing as four hundred and thirty,[6] and throughout the unity of Scripture is only maintained, as against the Jew, by the abundant reading of the New Testament into the Old. No one ever poured new wine into old bottles with less hesitation and sense of risk.

But converts to Judaism at that date were probably few, and the heretics gave more serious cause for alarm. The battle with Gnosticism was fought mainly on the

---

[1] *C. Cels.* ii. 38.
[2] *In Ep. ad. Rom.* vii. 18 ; Lomm. vii. 181.
[3] *In Gen.* Hom. xiii ; Lomm. viii, 240 *sqq.* ; B. vi. 113 *sqq.*
[4] *De Prin.* IV. iii. 14 ; B. v. 346.
[5] *In Jer.* Hom. xx. 2 ; Lomm. xv. 358-61 ; B. iii. 178-79.
[6] He will allow no discrepancy between Gen. xv. 13 ; Gal. iii.17. *Sel. in Gen.* Lomm. viii. 71.

field of exegesis and Marcion's distinction between the Creator God of the Old Testament and the good God of the New was a tenet common to most of the heretical schools. Hence Origen's chapter in the *De Principiis* on the identity of the God of the Law and of the Prophets with the Father of Jesus Christ.[1] Hence the constant attention given to passages in the Gospels and Epistles which appeal to the authority of the older books. Hence too the frequent assertion that justice and goodness are not really incompatible; God only punishes because he loves. Origen complained that heretical exegesis was not consistent,[2] and that even Heracleon must be criticized for his violent methods.[3] The teacher is a true peacemaker who can reconcile the apparent discrepancies between the Old Testament and the New. The position Origen has to defend leads him to underrate real distinctions and to ignore the actual differences which exist between the Gospel and the Law. The Gnostics however had asserted more than they could make good, and since the days when Marcion criticized the Gospels 'with a penknife' the argument had gone mainly in favour of the church.

From this principle of the unity of Scripture certain consequences followed. Plainly, if Scripture was a unity, it could not contradict itself. No small part of the task of the exegete was to reconcile the apparent discrepancies. We shall see later by what methods Origen achieved this. In any case there are not to be three tabernacles, as Peter suggested on the mount, for Law, Prophecy and Gospel, but one for all Scripture according to the divine ordinance.[4] Could Paul contradict himself?

---

[1] II. iv.
[2] *In Joann* x. 42; Lomm. i. 364–65; Br. i. 239; B. iv. 219.
[3] *Ibid.*, ii. 21; Lomm. i. 130; Br. i. 85; B. iv. 77.
[4] *In Lev.* Hom. vi. 2; Lomm. ix. 276; B. vi. 361.

Origen has only scorn for such a desperate assertion.[1] Passages might be complementary, but not in reality discordant. If they ever appear so, the cause lies with our human limitations.[2] On this point Origen's conviction knew no hesitation. The idea of a progressive revelation is not wholly strange to him, but he does not employ it, as we should do, in dealing with the difficulties of the earlier books. Rather, the truth of Scripture is one and abiding, could we but discover it.

It follows also that the interpreter may appeal from any one passage to any other. The Gospel may be explained by the teaching of the Apocrypha;[3] what the 'session' of Christ at God's right hand means is made clear by passages in the Psalms.[4] It is a favourite method with Origen, a method which in principle is entirely sound, to collect parallel passages when he has any difficult saying to explain. Paul had 'compared spiritual things with spiritual', and Origen justifies his practice by this authority. What are we to understand by the Great Trumpet, or by the Dies Irae, or by the Well whose praise was sung by princes? In each case the question is answered by the citation of other passages in which reference to the same subject is found.[5] Origen had a marvellous memory, and could also consult his texts, if he wished; hence that profusion of passages, 'similitudinis causa prolata', through which points of exegesis are made good.[6] Many of them would strike a modern commentator as not true parallels, but Origen

---

[1] *In Ep. ad Rom.* iii. 7 ; Lomm. vi. 197.
[2] § xxiii.
[3] *In Matt.* xiii. 4, Lomm. iii. 218.
[4] *In Matt. Com. Ser.* 111 ; Lomm. v. 9.
[5] *Ibid.*, 52 ; Lomm. iv. 320. *In Ep. ad Rom.* ii. 4 ; Lomm. vi. 76. § xxxvii
[6] *In Ep. ad Rom.* ix. 41 ; Lomm. vii. 355.

must be judged by the standards and methods of his day. The instinct of the student comes out in his recognition that difficulties can only be solved by diligent and laborious enquiry.

As for the cause and guarantee of this unity of the Scriptures, it lay in their divine inspiration. Man needs a revelation if he is to have the knowledge of God, for even Plato, in a well-known passage of the *Timaeus*, admits that 'it is a hard matter to discover the Maker and Father of this universe.'[1] It is the Scriptures that meet this want. Through them God makes himself known. If any one asks for evidence of their inspiration, they themselves contain it.[2] Their truth has carried conviction, for no teacher ever won converts so successfully as Moses and Jesus Christ. The predictions of the older books have been fulfilled, and the fulfilment of Prophecy is in Origen's view more conclusive than Miracles.[3] The very language of the Scriptures, devoid as it is of literary artifice, still bears for the candid reader the traces of inspiration.[4] So Origen will admit of no serious competition between the church's books and even the best in other literatures. And yet inspiration is no isolated and exceptional fact. There is a Law of Nature, as well as a Law of Moses.[5] The moral nature of man is in accord with the teachings of faith.[6] Some measure of truth God has given to us all.[7] Revelation therefore does but confirm reason, just as the temple sanctifies the gold.[8] Origen's high estimate of the

---

[1] *C. Cels.* vii. 42.
[2] *De Prin.* IV. i. 1.
[3] *In Joann*, ii 34. Lomm. i. 152 ; Br. i. 101 ; B. iv. 92.
[4] *De Prin.* IV. i. 6. ἴχνος ἐνθουσιασμοῦ.
[5] § xxvii.
[6] *C. Cels.* iii. 40.   [7] *Ibid.*, viii. 63.
[8] *In Matt. Com. Ser.* 18 ; Lomm. iv. 216.

inspired books does not make him unfair either to Plato or to average human nature. His admissions are often generous, even when he is dealing with Celsus.

In Origen's day the offices of the Divine Word and of the Holy Spirit were not clearly distinguished. This comes out in his theory of inspiration.[1] Both of the Word and of the Spirit may it be said that they ' spake by the Prophets '. The word of the Lord that came to Jeremiah is none other than the Word that was incarnate.[2] It is Christ who speaks in Deuteronomy.[3] Equally may it be said that the Scriptures owe their distinctive qualities to the inspiration of the Holy Spirit, or that in the account of the creation it is the Divine Spirit that speaks in Moses.[4] It is well to note such varying modes of expression, without making too much of the variation. In any case it is a higher power that speaks through ($\delta\iota\acute{a}$) the human writer. The Law was given by God through Moses.[5] The Prophets were not controlled and possessed after the manner of the Pythian priestess. Inspiration cleared rather than clouded their intelligence, which gives Prophecy an advantage over the oracles.[6] Moreover such inspiration varies in degree. The Spirit, which was abiding in Jesus, came and went intermittently in Moses and David.[7] Paul can build a whole house of truth, Luke and Timothy only add upper chambers.[8] Origen hesitates sometimes on this point, as when he asks the pertinent question, whether, when

---

[1] The early Liturgies afford a parallel. Sometimes the Word sometimes the Spirit, is invoked in the Epiclesis.
[2] § xv.
[3] *In Ep. ad Rom.* viii. 2 ; Lomm. vii. 200.
[4] *De Prin.* iv. ii. 2 ; *Sel. in Pss.* Lomm. xi. 376 ; *C. Cels.* iv. 55.
[5] *In Joann.* Frag. xii ; Br. ii. 223 ; B. iv. 494.
[6] *C. Cels.* vii. 3, 4.
[7] *In Num.* Hom. vi. 3 ; Lomm. x. 51 ; B. vii. 34.
[8] *In Jer.* Frag. xii ; Lomm. xv. 445 ; B. iii. 203.

Paul speaks of all Scripture as being inspired and profitable, he includes his own letters.[1] But, in the main, we accept the inspiration of Scripture as a whole, even when we find difficulties in the details. And so he draws his well-known parallel between Scripture and Nature.[2] Both are of God, yet there is much in both we cannot fully explain. The difficulties, frankly recognized, often left unsolved as beyond his range and measure, do not rob him of his conviction that every jot and tittle,[3] every use or omission of the Greek article,[4] the very letter of the Septuagint text,[5] are all designed for our instruction in the good order of Providence. All come down from a higher source. The very reading of the Scriptures, even when not understood, has influence.[6] Origen holds to his theory with wonderful courage and conviction, which we may admire even when he brings us very near to the border line of superstition.

These two principles then determine Origen's attitude to Scripture : Scripture is a unity ; Scripture is inspired. From the first it follows that the whole of Scripture must be accepted and defended ; there can be no selection and rejection of different elements. From the second it is clear that Scripture must contain nothing that is unworthy of God.[7] The position is apparently a simple one, but further consideration will show what difficulties it involved. For taken as a whole and in its literal sense Scripture did contain many things which it was hard to

---

[1] *In Joann.* i. 3 ; Lomm. i. 11 ; Br. i. 5 ; B. iv. 6.
[2] *Sel. in Pss.* Lomm. xi. 376 ; *De Prin.* IV. i. 7.
[3] *In Ep. ad Rom.* ii. 6 ; Lomm. vi. 89.
[4] *In Luc.* Hom. xxxv. Lomm. v. 220.
[5] *Ad Afric.* 4 ; *In Oseam.* Frag. i ; *In Isa.* ii. 1 ; Lomm. xiii. 249, 302 ; xvii. 26.
[6] *In Josuam* Hom. xx. 2 ; Lomm. xi. 168, 173 ; B. vii. 418-20.
[7] *De Prin.* II. iv. 4 ; cp. Siccine dignum est de Sancti Spiritus sentire Sermonibus ? *In Sam.* Hom. i. 9 ; Lomm. xi. 306.

justify. Origen had seen Jewish teachers reduced to sore straits in attempting to defend their law.[1] He had listened to educated and friendly Greeks who found grave offence in many statements of the Old Testament and even in certain passages in the New. Let alone such controversial exigencies, his own candid and penetrating spirit compelled him to realize the problem that was there. How was he to maintain the unity and inspiration of the church's books and yet to satisfy his own mind, the intelligence of students in the lecture room, the enquiries even of the more mixed congregation in the church? Let us realize a little more clearly the character of the difficulties he admitted.

To take the problem in its acutest form, certain statements in these books were not true. The book of Genesis says there were days before the sun existed, that God planted a garden and walked in it. The Gospels assert that Jesus saw all the kingdoms of the world from a high mountain.[2] None of these assertions is credible. Again, it is not invariably true that prophets are without honour in their own country, nor is it always a matter for blame and reprehension if men build and adorn their sepulchres.[3] Many predictions too of Scripture remain unfulfilled. The chariot had not been cut off from Ephraim, nor the horse from Jerusalem; and if Jesus was the Messiah promised of old, he had not eaten butter and honey, as Isaiah foretold.[4] Would it be claimed,

---

[1] E. g. 'Haec Judaei putent'. *In Gen.* Hom. vi. 3; *Vide quam inconveniens sit Judaica intelligentia. In Lev.* Hom. iii. 3; 'Judaeorum vero doctores et impossibilia haec et irrationabilia sequentes, literam faciant.' *In Lev.* Hom. iv. 7. Lomm. viii. 186; ix. 202, 230; B. vi. 70, 303, 327.

[2] *De Prin.* IV. iii. 1.

[3] *In Matt.* x. 18; *In Matt. Com. Ser.* 25; Lomm. iii. 48; iv. 226.

[4] *De Prin.* IV. ii. 1.

word for word, that the predictions of the Lord had come true? Some possibly, others not.[1] We cannot believe in a literal opening of the heavens at the baptism of Jesus, nor can we find it upon record that the hands of Judah were laid upon the neck of his enemies.[2] God has no eyes, as Scripture asserts, nor have spiritual beings knees to bend.[3]

It is a further difficulty that Scripture seems often to demand the impossible. This is especially true of the Law of Moses. At best the Law is often burdensome or absurd, and the legislators of Rome and Greece had on the whole done better than Moses.[4] But indeed in its literal sense the Law was often impossible and irrational. Many of its provisions, when read in church, for instance the law of the sin-offering, seemed to threaten disaster to the whole Christian religion.[5] To carry out all its prescriptions was an impossible task; it never had been nor ever could be fulfilled. Origen had discussed the Law with literalist Jews and only found them fall back upon the inadequate defence, 'Ita visum legislatori'.[6]

Nor in the letter was Scripture consistent. There were statements which could not be brought into harmony. The figures given of the dimensions of the Ark were quite incompatible with the numbers and bulk of the creatures it was said to have contained.[7] And as to the New Testament, he who should attempt to

---

[1] *In Matt. Com. Ser.* 54; Lomm. iv. 327.
[2] § xv.
[3] *Sel. in Gen*; *In Ep. ad Rom.* ix. 41; Lomm. vii. 360; viii. 50.
[4] *In Joann.* Frag. lvii; Br. ii. 271; B. iv. 530; *In Lev.* Hom. vii. 5; Lomm. ix. 307; B. vi. 388.
[5] *In Lev.* Hom. v. 1; Lomm. ix. 238; B. vi. 332.
[6] *In Ep. ad Rom.* ii. 9; Lomm. vi. 106
[7] *In Gen.* Hom. ii, Frag. 2; Lomm. viii. 102; *C. Cels.* iv. 41. Origen, following Jewish precedents, meets the difficulty by the drastic expedient of squaring all the numbers. The problem had been raised by the Gnostic Apelles, a disciple of Marcion.

reconcile all its discrepancies, more especially those between the Synoptists and John, could only grow bewildered and giddy at his task.[1] The recognition of these difficulties is surprisingly frank; it is small matter for wonder that many of Origen's hearers were troubled by his admissions.

Again there were many statements and commands of which, though not literally impossible or untrue, no sufficient explanation could be given. Why should God 'break the teeth of sinners'?[2] Why should the Christian 'salute no man by the way?'[3] Of what value, taken literally, were the law of circumcision on the eighth day, the prohibition to interweave flax with wool, the washing of others' feet, or the command that a captive woman should shave her head and pare her nails if one of her captors proposed to marry her?[4] Was it sense to bid man to grow, seeing that growth was not under man's control?[5] Was it moral for Abraham to tell lies?[6] And greater still was the difficulty when Scripture, in its more anthropomorphic passages, spoke or God as moving from place to place, or as inclining the fortunes of a battle field according as Moses' hands were raised or fell, or as giving way to such human passions as hatred, vengeance, wrath.[7] Hard indeed, or rather utterly impossible, was the task of the Christian exegete,

---

[1] § xliv.
[2] *Sel in Pss.* Lomm. xi. 410.
[3] *De Prin.* IV. iii. 3; § xxx.
[4] *In Ep. ad. Rom.* ii. 13; *Ibid.*, ii. 9; *In Joann.* xxxii. 8; *In Lev.* Hom. vii. 6; Lomm. ii. 404; vi. 106, 135; ix. 310; Br. ii. 164; B. iv. 439; vi. 391.
[5] *In Luc.* Hom. xi; Lomm. v. 123.
[6] *In Gen.* Hom. vi. 3; Lomm. viii. 186; B. vi. 70.
[7] *In Gen.* Hom. iv. 5; *Sel. in Pss.*; *In 1 Sam.* Hom. i. 9; *In Ezech.* Hom. i. 2; *In Jer.* Hom. xviii. 6; *In Mat.* xv. 11; *In Joann.* Frag. xiv; Lomm. iii. 349; viii. 167; xi. 306; xiii. 15; xiv 9; xv. 329; Br. ii. 225; B. iii. 160; iv. 496; vi. 55.

if all the statements and commands of Scripture must be justified in their literal meaning and defended as an inspired unity in which there is no discord and nothing unworthy of God.

This brings us of course to Origen's well-known solution of the problem, the method of Allegorical Interpretation. He does not find his remedy, as we might do, by assigning different spiritual value to different portions of Scripture, or by working out a theory of progress in revelation, or by expanding the great principle of the text, so often used by his master Clement, 'At sundry times and in divers manners.' These ideas were not wholly strange to him, but they were not exploited. His whole exegesis rests upon the principle that Scripture says one thing and means another; that every narrative, every injunction, is really a mystery, shrouding a secret sense which alone is of real value; that we may rise from the letter to the spirit, making our way from the poorer levels of the senses to a region in which the facts, as such, cease to be of any account. He was familiar with the Pauline distinction of 'body, soul and spirit.' He finds such a distinction in the senses of Scripture.[1] There too we have a bodily or historic sense; a moral sense, which—perhaps without any very special propriety—he classes with the soul; a higher element, the spiritual meaning. This three-fold distinction is helped by the LXX version of Proverbs xxii. 20–1, 'These things write out for thy use in a three-fold manner,'[2] though the original Hebrew has no hint of anything three-fold. Of the moral sense Origen makes no great use. We hear more of it, as is natural, in the Homilies than in the Commentaries, especially in

---

[1] *De Prin.* IV. ii. 5; *In Lev.* Frag. Lomm. ix. 171.
[2] *De Prin.* IV. ii. 4.

those on the Hexateuch. To take one example; Miriam's leprosy, incurred because she ' spake against Moses ', stands according to its moral sense for jealousy between brethren. But let us pass, he says, ' a moralibus ad intelligentiam mysticam ', from ethics to the mystic meaning. In this higher sense the heretics who attack the Old Testament are smitten with leprosy.[1] The distinction between these second and third senses is not always so clearly observed. Perhaps the moral sense need not detain us longer.

But the contrast between the literal and the spiritual or mystic sense of Scripture dominates Origen's exegesis. His references to ' the friends of the letter,' to the difficulties of the literalists, to the necessity for allegory, are constant and pronounced. In some passages there is no literal sense.[2] Thus waterpots containing two or three firkins apiece, the Ark with second and third stories, both indicate that the third, that is the literal sense, is in many cases not to be found.[3] Sometimes there are two firkins only; for some purposes the Ark has two stories. On the whole however the literal sense as a rule holds good and its value for the simpler class of believers is sometimes generously admitted.[4] He opposed the heretics who questioned the historic element in the Gospels.[5] He is not prepared, as Clement had been, to allegorize the hard demand made by the Lord of the young Ruler.[6]

---

[1] *In Num.* Hom. vii; Lomm. x. 53 *sqq.*; B. vii. 37.
[2] *De Prin.* IV. ii. 5.
[3] *Non semper in scripturis divinis historialis consequentia stare potest, sed non-nunquam deficit. In Gen.* Hom. ii. 6; Lomm. viii. 144; B. vi. 36-7; *De Prin. l. c.*
[4] *Si qui infirmi sunt et incapaces profundioris mysterii ædificentur ex litera. In Lev.* Hom. iv. 2; Lomm. ix. 219; B. vi. 317.
[5] *In Luc.* Hom. xvii; Lomm. v. 148.
[6] *In Matt.* xv. 15; Lomm. iii. 358. Origen must have had Clement's *Quis dives salvetur* in mind.

The unhistoric is only an element introduced into a historic whole.[1] And he strongly asserts, against all Docetic theories, the historic reality of the earthly life of the Lord.[2] But when all is said Origen has little of the historic instinct and his interest is not in facts. In the main he leaves them to the 'somatic' literalists, using them chiefly not for their intrinsic value but as a foil and contrast to the higher verities. So his constant practice and principle is 'the higher interpretation.'[3] We are to leave the letter and reach the mystic sense. Of the countless instances of this with which his pages are crowded a few may be selected to illustrate his method.

To begin with simple examples. Wine and gall mean the blending of orthodox opinion with a morally defective life.[4] Sarah follows Abraham because the flesh (woman) should follow reason (man).[5] To loose the latchet of the Lord is to make the meaning of His incarnation clear.[6] Pharaoh's daughter finding Moses is the Church discovering the meaning of the Law.[7] Isaac's wells are the scriptural sources of truth.[8] Moab is Epicurean teaching.[9] Camels and asses are stolid souls.[10] The frogs, lice, flies of the plagues are poets, dialectic

[1] μίγμα τοῦ ὡς ἀνιστορικοῦ. *In Joann*, Frag. lxxiv ; so Br. ii. 283 ; B. iv. 541 adopts a different text.
[2] § xix.
[3] Possibly as good a rendering as any of ἀναγωγή his frequent term. It does not mean induction in our sense, but rather the process by which exegesis is raised from the plane of letter and fact (*humilis locus literæ In Ex. Hom.* iii. 2 ; Lomm. ix. 27 ; B. vi. 165) to the higher plane of mystic and spiritual significance.
[4] *In Matt. Com. Ser.* 137 ; Lomm. v. 63.
[5] *In Gen.* Hom. iv. 4 ; Lomm. viii. 166 ; B. vi. 54.
[6] *In Joann.* Frag. xviii ; Br. ii. 235 ; B. iv. 498.
[7] *In Ex.* Hom. ii. 4 ; Lomm. ix. 20-21 ; B. vi. 159-60.
[8] *In Gen.* Hom. xiii. Lomm. viii. 240 ; B. vi. 113.
[9] *In Lib. Jud.* Hom. iv 1 ; Lomm. xi. 245.
[10] *In Lev.* Hom. xvi. 6 ; Lomm. ix. 441 ; B. vi. 503.

philosophers and cynics.[1] The list might be made indefinitely long. So Lazarus, Peter, Noah, Daniel, Job, are types of character and with us still.[2] There is a spiritual Babylonian, a spiritual Moses.[3] Barabbas is the Devil.[4] The kings of Egypt, of Tyre, of Babylon are spiritual powers who bring us into captivity.[5] Even for Salome's dance and for Lot and his daughters similar interpretations are found.[6] Sometimes the principle is applied on a wider scale. The book of Joshua is the book of Jesus who guides the church, the parallel being worked out with quick perception of all available similarities.[7] The Shulammite maiden of the Song of Songs is the Church or the Christian soul.[8] All the spiritual value of the Old Testament, especially of the Law, only becomes evident when Jesus removes the veil and its wealth of symbolism and imagery stands revealed and clear. It is along such lines that Origen solves his difficulties and finds treasure hidden even in the details of the sacred text. Spiritually interpreted the Law has its abundant justification. ' Secundum consilium, quod nos afferimus ad legem, possunt omnia spiritaliter fieri.'[9] Even in the case of the fourth Gospel he must translate the sensible Gospel into the spiritual, for nothing that comes of the senses is real and truth lies in the spiritual realm.[10] As he looks back over many years of exegetical labour

---

[1] *In Ex.* Hom. iv. 6 ; Lomm. ix. 42 ; B. vi. 178.
[2] §§ liv, xcviii ; *In Ezech.* Hom. iv. 4 ; Lomm. xiv. 63.
[3] *In Lam.* Frag. xciii ; Lomm. xiii. 206 ; B. iii. 269 ; § xxiv
[4] *In Matt.* xiv. 19 ; Lomm. iii. 313.
[5] *De Prin.* IV. iii. 9.
[6] *In Matt.* x. 22 ; *In Gen.* Hom. v. 5 ; Lomm. iii. 59 ; viii. 177 ; B. vi. 63.
[7] Cp. §§ xxiv-xxv.
[8] Cp. § xxxv.
[9] *In Ex.* Hom. xi. 6 ; Lomm. ix. 139 ; B. vi. 260.
[10] *In Joann.* i. 8, 26 ; Lomm. i. 21, 54 ; Br. i. 12, 32 ; B. iv. 13, 31 ; § xliv.

he feels that if he must not boast still he need not despair.[1] Christ, who is the wisdom of God, is his helper in this task.

We may enquire on what grounds Origen justified allegory, and how far we must commend or criticize him for his abundant use of it.

As to his justification, to some extent the question was one of degree. All believers, he claimed, admit some mystical element in Scripture.[2] Even the crudest literalist would not assert that God had wings.[3] The most devoted 'friend of the letter' would not bring ridicule on Paul by saying that it was mere physical beauty that he attributed to 'the feet of them that preach the gospel of peace.'[4] No one, then, whose opinion need be taken into account, would entirely and consistently deny the fundamental principle of allegory. Up to a certain point Origen could claim the consensus of reasonable Christians. But of course he went far beyond that point.

His appeal however would be to the few rather than to the many and great names may be cited in support of his method. Philo, as is well known, had allegorized the Pentateuch and reconciled Plato with Moses by such means. A school of allegorical exegetes must already have existed in Alexandria in Philo's time. There were even Jews prepared to neglect the ceremonial law on account of its spiritual significance. The legislation of the Mosaic books was frankly accepted in an allegorical sense.[5] And when we pass from Jewish to Christian interpretation, both Origen's predecessors in the School of Alexandria were committed to the same principle.

---

[1] *In Matt.* xiv. 6 ; Lomm. iii. 282.
[2] *De Prin.* IV. ii. 2.
[3] *Sel. in Gen.* ; Lomm. viii. 50 ; cp. Ps. xci. 4.
[4] *In Ep. ad Rom.* viii. 4 ; Lomm. vii. 212.
[5] See Drummond, *Philo Judæus* i. 18 *sqq*.

This seems clear even in the case of Pantaenus; he 'led the way in that method of spiritual or mystical interpretation of the Old Testament usually associated with his more famous followers.'[1] Clement of course has left his own records. In his interpretation of the Old Testament he was largely Philo's follower, but he carried over the same principle into the domain of the New. He was just as ready to interpret the long robe of the Lord as meaning the variegated beauty of the Scriptures, or to discern a reference to wealthy mine-owners in the foxes that have holes, as he was to find the heretics in those animals which chew the cud.[2] Philo, Pantænus, Clement all prepared Origen's way. He pushed his method to extremes but he marked no new departure.

Moreover the Jewish and Christian schools were in this matter not peculiar. Long before the date of Philo the difficulties of the old mythology had been explained by the very method which Origen employed in dealing with the problem of Scripture. Stories of the strifes and plots and amours of the gods were allegorized in Plato's time.[3] The Sophists and the Cynics brought the method into extended use. Its vogue and recognition reached their height in the Stoic school, from which source books on 'Homeric Allegories' and on 'the Nature of the Gods' are still extant.[4] Maximus of Tyre, a later Platonist who lectured in Rome when Origen was a boy, defended the myths as being full of symbolism: alike with poets and with philosophers 'everything is packed with hidden meanings.'[5] In few

---

[1] *D. C. B.* art. Pantaenus.
[2] See the present writer's *Clement of Alexandria* ii. 210 *sqq.*
[3] *Republic*, 378.
[4] Drummond, *op. cit.* i. 121; Zeller, *Philosophie der Griechen* iii (i) pp. 321 *sqq.*
[5] Or. iv. 4.

instances does Origen offer to the argument of Celsus a more telling retort than when he says in effect, ' You criticize our allegories, but do you not allegorize Hesiod and Homer yourselves? What of Chrysippus? What of Plato? What of Numenius? If Greeks may use allegory, why should it be forbidden to the Christian interpreter?'[1] Certainly Celsus had little right to raise the objection.

But probably the more difficult, certainly the more insistent critics, were the literalists within the church, for whom the names of Chrysippus or Philo or even of Clement would carry little authority. For such, if Scripture said animals it meant animals, and if Paul the Apostle made statements it was no business of Origen to twist them out of their plain sense.[2] When such persons attacked him, or when in his own heart he wondered whether he had ventured on a dangerous path,[3] his most effective appeal was doubtless to the example set by Paul. The incidents of Israel's journey and the story of Hagar had been definitely allegorized in the Epistles. To these precedents Origen refers. He dare not, he says, venture upon the new and difficult ascent to the heights of allegory alone.[4] But Paul has shown him the

---

[1] Much is said on this subject in *C. Cels.* iv.

[2] *In Lev.* Hom. vii. 4 ; *In Ep. ad Rom.* iii. 7. Other criticisms were *Noli allegorizare* ; *noli per figuram exponere* ; *Cur vim facis scripturæ? Quid iterum hic euresilogus agit? Adhuc detrahunt iis,* he complains, *qui Christo consurrexerunt et quæ sursum sunt in Scripturis requirunt. Ea sentire nos criminantur quæ nunquam sensisse nos novimus. In Ezech.* Hom. vi. 8 ; *In Lev.* Hom. xvi. 4 ; *In Matt. Com. Ser.* 15 ; *In Luc.* Hom. xxv. Lomm. iv. 210 ; v. 182 ; vi. 196 ; ix. 300, 434 ; xiv. 90 ; B. vi. 382, 497.

[3] *Utinam . . . non videamur temere et periculose dixisse. In Matt. Com. Ser.* 16, Lomm. iv. 213.

[4] C. Cels. iv. 49 ; *In Num.* Hom. iii. 3 ; Lomm. x. 28 ; B. vii. 16-17. Cp. 1 Cor. x. 1-4 ; Gal. iv. 21-4. Other references to the Apostle's authority for allegory may be found in Lomm. viii. 155, 181, 187, 225 ; ix. 300 ; x. 56 ; B. vi. 45, 66, 71, 100, 382 ; vii. 39.

way. This appeal to the Apostle's authority occurs with marked frequency. Here at any rate Origen speaks with confidence and feels that his ground is sure.

Thus when his critics, whether within or without the church, attacked Origen for his use of allegory, he had arguments of considerable defensive force to urge in reply. But they did not convince everyone, either in the third or in the next following centuries. What should be our own estimate of this marked feature in his writings? The point has been very fully discussed by all modern writers on Origen.[1] It will be sufficient here to make two admissions and two claims.

He failed no doubt in the first duty of every exegete, which is to ascertain, as exactly as available information admits, what in a given passage a given writer intended to say. With all his acuteness, with all his insistence upon the accuracy of Scripture, he does not make his way to the heart of an author's meaning, partly because it is what he takes to be the mind of the Spirit as expressed through the author—not the author's own thought—that has his real interest and concern. No doubt it is a legitimate task of exegesis to expand the meaning of Scripture, and to recognize where its teaching can be applied to other conditions with good result. But this process should always start from a right understanding of the primary sense. This Origen missed. He found in Scripture what he wished to find, and was very far from 'letting the Bible speak for itself.' He was not without principles in his exegesis,

---

[1] See Huet ii. 13. Redepenning i. 290 *sqq*.; Denis 33 *sqq*.; Bigg. *Platonists*, Lect. iv; DeFaye, *Origène*, vol. i. ch. vii. Westcott in *D. C. B.* art. Origenes, section on 'Origen as critic and interpreter'.

but one can understand what Denis means by describing his method as 'ce jeu d'imagination'.[1]

And if, negatively, Origen failed by his indifference to the primary meaning of his texts, his positive error in misconceiving the method of inspiration was not less serious. Truth is sometimes concealed under literal statements and figures of sense. In the parables of the Lord this was done with deliberate intent. But the belief that throughout Scripture a hidden mystic sense underlies all narratives and all details and is there buried in concealment by the divine purpose, is sheer misconception of the method of revelation. It was the belief of the age and Origen is not alone responsible for it. Clement before him had devoted the greater part of the fifth book of the *Stromateis* to a defence of this doctrine of 'concealment' and Origen may have heard it all in Clement's lectures. But excuse or explain it as we may, this false principle is there and is operative. It dominates and vitiates Origen's exegesis.

Yet there is another side to the account. Allegory saved the Scriptures for the Church. Taken literally the Old Testament could not have been shown as against Jewish controversialists to be Christian literature, nor could either Testament have been defended against the criticisms of educated Greeks. The answer to each lay in allegorical exegesis. The method had been worked to excess in the Gnostic schools,[2] and Origen has often to plead for consistency and balance in contrast to what he deemed their errors. It was because he could use this method on his own lines that in church or lecture room he addressed his many audiences with an entire

---

[1] *Op. cit.*, p. 33.
[2] Heretics rejoice in allegory. *In Joann.* xx. 20 ; Lomm. ii. 240 ; Br. ii. 63 ; B. iv. 352.

and unhesitating confidence in the spiritual value of the Scriptures which it was his lifelong service to expound. The 'simpliciores' were troubled but the competent few were attracted and multiplied.

Further, allegory meant freedom. It was escape from the bondage of the letter. It meant that outside the church's Rule of Faith, which Origen held to be sacred and inviolable and never consciously infringed,[1] it was open to him to read his own convictions into the language of the canonical books. With what wide liberty of speculation he pursued this method, some of the extracts in this volume will adequately show. Was it well, or was it not well, was it laudable synthesis or in Harnack's phrase, deplorable 'secularization', that the church should assimilate the teaching of Plato and the Stoics? The question may be variously answered. In any case Origen was the greatest of the many teachers who brought Hellenic culture into the religion of the Man of Nazareth. Allegory made this possible. The letter remains unaltered, but the spirit of the philosophers is blended in exegesis with the spirit of the prophets. The method was the method of the age. Through it the Alexandrine master secured a large measure of intellectual freedom.[2] Must we blame him that he accepted the conditions and opportunities of his time?

Allegory then was the dominant feature of Origen's exegesis. It supplied the form and enlarged the possibilities of his interpretation. It remains to notice certain other elements in his work.

---

[1] Cp. Introduction to the *De Principiis*.
[2] So Drummond finely says about Philo. 'His method of exegesis belonged to the time in which he lived, and we must not allow the tedium of his exposition to hide from us the beauty of his religious conceptions and the just balance of his ethical ideals.' *Op. cit.* i. 22-3.

In strict order criticism precedes interpretation. He who would expound the text, must know what the text is. The two in Origen proceed side by side. He was the first great textual critic, and the *Hexapla* was indeed a monument of laborious learning. His interest in textual questions was already formed when he wrote his earliest Commentaries.[1] Throughout it was his practice to refer to MSS. variations and to the different Greek versions of the Old Testament, those of the LXX, of Aquila, Theodotion and Symmachus and a fifth, which he had found on the shore at Actium, strange place indeed for the discovery of such a literary prize.[2] Of certain books of Scripture he himself possessed more than one copy.[3] It is sometimes said that his criticism is vitiated by his reliance upon the mere number of manuscripts, rather than upon their trustworthiness. This is not true without qualification. He would on occasion reject a reading which most of the copies known to him supported.[4] He speaks, whatever exactly the expression means, of 'the more accurate copies'.[5] Carelessness in copyists he admits with good reason, and in some cases he refers to intentional alterations of the text.[6] But these as a rule were of heretical origin, Marcion being the great offender, and Origen expressly repudiates the

---

[1] *In Joann., In Gen., In Pss.* Cp. ὠβελίσαμεν, *In Joann.* xxviii. 16; Lomm. ii. 348; Br. ii. 131; B. iv. 410, and the frequent references to the five Greek versions in the *In Gen.* and *In Pss.*

[2] Jerome, *Prologue ad Damasum*; Lomm. xiv. 235; cp. *H.E.* vi. 16 where even a sixth and a seventh version are mentioned.

[3] *Ad Afric.* 2; τὰ παρ᾽ ἡμῖν ἀντίγραφα. Lomm. xvii. 22-3.

[4] E.g. he prefers in John i. 28. Bethabara to Bethany from personal knowledge of the place, as against MS. authority. He says of a certain reading '*in plerisque codicibus legitur*', but accepts another. *In Joann.* vi. 40; *In Cant. Cantic.* Hom. i. 6; Lomm. i. 238; xiv. 249; Br. i. 157; B. iv. 149; viii. 36.

[5] *In Jer.* Hom. viii. 1; Lomm. xv. 192; B. iii. 55.

[6] § lxxxiv.

charge of Celsus that the church had tampered with her texts.[1] It is well known that Origen studied Hebrew, contrary to the custom of Christian teachers in his time,[2] and though his mastery of the language was probably never very complete, he could at least refer to his Hebrew text for elucidation of the Greek, or use it on occasion for the settlement of a debated reading.[3] His acknowledgment of his debts to Hebrew teachers is frequent. No great exegete has wandered further from the actual letter of Scripture than Origen. It is a different feature in his work which confronts us, as we watch him comparing copy with copy, version with version; as we note his efforts to understand the causes of variation in manuscripts; as we picture the labour which had gone to the making of those fifty rolls of papyrus, which remained for the use of students in the library of Pamphilus at Cæsarea.[4]

But if Origen did much for the text of the Septuagint, it is also true that the Septuagint influenced Origen's exegesis. The Old Testament with which he was familiar was the Old Testament in Greek. Like the other Christian teachers of his age he accepted the Greek version as inspired.[5] That is his general principle, and justifies his careful examination of its phrases and his desire for a reliable text. If he often fails to apprehend the genius of the Hebrew Scriptures, this is largely the

[1] *Sel. in Pss. In Matt. Com. Ser.* 121 ; Lomm. v. 35 ; xi. 408 ; *C. Cels.* ii. 27.
[2] '*Contra ætatis gentisque suæ naturam*'. Jerome, *De Vir. Illust.* liv.
[3] *In Matt.* xiv. 16 ; xvi. 19 ; *In 1 Sam.* Hom. i. 4 ; Lomm. iii. 306 ; iv. 58 ; xi. 293 ; B. viii. 5.
[4] '*Die Hexaplen, mindestens fünfzig sehr starke Bücherrollen*' Redepenning. ii. 177. The work 'would have filled 3,250 leaves or 6,500 pages'. Swete, *Introd. to O.T. in Greek*, 2nd edition, p. 74.
[5] *In Luc.* Hom. xxxv ; *In Cant. Cantic. 1* ; Lomm. v. 220 ; xiv. 344 ; B. viii. 101.

result of his knowing them best in their Greek version. His memory is rarely at fault in quoting them,[1] but he is not always conscious of the wide difference in value which must separate an original from any translation. His desire to discover the New Testament symbolically foreshadowed in the Old was greatly assisted by the fact that both were known to him in the same language. He could find the terms most discussed in current controversies already used in the versions of Genesis, Proverbs or the Psalms.[2] And in some instances he devotes considerable space to the exegesis of a phrase which does not occur at all in the Hebrew text.[3] Probably the content of his teaching was in the main determined by quite other influences, but no true estimate of his interpretation of Scripture can be formed without some reference to the fact that, even when he is dealing with Ezekiel or Leviticus, it is mainly the Greek version that he has in mind.

Again, in exegesis he is much concerned with details. In part this is due to his estimate of their purpose and value; in part it results from the custom, whether in written books or in lectures and sermons, of dealing with each passage of Scripture in its turn. The teacher did not choose his text, and something had to be said even if the day's lesson were a list of names.[4] Some things he

---

[1] But Micah is quoted as Hosea; *In Matt.* xvi. 21; and εὐνοῦχος given for οἰνοόχοος, *In Matt.* xv. 5, where it is significant. Lomm. iii. 335; iv. 62.

[2] E.g. ἐξανάστασις in Genesis. *In Joan.* vi. 10; λόγος in Pss. *ib.* i. 24; ἀρχή in Prov. *ib.* xix. 9; Lomm. i. 50, 192; ii. 157; Br. i. 29, 123; ii. 13; B. iv. 29, 120, 309.

[3] *De Prin.* IV. ii. 4; *In Josuam.* Hom. viii. 1; xxii. 3; Lomm. xi. 75, 195; B. vii. 336, 443.

[4] There was an '*ordo lectionum*' but the sermon might disregard it occasionally at the request of the congregation. *In Num.* Hom. xv; Lomm. x. 168; B. vii. 128.

might hurry over; on some points he might go back to an earlier passage.[1] But each day brought its portion,[2] and the less obvious its spiritual value, the greater the obligation upon the exegete to prove that this was really there. Origen's mind was extraordinarily quick to see points and to anticipate objections, and his treatment of details often has much value. He draws attention, especially in the Old Testament, to the importance of determining who is the speaker.[3] He insists with conviction upon the minute accuracy of Scripture, bidding us mark with what precision a particular term is used. We are not to confuse the feeding of the five thousand with the feeding of the four.[4] He will have no 'doublets', and the same principle is applied to the two versions of the Lord's Prayer.[5] Especially in his *Commentaries* on the Romans he pays attention to points of grammar, punctuation and terminology. Throughout he will devote minute care to the exact meaning of a word, quoting parallels, noting different possible senses, propounding etymologies true or false. His mastery of such subjects is admirable. We feel the great mind at work in little things. But no doubt there is a corresponding loss. He is liable to be unduly influenced by particular texts and particular words. The details tend to monopolize him. When he deals with the *True Word* of Celsus, it is section by section that he discusses it. The underlying principles do not emerge in their true proportion. Attention to the small error tends to diminish the significance of the great.

[1] *In Num.* Hom. xxvii. 12 ; *In Lev.* Hom. ii. 1 ; Lomm. ix. 185 ; x 354 ; B. vi. 290 ; vii. 272.
[2] Cp. '*Hesterno die dixeramus*', etc. *In Num.* Hom. xiii. 1. Lomm. x. 142 ; B. vii. 107, and the note in Redepenning ii. 229.
[3] 'Persona dicentis magnopere consideranda est'. *In Num.* Hom. xxvi. 3 ; Lomm. x. 321 ; B. vii. 246.
[4] *In Matt.* xi. 19. Lomm. iii. 123.
[5] *De Orat.* xviii.

To some extent it is the same with his treatment of Scripture. He deals with each given book in passages, one by one. It does not follow that its characteristics as a whole are therefore entirely missed, for he has clear ideas on the general trend and significance of the fourth Gospel and of the book of Joshua and of the Song of Songs, and he also discerns the affinity between Jeremiah and Jesus Christ.[1] But the details take most of his attention. He speaks of distinguishing between the Old and the New Testaments,[2] but this is only imperfectly accomplished. He has little sense of the peculiar spiritual beauty of the Psalms. He understands something of Paul, for whom he had both affinity and admiration, but he has little appreciation of the human characteristics of the Son of Man, and such as he has is always of the doctrinal order. Herein we note a limitation, but after all what master is without them? or would be a master if he were?

One phase of this characteristic is seen in the attention Origen pays to names and to numbers. Both, as he held, had a mystic significance. Philo, Clement and the Gnostics had here preceded him, so that once again he is no innovator. Number was believed to exert influence on events.[3] Names were of such effective potency that an invocation lost its force if translated into another tongue.[4] It is clear that much ingenuity and attention were devoted to these subjects; there was a sort of science of names and the old question was still debated, whether names were by nature or by arrangement.[5] On

---

[1] § lxvii.
[2] 'Instrumenta distinguere', *In Ezech.* Hom. i. 9; Lomm. xiv. 21. B. viii. 333.
[3] Number has δύναμίν τινα ἐν τοῖς οὖσιν. *Sel. in Pss.* Lomm. xi. 377.
[4] *C. Cels.* v. 45.
[5] φύσει or θέσει *De Martyr.* xlvi.

ORIGEN AS EXEGETE

these lines Origen refers to place names such as Capernaum and Gerizim; to personal names, Hophni, Elizabeth, possibly Pontius Pilate.[1] On the name Jesus he has much to say, and Bethabar ais preferred as a reading to Bethany in part because of its significance.[2] So with number. He is encouraged in commencing the twenty-eighth book of his *Commentaries* on John's Gospel by the fact that twenty-eight was held to be a perfect number. There was a correspondence between the numbers and the contents of the Psalms.[3] The number seven stood for this world; eight, the ogdoad, for the next.[4] Nor is it without significance that God knows the numbers of the stars of heaven and of the hairs of our head.[5] On the other hand Origen quaintly remarks that 'things creeping innumerable' were appropriately without number, for this privilege would not be given to creatures that crawled upon their bellies.[6] These are examples of his fanciful interest in a field where etymology and arithmetic did not greatly restrict the imagination. It was a tradition, no doubt, but it was a tradition which suited Origen's bent.

So this great exegete left abundant scope alike for his successors and for his critics. We do him no wrong when we recognize his limitations, some of them personal, some of them the conditions of his age. It is of the latter that we are more conscious. 'This was all right in its time', we say; or, 'Our view of inspiration is not his.' Yet we rarely feel that he is positively wrong.

---

[1] *In Matt.* xiii. 11; *In Matt. Com. Ser.* 116; *In Joann.* ii. 33; xiii. 13; *In 1 Sam.* Hom. i. 7; Lomm. i. 150; ii. 23; iii. 232; v. 22; xi. 301; Br. i. 99, 260; B. iv. 90, 237; viii. 12.
[2] *In Joann.* vi. 40; Lomm. i. 238; Br. i. 158; B. iv. 149.
[3] § xl.
[4] *Sel. in Pss.* Lomm. xiii. 102-3.
[5] *In Num.* Hom. i. 1; Lomm. x. 12-13; B. vii. 3-4.
[6] *Sel. in Pss.*; Lomm. xiii. 156; lxx. ὧν οὐκ ἔστιν ἀριθμός

From one point of view, if not from another, the thing he meant was true. Now and again his exegesis is very strained, and he frankly allows that so it must seem to some.[1] He knew the interpreter might be too venturesome.[2] At times he twists statements into consistency. At times he gives us a very lame theodicy.[3] And now and again we meet a frankly impossible suggestion and wonder that so acute an intelligence could have propounded it. But considering the bulk of his work and the haste with which much of it must have been accomplished, these defects meet us with surprising infrequency. The labour of his achievement, the combination of moral earnestness with mental alertness, the sincerity of conviction, the sense of possessing a great heritage—these are the features which arrest us constantly. And there remain also one or two other qualities in his work with a mention of which this estimate may close.

Origen has the humility which characterizes true greatness. On certain points he is quite clear, almost dogmatic. Beyond them he is often only the enquirer, seeking for truth, admitting hesitation. He will allow no infringement of the Church's Rule of Faith. He is quite certain that the case of Celsus could not be maintained. He does not admit the possibility of matter being a first cause equally with God. And literalism in exegesis is definitely wrong. On all these points he speaks affirmatively and decisively. They are not open

---

[1] Exegesis, he held, should not be '$\beta\iota\alpha\iota o\varsigma$'. He uses this term (*supra* p. xviii) of Heracleon and fears it may be urged against himself. *In Matt.* xv. 7, 18, 22; Lomm. iii. 340, 364, 374.

[2] Cp. $\tau o\lambda\mu\eta\rho\hat{\omega}\varsigma$. *In Joann.* xxviii. 15. Lomm. ii. 345; Br. ii. 130; B. iv. 409.

[3] E. g. his Exegesis of 1 Sam. ii. 30 in *Com. in Ep. ad Rom.* ii. 6; Lomm. vi. 90; also his explanation of 'Let this cup pass' in *De Martyr.* xxix.

questions. But side by side with this decision runs through all his writings another strain. He speaks 'as he is able'. This point demands 'qualifications greater than I possess'. This is a subject for the truly learned, 'of whom I well know that I am not one'. To this question 'it is not easy to find an answer'. Repeatedly he leaves matters for hearers or readers to decide. 'It is for the reader to judge.' 'He who is able must consider.' 'Some one else may suggest a better explanation.'[1] He is glad to convince but he does not seek to control the minds of others. Hence his common practice of giving two or more interpretations and leaving to others the choice between them. He is ready to acknowledge the help which a teacher receives from his pupils; he is in their debt as well as they in his.[2] And there are subjects in which a true teacher must advance with caution, 'suspenso pede', for a false step may bring disaster.[3] When his bold speculations brought, especially after his death, the swarm of critics and objectors upon his memory, Pamphilus, his loyal admirer, could reply that Origen had made suggestions rather than assertions. On many points his ideas were put forward for discussion and enquiry.[4] The church had given no decision on the pre-existence of the soul or on the nature of the stars. It was therefore open to Origen to consider the anterior reasons which made Esau different from Jacob and the evidence which went to show that the stars were living

---

[1] *In Matt.* xvi. 19; xvii. 7; *In Matt. Com. Ser.* 96, 116; *In Joann.* xiii. 58; *In Ep. ad Rom.* vi. 12; vii. 17; viii. 8; x. 42; Lomm. ii. 118; iv. 59, 103, 442; v. 22; vii. 74, 173, 251, 452; Br. i. 317; B. iv. 288.

[2] § lxvii.

[3] *In Ep. ad Rom.* vii. 16; Lomm. vii. 165.

[4] '*Discutiens et pertractans potius quam affirmans.*' '*Haec quantum ad nos pertinet, non sint dogmata; sed discussionis gratia dicta sint.*' Pamphilus, *Apologia* i. ix; Lomm. xxiv. 312, 404-5. What remains of this Apologia is well worth attention.

beings. But he claims no finality. These things are 'discussionis gratia dicta'. And so, along with his daring flights of imagination, which carry us backwards into dim beginnings and forwards into the long series of the worlds to be, there remains not less evident the spirit of the seeker and of the learner, which makes tentative answers, and follows up hints, and has respect for other minds, and is not ashamed to acknowledge ignorance. He is no sceptic. But he is even further removed from being an autocrat in exegesis.

All the best characteristics of Origen, his thoroughness, his patience, his courage, his humility, come out with singular distinctness in his conception of the teacher's vocation. Whatever the value of his own personal work, the dignity of his high calling admits for him no question. 'First apostles, secondarily prophets, thirdly teachers'— so high does the teacher stand in the church's grades of precedence.[1] He is the guide of the few who are called to carry their search for truth 'above that which is written.'[2] He is to be a true 'master', however little he must insist upon his right to claim the title. His position is of divine appointment, and when error is proved false, when, in Origen's quaint adaptation of Scripture, five doctors put to flight a hundred demons, the teacher's service abounds to the glory of God.[3] And yet, high as is the calling, the true teacher never loses sight of his many limitations or of his overwhelming responsibilities. For he is limited first by his own inadequacy. He doubts whether he is the able minister of the New Testament.[4] He must not despair,

[1] *In Joann.* xxxii. 10 ; Lomm. ii. 411 ; Br. ii. 168 ; B. iv. 443.
[2] *Ibid.* xii. 5 ; Lomm. ii. 10 ; Br. i. 252 ; B. iv. 230.
[3] *In Matt. Com. Ser.* 12 ; *In Matt.* xiii. 15 ; *In Ep. ad Rom.* iii. 1 ; *In Lev.* Hom. xvi. 7 ; Lomm. iii. 236 ; iv. 203 ; vi. 170 ; ix. 443 ; B. vi. 504.
[4] *In Joann.* Frag xvi ; Br. ii. 233 ; B. iv. 105.

ORIGEN AS EXEGETE

but he must make no great claim to success.[1] Often he is puzzled and in difficulty, so that he must needs turn to God for guidance.[2] Then time was short, and though, like Augustine after him, he delivered a daily sermon, still it was difficult to say all he wished and even in the second century congregations liked short sermons, 'brevitatem auditores ecclesiae diligunt.'[3] For his hearers also and probably his readers as well had their own limitations, their indifference, their irregularity, their lack of insight, their rooted prejudices.[4] He warns them that they too have their responsibilities, and that the greatest care is necessary in the choice of our religious guides.[5] The wise are a small company, 'valde rari.'[6] These things at times make Origen shrink and hesitate in face of the teacher's responsibilities. Woe to the lazy teacher who hid his talents.[7] Harm and discredit came upon the church through the incompetence of her appointed instructors.[8] Hardly less harm through those who divulged all mysteries and revealed the inner secrets of faith to minds as yet unfitted to receive them—'pearls before swine,' as the often quoted text might have reminded them.[9] For wise reserve was in many cases necessary.[10] The true teacher must discriminate between

---

[1] *In Matt.* xiv. 6; Lomm. iii. 282.
[2] *In Lev.* Hom. vi. 1; Lomm. ix. 272; B. vi. 359.
[3] *In Num.* Hom. xxvii. 12; *In Lib. Jud.* Hom. vi. 1; Lomm. x. 354; xi. 256. In Augustine's day sermons on Sunday were short. *In Joann*, Tract. xlvii. 9.
[4] *In Ex.* Hom. xiii. 3; Lomm. ix. 154; B. vi. 272-3; Bigg, *Platonists*, 129.
[5] *In Lev.* Hom. xvi. 2; *In Matt.* xi. 14; Lomm. iii. 104; ix. 432; B. vi. 495.
[6] *In Josuam.* xvii. 2; Lomm. xi. 154; B. vii. 402.
[7] *In Matt. Com. Ser.* 66; Lomm. iv. 366.
[8] *In Num.* Hom. vii. 2; Lomm. x. 57; B. vii. 40.
[9] *In Lev.* Hom. vi. 6; xii. 7; *In Num.* Hom. iv. 3; Lomm. ix. 285, 396; x. 36; B. vi. 369, 466; vii. 23, § lv.
[10] *In Num.* Hom. iii. 1; Lomm. x. 24; B. vii. 13.

his pupils, exercising the most considerate care over those who, male or female, were still catechumens only, yet not neglecting the educated or laying himself open to the ridicule of the intellectuals.[1] Nor indeed was his task wholly one of instruction. Both by his preaching and his living he must set forth the Word and show it accordingly. Along with doctrine must go the *vitæ exemplum*, and his teaching must arouse the conscience as well as inform the mind.[2] God's fire is to be in his heart and it is the fire which kindles as well as illuminates.[3] Sometimes the temptations of popularity beset him.[4] Sometimes he was tempted to shirk his task.[5] And for lack of wisdom he might fail to discriminate between what should and what should not be said.[6] The office was high and honourable but who would seek it?[7] For both intellectually and morally it was strenuous and exacting. All his sermons, he expects, will be criticized at the day of judgment, when apparently there will be no lack of time.[8] To all teachers, himself included, were Ezekiel's warnings to prophets and false prophets addressed. Hence the need for him to appeal to his congregation, asking their prayers for his enlightenment; or to the 'Lector benevolus' with a request for his patience and kindly judgment.[9] Throughout his works these references to his own calling are frequent and evidently sincere. They help us to understand his influence and

---

[1] *In Luc.* Hom. vii, xxii; *In Matt. Com. Ser.* 49, 134; Lomm. iv, 303; v. 55, 110, 169.
[2] *In Ep. ad Rom.* x. 11; *Sel. in Pss.* Lomm. vii. 410; xii. 245.
[3] *Sel. in Pss.* 7; *In Ex.* Hom. xiii. 4; Lomm. ix. 158; xii. 283; B. vi. 276.
[4] *In Luc.* Hom. xxv; Lomm. v. 182.
[5] *In Josuam.* Hom. xx. 2; Lomm. xi. 175; B. vii. 420.
[6] *In Ezech.* Hom. i. 11; Lomm. xiv. 25; B. viii. 335.
[7] § lviii.
[8] *In Ezech.* Hom. ii. 3; Lomm. xiv. 34; B. viii. 343.
[9] *In Ep. ad Rom.* iv. 2; vii. 15; Lomm. vi. 250; vii. 163.

to appreciate the characteristics which attracted crowds to the house in which he taught as a young man in Alexandria and elicited twenty years later the enthusiastic panegyric from Gregory in Cæsarea. Through all that is untenable, eccentric, past and over in the details of his exegesis, there still shines clear, for everyone who will study him with sympathy and insight, the great conception of a noble vocation. He is God's banker, distinguishing between the true and counterfeit metal, loaning out the golden coin of truth to souls who will repay it with interest in reasonable service and intelligent devotion. In our own days, when knowledge is increased and the making of many books goes on without cessation, no single teacher is likely to occupy a position in exegesis so eminent as that of Origen in his century. But it is well for the Church when among our 'many masters' Origen's diligence, Origen's candour, Origen's reverence do not fail.

BIBLIOGRAPHY

The following list of books, though it does not claim to be complete, may be of service to the reader. Some of the works named are out of print. Several are included which do not deal exclusively with Origen.

ORIGENIS OPERA OMNIA. Ed. Carol. Henric. Edouard Lommatzsch. Vols. i–xxv. Berlin, 1831–48.

ORIGENES WERKE, by various editors, in the series ' Die griechischen christlichen Schriftsteller der ersten drei Jahrhunderte herausgegeben von der kirchen-väter Commission der königl. preussischen Akademie der Wissenschaften '. Leipsig, 1891, etc., in progress. Vols. i–viii have appeared.

THE COMMENTARY OF ORIGEN ON S. JOHN'S GOSPEL. By A. E. Brooke. 2 vols. Cambridge, 1896.

THE PHILOCALIA OF ORIGEN. By J. Armitage Robinson. Cambridge, 1893.

THE WRITINGS OF ORIGEN. Translated by Frederick Crombie. In the Ante-Nicene Christian Library. 2 vols. Edinburgh, 1869.

ORIGENIANA. By Peter Daniel Huet, Bishop of Avranches. 4 vols. 1733. Reprinted in Migne, Origenes, vol. vii (Patrologiae Graecae Tomus XVII) and in Lommatzsch, vols. xxii–xxiv.

ORIGENES. Eine Darstellung seines Lebens und seiner Lehre. By Ernst Rud. Redepenning. Bonn, 1841–46.

DE LA PHILOSOPHIE D'ORIGÈNE. By M. J. Denis. Paris, 1884.

ORIGÈNE, SA VIE, SON OEUVRE, SA PENSÈE. Vol. I. By Eugène de Faye. Paris, 1923.

ORIGEN AND HIS WORK. The English Translation of Lectures delivered at the University of Upsala in 1925. By the same. London, 1926.

THE CHRISTIAN PLATONISTS OF ALEXANDRIA. Being the Bampton Lectures for 1886. By Charles Bigg. Oxford, 1886. Reprinted, with some additions and corrections. ED. F. E. Brightman, 1913.

DICTIONARY OF CHRISTIAN BIOGRAPHY. Article 'Origenes'. By B. F. Westcott. One volume edition. London, 1911.

REALENCYKLOPÄDIE FUR PROTESTANTISCHE THEOLOGIE AND KIRCHE. Founded by J. J. Herzog. Enlarged edition by A. Hauck. Article 'Origenes'. By E. Preuschen. Leipsig, 1904.

PATROLOGIE. By Otto Bardenhewer. 3rd edition. Freiburg in Breisgau, 1910.

PATROLOGY. Translation of 2nd edition in English. By T. J. Strahan. Freiburg in B. and St. Louis, 1908.

GESCHICHTE DER ALTCHRISTLICHEN LITTERATUR BIS EUSEBIUS. By Adolf Harnack. 4 vols. Leipsig, 1893.

HISTORY OF DOGMA. By Adolf Harnack. Translated by Neil Buchanan and others. Vols. i–viii (for Origen see vol. ii). London, 1896–1899.

THE APOLOGY OF ORIGEN IN REPLY TO CELSUS. By John Patrick. Edinburgh and London, 1892.

RECHERCHES SUR L'HISTOIRE DU TEXTE ET DES VERSIONS LATINES DU DE PRINCIPIIS D'ORIGÉNE. By Gustave Bardy. Paris, 1923.

SIX LECTURES ON THE ANTE-NICENE FATHERS. By Fenton John Anthony Hort. London, 1895.

DES GREGORIOS THAUMATURGOS DANKREDE AN ORIGENES. Edited by Paul Koetschau. Freiburg in B. and Leipsig, 1894.

ORIGEN THE TEACHER. Being the Address of Gregory translated. By William Metcalfe. London, 1907.

PATRISTIC STUDY. In the series, ' Handbooks for the Clergy '. By Henry Barclay Swete. London, 1904.

LIVES OF THE FATHERS. By Frederick W. Farrar. 2 vols., Edinburgh, 1889.

THE ORIGINS OF CHRISTIANITY. By Charles Bigg, edited by T. B. Strong. Oxford, 1909.

EARLY CHURCH HISTORY TO A.D. 313. By Henry Melvill Gwatkin. 2 vols. London, 1909.

MARC AURÈLE ET LA FIN DU MONDE ANTIQUE. By Ernst Renan. Paris, 1899.

TEXTE UND UNTERSUCHUNGEN ZUR GESCHICHTE DER ALTCHRISTLICHEN LITTERATUR. Edited by Oscar von Gebhardt, Adolf Harnack and C. Schmidt. Leipsig, 1882, etc. See Indices for items dealing with Origen.

ABBREVIATIONS.

Lomm. ... The Edition of Lommatzsch.
B. .. The Berlin Edition, *Origenes Werke*, as in the foregoing list.
Br. ... Brooke's edition of the *Commentary on St. John*.
D.C.B. ... *Dictionary of Christian Biography*.
H.E. ... Eusebius' *Ecclesiastical History*.
§ ... The passages translated as numbered in this volume.

LIST OF PASSAGES TRANSLATED

I

THE BEING AND NATURE OF GOD

I.	God's absolute Existence	*In Lib. 1 Sam.* Hom. i. 11.	1
II.	God as Spirit, Light and Fire	*Comm. in Joann.* xiii. 21-3.	2
III.	Degrees of Deity	*Sel. in Psalmos.*	7
IV.	One God; gods many	*In Exod.*, Hom. viii. 2.	8
V.	God made good, not evil	*In Jerem.* Hom. ii. 1.	11
VI.	God's Foreknowledge	*Comm. in Ep. ad Rom.* vii. 7.	12
VII.	Pater non impassibilis	*In Ezech.* Hom. vi. 6.	15
VIII.	Divine Condescension	*Comm. in Matt.* xvii. 19-20.	16
IX.	God's Converse with Man	*In Jerem.* Hom. xviii. 6.	19
X.	Eternal Generation	*In Jerem.* Hom. ix. 4.	23
XI.	Eternal Generation	*In Ep. ad Heb.* Frag.	24

II

THE WORK AND OFFICE OF THE DIVINE WORD

XII.	'By Whom all things are made'	*Comm. in Joann.* ii. 10.	25
XIII.	The Creative Activity of the Word.	*Comm. in Joann.* Frag. i.	28
XIV.	The Bread and Wine	*Comm. Ser. in Matt.* 85.	31
XV.	The Word which came to the Prophets	*In Jerem.* Hom. ix. 1.	33
XVI.	Human Nature and the Word	*Comm. in Joann.* xxxii. 25.	36
XVII.	The Son of Man	*Sel. in Psalmos.*	38
XVIII.	The varied Work of the Saviour	*Comm. in Joann.* i. 20.	40
XIX.	The Lord's natural Body	*Frag. in Ep. ad Gal.*	41
XX.	The greatness of the Saviour	*In Luc.* Hom. vi.	45

III

THE HOLY SCRIPTURES. PRINCIPLES AND EXAMPLES OF EXEGESIS

XXI.	Many Interpreters.	*Sel. in Psalmos.*	47
XXII.	Scripture a whole..	*Comm. in Matt.* ii.	47
XXIII.	All Scripture has meaning	*In Jerem.* Hom. xxxix.	49

LIST OF PASSAGES TRANSLATED

XXIV.	Joshua, Jesus	*In Josuam.* Hom. ii. 1.	51
XXV.	Jesus interprets the Law	*In Josuam.* Hom. ix. 8.	53
XXVI.	The Law of Nature	*Comm. in Ep. ad Rom.* ii. 9.	55
XXVII.	The Universal Law	*Comm. in Ep. ad Rom.* iii. 6.	58
XXVIII.	Several kinds of Law	*Comm. in Ep. ad Rom.* vi. 12.	63
XXIX.	The inward Gospel	*Comm. in Joann.* i. 7–8.	64
XXX.	Some Commands not intended literally	*Comm. in Matt.* xv. 2.	67
XXXI.	Testimony of the Baptist	*In Joann.* Frag. xx.	69
XXXII.	Allegory in Paul	*In Exod.* Hom. v. 1.	72
XXXIII.	The Palace of Truth	*Comm. in Ep. ad Rom.* v. 1.	75
XXXIV.	Praise and Blame for Heracleon	*Comm. in Joann.* xiii. 10.	77
XXXV.	The Song of Songs.	*In Cant. Cantic.* i.	79
XXXVI.	Shadows	*In Cant. Cantic.* iii.	84
XXXVII.	The Song of the Well	*In Num.* Hom. xii. 1.	87

IV

THE HOLY SCRIPTURES. PROBLEMS AND CRITICISM

XXXVIII.	Scripture and Nature	*Sel. in Psalmos.*	94
XXXIX.	Eleven Psalms of Moses	*Sel. in Psalmos.*	96

XL.	The Order of the Psalms	... *Sel. in Psalmos.*	98
XLI.	The Songs of Ascents (Pss. cxx–cxxxiv).	*Sel. in Psalmos.*	99
XLII.	The Ages of the Soul	... *Sel. in Psalmos* Hom. iv. 3.	101
XLIII.	Four Gospels	... *In Luc.* Hom. 1.	104
XLIV.	Discrepancies	... *Comm. in Joann.* x. 3.	105
XLV.	An Addition to the Text	... *Comm. in Matt.* xv. 13–14.	107
XLVI.	Apocryphal Books	... *Comm. Ser. in Matt.* 28.	111
XLVII.	The Darkness at the Crucifixion	... *Comm. Ser. in Matt.* 134.	114
XLVIII.	God not tempted	... *In Luc.* Hom. 29.	119
XLIX.	The Epistle to the Romans	... *In Ep. ad Rom. Prefat.*	120
L.	The Epistle to the Hebrews	... *In Ep. ad Heb. Frag.*	124
LI.	The word 'Eternal'	*Comm. in Ep. ad Rom.* vi. 5.	125
LII.	Spirit, Soul, Body	... *Sel. in Psalmos.*	126

V

THE CHRISTIAN CHURCH

| LIII. | Order in the Church... | *In Num.* Hom. ii. 1. | 128 |
| LIV. | The Blessing of Peter. | *Comm. in Matt.* xii. 10–11. | 130 |

LV.	Fidelity and Wisdom...	*Comm. Ser. in Matt.* 61.	134
LVI.	Corban	... *Comm. in Matt.* xi. 9.	137
LVII.	Office not to be sought.	*In Isai.* Hom. vi. 1.	139
LVIII.	The Leader's responsibility	... *In Num.* Hom. xx. 4.	142
LIX.	The Standard of Faith.	*In Jerem.* Hom. iv. 2–3.	145
LX.	Tares and Wheat	... *In Josuam.* Hom. xxi. 1.	147
LXI.	Heretics	... *In Ep. ad Titum.*	149
LXII.	The false Faith of Heretics	... *Comm. in Ep. ad Rom.* x. 5.	153

VI

THE TEACHER AND HIS TASK

LXIII.	The Christian Scribe...	*Comm. in Matt.* x. 15.	156
LXIV.	Right Enquiry	... *Comm. in Ep. ad Rom.* vii. 17.	158
LXV.	Quiet for Work	... *Comm. in Joann.* vi. 1–2.	160
LXVI.	The Buyer of Truth	... *In Luc.* Hom. xxxviii.	164
LXVII.	Ingratitude the Prophet's Lot	... *In Jerem.* Hom. xiv. 1–5.	165
LXVIII.	The Disciples and the Multitude	... *Comm. in Matt.* xi. 4.	172

LIST OF PASSAGES TRANSLATED

LXIX.	Seductive Rhetoric	*In Ezech.* Hom. iii. 3.	174
LXX.	Stale Teaching	*In Levit.* Hom. v. 8.	177
LXXI.	Diversity of Spiritual Fare	*In Num.* Hom. xxvii. 1.	180
LXXII.	The Value of Faith	*Sel. in Psalmos* Hom. iii. 6.	184
LXXIII.	Truth welcome wherever found.	*In Exod.* Hom. xi. 6.	188
LXXIV.	Christianity and Philosophy	*In Gen.* Hom. xiv. 3.	190

VII

SPECULATIONS AND ENQUIRIES

LXXV.	The Nature of the Soul	*In Cant. Cantic.* Lib. ii.	194
LXXVI.	The Causes of Disaster	*Comm. Ser. in Matt.* 36.	197
LXXVII.	God the Source of Good	*Comm. Ser. in Matt.* 72.	199
LXXVIII.	The Fire that purifies	*In Exod.* Hom. vi. 4.	201
LXXIX.	Astrology	*Comm. in Gen.* iii. 9.	203
LXXX.	The causes of Lunacy	*Comm. in Matt.* xiii. 6.	206

LIST OF PASSAGES TRANSLATED   lvii

LXXXI.	Sin and Birth	... *In Levit.* Hom. viii. 3.	208
LXXXII.	Reincarnation	... *Comm. in Joann.* vi. 10–13.	212
LXXXIII.	Samuel at Endor ...	*In Lib. 1 Sam.* Hom. 4–5.	217
LXXXIV.	Hades or Paradise?	... *Comm. in Joann.* xxxii. 32.	220
LXXXV.	Spiritual Publicans	*In Luc.* Hom. xxiii.	223
LXXXVI.	The Second Advent	*Comm. Ser. in Matt.* 70.	226
LXXXVII.	The Resurrection...	*Frag. Sup. Isai.*	228
LXXXVIII.	The Resurrection...	*Sel. in Psalmos.*	230
LXXXIX.	Resurrection or Survival?	... *Comm. in Matt.* xvii. 29.	236
XC.	The Future State...	*Comm. in Ep. ad Rom.* v. 10.	238
XCI.	Diversity in Heaven	... *In Num.* Hom. xxviii. 2.	241
XCII.	No Family Relationships in Heaven	... *Comm. in Matt.* xvii. 33.	244

VIII

THE CHRISTIAN LIFE

XCIII.	Perfect Faith	.. *Comm. in Joann.* xxxii. 16.	249
XCIV.	Knowledge	... *Comm. in Ep. ad Rom.* viii. 1.	252

XCV.	Degrees of Sin	... *Comm. in Joann.* xix. 14.	255
XCVI.	Other Gods	... *In Lib. Jud.* Hom. ii. 3.	257
XCVII.	Illumination according to capacity	... *In Gen.* Hom. i. 7.	260
XCVIII.	Lazarus	... *Comm. in Joann.* xxviii. 7.	262
XCIX.	Fasting	... *In Levit.* Hom. x. 2.	265
C.	The Field within	... *Sel. in Psalmos.*	267

PART I

THE BEING AND NATURE OF GOD

I

Absolute being belongs to God alone.—(*In Lib. 1 Sam.*
Hom. i. 11; Lomm. xi. 310–11; B. viii. 20–21.
From the Latin.)

Thus many may be made holy, as also the commandment of God says, Be ye holy, for I also am holy.[1] But howsoever any one may advance in holiness, and whatever measure of purity and integrity he may gain, a man cannot be so holy as the Lord is, for the Lord is the giver of holiness, he the recipient; the Lord is the fount of holiness, he is the drinker at the holy fount; the Lord is the light of holiness, he is the beholder of the holy light. Therefore, There is none holy as the Lord and there is none beside Thee.[2]

I do not clearly understand what is the meaning of the words, There is none beside Thee. If it had said, There is no God beside Thee, or, There is no Creator beside Thee, or added any other like term, no enquiry would have seemed necessary. As it stands, with the words, There is none beside Thee, the implication of the passage seems to be that nothing that exists has existence by virtue of its own nature. It is Thou alone to whom existence is given by none. For we all, that is the whole creation, did not exist before we were created, and thus our existence is by the will of the Creator.

[1] Lev. xx. 26. [2] 1 Sam. ii. 2.

And since we once did not exist, if it be said of us that we are, the statement is not absolutely true, in so far as the period when we did not exist comes in question. It is God alone who always had existence and never received any beginning of being. For instance, when Moses desired to learn of God what was his name, God taught him and said, I am that I am and this is my Name.[1] Now if there were in all creation any other thing that could be designated by this name and this description, the Lord would never have said that this was His name. He knew that He alone was, and that all creatures had received existence from Himself. A shadow does not exist by comparison with a body; smoke does not exist by comparison with fire. Likewise the things that are in heaven and the things that are on earth, things visible and things invisible, in relation to the nature of God have no existence. In relation to the will of the Creator they are what He who made them willed that they should be. Therefore it is said, There is none beside Thee.[2]

II

God is a spirit. So also is God described as light and as fire. We must not interpret these terms in a literal sense. They have each a spiritual significance.—(Comm. in Joann. xiii. 21–3; Lomm. ii. 34–40; Br. i. 267–70; B. iv. 244–47. From the Greek.)

God is a spirit: and they that worship Him must worship in spirit and truth.[3] Many men have expressed

---

[1] Ex. iii. 14–15.
[2] For Origen's conception of God, compare the opening chapter of the *De Principiis*; Denis, *De la Philosophie d'Origène*, pp. 81–8
[3] John iv. 24.

many views about God and His being. Some have said that He is of a corporeal nature, rarified, and ethereal; some that His nature is incorporeal; others [1] that in precedence and power He is above being. So it is right we should consider whether we have grounds in the divine Scriptures for any statement in regard to the being of God. Now in this passage it is said that spirit is, so to say, His essence. God is a spirit, it says. In the law He is fire; for it is written, Our God is a consuming fire.[2] With John He is light; God, he says, is light, and in Him is no darkness at all.[3] Now if we are to take these passages in their simpler sense, never pushing our enquiry beyond the text, we must say at once that God is a body, though what strange consequences await us after this statement, is not for the many to comprehend. Few indeed, and specially few of those whom reason and providence have well equipped, have undertaken enquiries about the nature of bodies. However, as a general statement, they describe Providence as of the same essence as those for whom it provides, perfect, but such in nature as its objects. Those who will have it that God is a body admit the difficulties which confront their argument, being quite unable to contest its evident implications. In saying this, however, I exclude those who assert that there is a fifth nature among bodies, one distinct from the elements.[4]

Now if every material body has a nature which is, in

---

[1] Retaining with Br. the ἄλλους of the MSS.
[2] Deut. iv. 24; Heb. xii. 29.
[3] 1 John i. 5.
[4] The reference is to Aristotle's theory of a πέμπτον σῶμα, quinta essentia. Cp. Cicero, *Post. Acad.* I. vii. 26; Eus. *Præp. Ev.* xv. 7. Origen rejects this theory. *De Prin.* III. vi. 6. Cp. *C. Cels.* iv. 60.

its proper character, something devoid of qualities, yet a nature alterable and variable and throughout capable of change and receptive of any qualities with which the Creator may wish to endow it,[1] necessarily it follows that God, if He be material, is alterable and variable and capable of change. Those I have in mind feel no shame in saying that God, being a body, [2] is even destructible; but He is a body spiritual and ethereal, they say, more especially so in His ruling element. And though destructible, God is not, they hold, destroyed, since there is no one to destroy Him. But we, by reason of our failure to see the consequences, if we say God is a body and, on scriptural grounds, a body of a certain kind, spirit or breath,[3] consuming fire, light, on our refusal to admit the necessary consequences of this, shall appear foolish and awkward, as men who dispute what is quite evident. For all fire, needing to be fed, is destructible and all breath or spirit, if we take the term in its simpler sense,[4] being a body, is of its own nature capable of change to greater density. Thus in these matters we must either keep to the letter and admit these incongruous and blasphemous inferences about God; or else look around, as we do in many other cases, and consider what may be the intended meaning of calling God spirit or fire or light.

And first let me observe that just as, when we find mention made in Scripture of eyes, eyelids, ears, hands, arms, feet and even of wings of God, we give the terms an allegorical meaning, censuring those who assign to

---

[1] The distinction drawn is similar to, yet not quite identical with, that between 'substance' and 'accidents'.

[2] He is thinking of the Stoics. Cp. Clem. Alex. *Strom*, I. xi. 51.

[3] $\pi\nu\epsilon\hat{v}\mu a$. It is unfortunate that we have no one term that covers all the meanings of this word.

[4] i.e. as meaning air or wind. Cp. John iii. 8.

God a form like the form of men, and doing so with good reason; similarly we must take in regard to the terms I have named a corresponding course. This indeed is clear from what we recognize as common usage. For according to John, God is light and in Him is no darkness [1] at all. Let us then consider with truer insight, to the best of our ability, in what sense we are to conceive of God as light. For the term light is used in two senses, in a bodily sense and in a spiritual. The latter is the intelligible light, invisible, as the Scripture would say; incorporeal, as the Greeks would term it. There is an instance of the bodily light, admitted by all who accept the narrative, in the words, All the children of Israel had light in all their dwellings.[2] Of the intelligible and spiritual light an example occurs in one of the Twelve Prophets; Sow to yourselves in righteousness, reap unto the fruit of life, illuminate yourselves with the light of knowledge.[3] Correspondingly, in the same manner, the term darkness will have two senses. Of the ordinary use of the term an instance is, God called the light day and the darkness He called night.[4] Of the intelligible sense, The people which sat in darkness and in the shadow of death, to them did light spring up.[5]

On this principle it is right to see what conception it befits us to hold of God, who is called light, in whom is no darkness at all.[6] Is God light because He enlightens our bodily eyes, or our spiritual eyes, concerning which the prophet also says, Lighten mine eyes that I sleep not in death?[7] It is, I think, clear to every one that we should never say that God does the work of the sun

---

[1] 1 John i. 5.
[2] Ex. x. 23.
[3] Hos. x. 12. From the LXX.
[4] Gen. i. 5.
[5] Matt. iv. 16; Isa. ix. 2.
[6] 1 John i. 5.
[7] Ps. xiii. 3.

while He allows some other to enlighten the eyes of those who shall not sleep unto death. God therefore does enlighten the mind of those whom He judges worthy of His special enlightenment. If He is illuminating Mind, according to the saying, The Lord is my light,[1] necessarily being intelligible and invisible and incorporeal it is of this, that is of mind, that we must suppose Him to be the light.[2] Further I ask whether He be not consuming fire in the same sense. For physical fire too has consuming power, consuming for example wood and hay and stubble.[3] But if it consumes wood, hay, stubble, then it is on such things as wood, hay, stubble that it exercises consuming power. Whereas if wood and hay and stubble have an allegorical sense, then it is surely of material so understood that our God is the consuming fire, when we find Him so described.[4]

And right it is that the Lord should consume such things and abolish what is bad. In this process there result, I suppose, pangs and pains, though not from any physical attack, in our inmost personality, where the structure that deserves to be consumed was put together.

God then is named light by a transference of the term from physical light to the light invisible and incorporeal. He has the name by reason of His power to enlighten our spiritual eyes. He is too described as consuming fire, the term being understood from the physical fire which consumes physical material. Such seems to me to be the truth in regard to, God is a spirit.[5] For since we derive our life, this mediocre thing we commonly mean by the term, from the breath or spirit, as the

---

[1] Ps. xxvii. 1.   [2] The text here is uncertain.
[3] 1 Cor. iii. 12.   [4] Heb. xii. 29.
[5] John iv. 24.

spirit or air about us breathes what we call in a bodily sense the breath of life;[1] from that fact, I suppose, we have derived the use of the term spirit for God, who leads us into the real life. For the spirit is said in Scripture to give life,[2] and plainly it means the giving not of this middle life but of the more divine. For the letter kills and causes death, not the separation of the soul from the body, but the separation of the soul from God and from His Lord and from the Holy Spirit.

III

There are Degrees of Deity.—(Selecta in Psalmos ; Lomm. xiii. 134. From the Greek.)

Give thanks unto the God of gods, for His mercy endureth for ever.[3] This term (ἐξομολόγησις) signifies the giving of thanks and ascription of praise. It is also used for the confession of sins, as here.[4]

From the same writer. He is the God of those gods unto whom the word of the Lord came, according to the Scripture which says, I said ye are gods;[5] also, I am the God of Abraham, and the God of Isaac, and the God of Jacob[6]—clearly because of His great love and affinity for them. Of the demons He is God by reason of His creative power. The Apostle also says, If there be gods many and lords many in heaven or on earth.[7] But those who in addition to the Trinity are termed gods are so by

---

[1] Gen. ii. 7.   [2] 2 Cor. iii. 6.   [3] Ps. cxxxvi. 2.
[4] Probably R.V. rendering 'give thanks' as above is the truer meaning.
[5] Ps. lxxxii. 6.
[6] Ex. iii. 6.
[7] 1 Cor. viii. 5. The existence of these other and lesser gods is admitted even in *C. Celsum.* See viii. 1-5; also the next section.

participation in the godhead. But the Saviour is not God by participation but in virtue of His own being. The words, For His mercy endureth for ever, are a sort of concluding refrain of praise. Since He is ever merciful, those who praise Him say naturally, Endureth for ever, and so on.

IV

For us there is one God. Yet there exist also gods many and lords many, as both the Old and New Testaments declare.—(In Exod. Hom. viii. 2 ; Lomm. ix. 91–4; B. vi. 219–21. From the Latin.)

Let us begin then with the first commandment. Yet do I need the help of the God who gave the commandments for speaking, and you require purified ears for hearing. Whoever then among you has ears to hear, let him hear how it is said, Thou shalt not have other gods beside me.[1] If he had said, There are not other gods beside me, the saying would appear more universal. But as it says, Thou shalt not have other gods beside me, their existence is not denied, but the man to whom these commandments are given is forbidden to make them his gods. This, I suppose, is the source from which the Apostle Paul derived what he wrote to the Corinthians, saying, Though there be that are called gods, whether in heaven or on earth. Also he adds, And as there are gods many and lords many, yet to us there is one God, the Father, of whom are all things and we unto him ; and one Lord, Jesus Christ, through whom are all things and we through him.[2] And in many other passages of Scripture you will find the name 'gods' is used, as it

---

[1] Exod. xx. 3.   [2] 1 Cor. viii. 5.

says in another place, The Lord Most High is terrible and He is a great king over all gods;[1] also, The Lord, the God of gods, hath spoken;[2] also, He judgeth among the gods.[3] Of lords the same Apostle says, Whether they be thrones or dominions or powers, all things are through Him and in Him were all things created.[4] Now lordships or dominions mean nothing but a certain rank and number of lords. In this point, as I think, the Apostle Paul has made the meaning of the law more clear. What he says is something of this kind ; Though there be many lords which have lordship over other nations, and many gods which are worshipped by others, yet for us there is one God and one Lord.

As to the reason for there being gods many and lords many, Scripture itself, if you listen with attention and patience, will be able to instruct us. This very Moses says in the psalm in Deuteronomy, When the Most High—these are his words—divided the nations and separated the sons of Adam, He set the bounds of the peoples according to the number of the angels of God. And His people Jacob became the Lord's portion, Israel was the lot of His inheritance.[5] Thus it is clear that the angels, to whom the Most High entrusted the government of the nations, are called gods and lords—gods as appointed by God, lords as obtaining authority from the Lord. Thus also the Lord said to the angels who did not preserve their high estate, I said, Ye are gods, and all the sons of the Most High. Nevertheless ye shall

---

[1] Ps. xlvii. 2. Where ' over all the earth ' is the reading. Probably Origen quoted from memory and had Ps. xcv. 3, in mind.
[2] Ps. l. 1. See lxx and R.V. margin.
[3] Ps. lxxxii. 1.
[4] Col. i. 16.
[5] Deut. xxxii. 8, 9.' Angels of God ' is from LXX. See Driver *in loc.* and Cheyne, *Job and Solomon*, p. 81.

die like men and fall like one of the princes;[1] following no doubt the example of the devil, who came to perdition first of all. This makes it evident that transgression, not nature,[2] brought the curse upon them. Therefore, O my people Israel, who art a portion of God, who hast become the lot of His inheritance, shalt thou not have, he says, other gods besides me, because one God is truly God, and one Lord is truly Lord. But to the others, who are created by Him, it is not nature but favour that gives the name.

But do not think that these things are said only to the Israel which is after the flesh. Far more are these things said to thee, who art made Israel by the inward vision of God, and art circumcised in the heart not in the flesh. For though we be Gentiles in the flesh, yet in spirit we are Israel, by reason of Him who said, Ask of me and I will give thee the nations for thine inheritance and the uttermost parts of the earth for thy possession;[3] and by reason of Him who said again, Father, all things that are mine are thine and thine are mine, and I am glorified in them.[4] Provided, that is, thou so livest as to deserve to be a portion of God and to be measured in the lot of His inheritance. Otherwise, if thy life is unworthy, let them be a warning to thee who had been called to be God's portion and through their sins deserved only to be scattered among all the nations. They who once were led out of the house of bondage now again, since whosoever committeth sin is the servant of sin, serve not the Egyptians only but all the nations. Therefore to thee also who through Jesus Christ art come out of Egypt and hast been led forth from the house of bondage, it is said, Thou shalt have none other gods but me.

---

[1] Ps. lxxxii. 6-7.
[2] As the Gnostics maintained.
[3] Ps. ii. 8.
[4] John xvii. 10.

V

God made all things good. Sin and wickedness are of our making.—(*In Jerem.* Hom. ii. 1; Lomm. xv. 128–30; B. iii. 16–17. From the Greek.)

On the passage, How art thou, a degenerate vine, turned unto bitterness? *So far as* Though thou wash thee with soda and take thee much soap, yet art thou stained in thine iniquity before me, saith the Lord.[1] God made not death; neither delighteth He when the living perish. For he created all things that they might have being, and the generative powers of the world are healthsome, and there is no poison of destruction in them, nor hath Hades royal dominion upon earth.[2] Then, passing a little further on, I will say, Whence then came death? By the envy of the devil death entered into the world.[3] Thus whatever excellence we possess, God was its maker; wickedness and sin we formed for ourselves. On this account too, in these verses, the opening of the passage of the prophet which was read addresses in a tone of surprise those who have bitterness in their soul, the opposite of the sweetness God formed in it. How art thou, a degenerate vine, turned unto bitterness? It is as if he said, God did not make lameness but made all men sound of limb. What is the cause that has arisen for the lame being lame? And God made of clear purpose all our members sound; what has been the cause of their infirmities? In like manner the soul, not of the first man only but of every man, was made in God's image. For the words, Let us make man in our image, after our likeness,[4] extend to all men. And this, like God's image in Adam, as the many understand it, is prior

---

[1] Jer. ii. 21–2.
[2] Wisdom i. 13–14.
[3] *Ibid.*, ii. 24.
[4] Gen. i. 26.

to what he afterwards assumed when, because of sin, he bore the image of the earthly. So in all cases is God's image prior to the image of the worse. Being sinners we once bore the image of the earthly: let us repent and bear the image of the heavenly. Nay, creation was made after the image of the heavenly.

Therefore here does the Word express surprise at those who sin, and says, with reproof, How art thou, a degenerate vine, turned unto bitterness? For I planted thee a fruitful vine, all sound. It has been already said, and reverting a moment I will convince you, that God planted the soul of man as a fair vine, but each has turned and become the opposite of his Maker's will. I planted thee a fruitful vine, altogether—not partially—sound. Nor was one sound and another false, but I planted thee a fruitful vine, all sound. How art thou turned, after I made thee a vine wholly sound? How art thou turned unto bitterness and become a degenerate vine?[1]

VI

God foreknows and foreordains the good but not the evil. The soul of Jesus is that image of His Son to which we are to be conformed.—(Comm. in Ep. ad Rom. vii. 7; Lomm. vii. 122-25. From the Latin).

We must not follow the general opinion of the crowd and suppose that God foreknows both the good and the evil, but our views must be formed in accordance with the usage of holy Scripture. For let the careful student

---

[1] This passage is one of many in which Origen refers to the nature and origin of evil. His general position is that God did not make evil. It comes through the wrong use of freedom. Even the devil fell by his own will. God permits evil, using it for good. The extent of it varies. It is 'the rubbish round the building.' Whether it will finally cease, he hesitates to say. There is a good deal on the subject in the *C. Celsum*.

of Scripture take note whether he has found Scripture in any passage assert that God foreknows the wicked, as in the present passage it does plainly declare with regard to the good that, Whom He foreknew He also foreordained to be conformed to the image of His Son [1] For if those whom He foreknew He also foreordained to be conformed to the image of his Son, whereas no wicked man can be conformed to the image of the Son of God ; it is evident that the writer is speaking only of the good. He foreknew those whom He also foreordained to be conformed to the image of His Son, but the rest God is not said merely not to foreknow but not even to know. For God, Knoweth them that are His,[2] but to those who do not deserve to be known by God the Saviour says, Depart from me for I never knew you, ye that work iniquity.[3] Similarly then in the present passage also, Whom God foreknew, them He foreordained to be conformed to the image of His Son. But the rest are not said to be foreknown, not because anything can evade the notice of that nature which everywhere is and is nowhere absent, but because all that is evil is accounted unworthy of His knowledge or foreknowledge. Whom He foreknew He also foreordained. Consider also this point ; Can God be said to foreknow or to foreordain in regard to those who are not yet in existence ; or in regard to those who exist indeed but are not yet conformed to the image of His Son ? Is not foreknowledge more appropriate in the former case than in regard to that which shall be that which as yet it is not ?[4] For this is more a matter of the will than of the foreknowledge of the Creator. Where will foreknowledge display itself

---

[1] Rom. viii. 29.
[2] 2 Tim. ii. 19 ; cp. Num. xvi. 5
[3] Matt. vii. 23.
[4] The text has been suspected.

when that which is to be depends upon the will of the doer?[1]

Attentive readers will perhaps also notice that the question may be raised, Why did it not say, Conformed to His Son, but, Conformed to the image of His Son? Whoever raises this question will point out that, just as the Son Himself, who is called The image of the invisible God,[2] is distinct in regard to His person from Him of whom He is the image; so here too what is termed the image of His Son must be something distinct from that of which it is the image. Hard and difficult as this subject seems, still consider if we may not say this; Though every man who has developed his nature towards that standard which, as we laid down above, is an image of God, that is an image of the Son of God, still it is the very soul of Jesus that must be called peculiarly and distinctively His image, for this fully and entirely received Him and fashioned Him inwardly; this soul so in all things united itself with the Word and Wisdom of God, that in no single point could it be regarded as in contrast with His likeness.[3] Thus whoever makes for the height of perfection and blessedness is in progress towards the image and likeness of that soul which, primarily and before all others, is the image of the Son of God, so that He is himself The firstborn among many brethren,[4] I mean among those whose chief He is in the fashioning of the image of the Son of God.

---

[1] Elsewhere however he speaks of the divine foreknowledge as quite compatible with human freedom. Cp. *In Ep. ad Rom.* i. 3; Lomm. vi. 17; also § ix.

[2] Col. i. 15.

[3] Cp. § xvi, *infra*. The meaning of the present passage is, that just as the Son or Word is the image of God, so is the human Soul of Jesus the image of the Son or Word.

[4] Rom. viii. 29.

VII

IPSE PATER NON EST IMPASSIBILIS

(*In Ezech.* Hom. vi. 6; Lomm. xiv. 87-8; B. viii. 384-85. From the Latin.)

None eye pitied thee, to do any of these things unto thee.[1] Therefore, saith the Lord, have I done none of these things unto thee, that I should be affected on thy behalf.[2] I will take a parallel from men; then, if the Holy Spirit grants it, I will pass on to Jesus Christ and to God the Father. When I speak to a man and entreat him on some account to have pity on me, if he is a man without pity, he is quite unaffected by the things I say. But if he is a man of gentle spirit, and no callousness of heart has grown hard within him, he hears me and has pity upon me; his feelings are softened at my prayer. Something of the kind I pray you imagine with regard to the Saviour. He came down to earth in pity for the race of men. By our affections He was affected, before He was affected by the sufferings of the cross and condescended to take our flesh upon him. Had He not been affected, He would not have entered into association with the life of men. First He is affected; then He comes down and is seen. What is that affection whereby on our account He is affected? It is the affection of love. The Father Himself, too, the God of the Universe, long suffering, and of great compassion, full of pity, is not He in a manner liable to affection? Are you unaware that, when He

---

[1] Ezek. xvi. 5. There are slight differences in the text. R.V is here printed.

[2] The Latin is, '*Ut paterer aliquid super te*': The LXX is 'τοῦ παθεῖν τι ἐπί σοι. I have used 'affect', 'affection' in this translation. It is probably better than 'passion'. But we have no real English equivalent for πάθος and its cognates.

orders the affairs of men, He is subject to the affections of humanity ? The Lord thy God bare with thy ways, as if a man should bear with his own son.[1] God then bears with our ways, just as the Son of God bears with our affections. The very Father is not impassible, without affection. If we pray to him, He feels pity and sympathy. He experiences an affection of love. He concerns himself with things in which, by the majesty of His nature, He can have no concern, and for our sakes He bears the affections of men.[2]

VIII

It is only by coming within human limitations that God influences human affairs. He deals with us not on the level of His own true being but on that of our state and capacity. In this sense should we understand the phrase ' Son of Man '.—(Comm. in Matt. xvii. 19–20 ; Lomm. iv. 126–29. From the Greek.)

Inasmuch then as we are men, and it is not for our good to behold the riches of the goodness of God[3] and the great abundance of His goodness, concealed by Him lest we should suffer hurt, of necessity the kingdom of Heaven was likened unto a man that was a king,[4] that God might speak as a man to men and regulate the affairs of men—whose affairs could not be so regulated if God remained God absolutely—both by speaking through the

---

[1] Deut. i. 31.
[2] Compare with this passage *De Prin.* II. iv. 4 ; *In Num.* Hom. xxiii. 2 ; *In Joann*, Frag li ; Lomm. x. 276; Br. ii. 266 ; B. iv. 525-26 ; vii. 211-12. As a rule his position is that no ' $\pi\acute{a}\theta os$ ' must be attributed to the divine nature. But his expressions are difficult to reconcile.
[3] Rom. ii. 4.
[4] Matt. xxii. 2. $\mathring{a}\nu\theta\rho\acute{\omega}\pi\varphi\ \beta\alpha\sigma\iota\lambda\epsilon\hat{\iota}$.

prophets and by otherwise regulating men's affairs. The kingdom of Heaven will cease to be likened unto a man when there is an end of jealousy, of strife,[1] and of other passions and of sins, an end of walking after the manner of men, and we become fit to hear from God the words, I said ye are gods and all of you sons of the Most High,[2] or of His Christ, and no longer commit deeds for which it might be said, Ye shall die like men.

Also I believe that not only will the likening of the kingdom of Heaven to a man that is a king cease, but also a thousand other things, which for sinful men are necessary. As, for example, it is written in Hosea, I am unto Ephraim as a panther, and as a lion to the house of Judah.[3] And in another place, I will meet them as a she-bear that is bereaved. God will cease to act as a panther, or a lion, or a bear bereaved,[4] when He shows Himself as He is. Those whose conduct was evil will cease to need Him as panther, lion or bear, and He will thus no longer have any who need Him in such capacities. In that sense I also understand the saying, Our God is a consuming fire.[5] So long as there are things which deserve to be consumed, so long is our God the fire that consumes them. When everything that should by nature be thereby consumed has been consumed by the consuming fire, then our God will be no longer a consuming fire but only light, as John said in the words, God is light.[6] And as these points have been raised, consider if you can interpret in the same fashion the passage in the General Epistle of John. It runs thus: Beloved, now are we children of God, and it is not yet made manifest what we shall be. We know that if He shall be manifested, we

---

[1] 1 Cor. iii. 3.
[2] Ps. lxxxii. 6–7.
[3] Hos. v. 14 ; LXX.
[4] Hos. xiii. 8.
[5] Deut. iv. 24 ; Heb. xii. 29.
[6] 1 John i. 5.

shall be like Him, for we shall see Him even as He is.[1] For now, even if we are accounted worthy to see God with mind and heart, still we do not see Him as He is, but as He comes to us for our advantage. But at the end of the world, at the final restoration of all that He hath spoken by the mouth of His holy prophets since the world began,[2] we shall behold Him, not as now for what He is not, but, as then will be right, for what He is.

These observations once made on the text, The kingdom of heaven is likened unto a man that is a king, we can also discover the reason for the Saviour constantly naming Himself Son of man, or Son of a man. Just as God, regulating the affairs of men, is termed in parable man, and perhaps in a sense becomes man, so evidently the Saviour in His true character is Son of God, and God, and Son of His Love, and Image of the invisible God.[3] But He does not remain in His true character. He becomes Son of man, through the dispensation of Him who is termed man in parables but is really God. So, in dealing with the affairs of men, does He imitate God, who is called in parables, and in a sense becomes, man. One must not look for some particular man and say that the Saviour is this man's son, but taking one's stand upon the conception of God, and upon the parables which say that He is man, give intelligent interpretation to the statement that He is Son of man.[4] Amongst us then, who are men, The kingdom of heaven is likened unto a

---

[1] 1 John iii. 2.
[2] Luke i. 70 ; Acts iii. 21. Final restoration is a favourite idea with Origen. Cp. *De. Prin.* II. iii. 5. *In restitutione omnium, cum ad perfectum finem universa pervenient* ; also his frequent use of ἀποκαθιστάνειν. ἀποκατάστασις.
[3] Col. i. 13–15.
[4] Cp. § xvii.

man that is a king.¹ But amongst those who in Scripture are called gods—God standeth in their congregation, He judgeth among the gods²—the kingdom of heaven is like unto God the King.³

IX

In His converse with men, God assumes human characteristics which are not properly His own.—(*In Jerem.* Hom. xviii. 6; Lomm. xv. 325-29; B. iii. 157-60. From the Greek.)

How then the Scripture came to introduce God as saying, I will repent,⁴ for the moment I do not explain. There is also the passage in the Kings, It repenteth me that I anointed Saul to be king.⁵ It is said too of God in general that He repents of evil.⁶

Consider however what in general principles we are taught about God. In one passage, God is not as man, that He should be deceived, nor as a son of man that He should be threatened.⁷ By this statement we learn that God is not as man, yet by another that God is as man, where it says, the Lord thy God correcteth thee as a man might correct his son.⁸ Also again, He bare with thy

---

¹ Matt. xxii. 2.
² Ps. lxxxii. 1.
³ It is characteristic of Origen to base this long discussion upon a word ($\mathring{a}\nu\theta\rho\omega\pi os$) which in the passage expounded is quite without emphasis. Also it is characteristic of the Alexandrine fathers generally to regard God theoretically as far removed from human life and yet to teach His close relation in practice with all the affairs of men. Correspondingly they believe that man can even rise to be divine. Cp. my *Clement of Alexandria* i, 335 *sqq.*; ii. 91 *sqq.*
⁴ Jer. xviii. 7-8.
⁵ 1 Sam. xv. 11.
⁶ *e.g.* Joel ii. 13.
⁷ Num. xxiii. 19; LXX.
⁸ Prov. iii. 12.

ways, as a man with his son.[1] Thus when the Scriptures refer to God as God, and do not regard His administration of human affairs as involved, they say that He is not as man. Of his greatness there is no end.[2] And, He is to be feared above all gods.[3] Also, Praise ye Him, all ye angels of God; praise ye Him, all His powers; praise ye Him, sun and moon; praise ye Him, all ye stars and light.[4] Picking them out, you might discover a thousand other passages from the holy Scriptures, with which to class the saying, God is not as man. But when the divine activity is concerned with the affairs of men, then it takes on the mind of a man, his character, his ways of speech. In like manner, if we are talking to a child of two years old, we use baby language for the child's sake. For it is impossible, if we preserve the style appropriate to the age of a full grown man and speak to children without any condescension to their ways of talking, for children to understand. Conceive, I pray you, something of this sort in regard to God in His dealings with the race of men and especially with men who still are children. Observe how we full grown men do change our terms in addressing babes. Bread we describe to them by some special term. Drinking we call by another name. We do not employ the language of the grown up, as we do to our full grown contemporaries, but a style that is childish and babylike. If we speak to children of their clothes, we give them other names, devising as it were some childish term. Are we then at such times not grown up? If any one hears us talking to children, will he say, This old fellow has grown silly? This man has forgotten his beard, man's badge of maturity? Or is it allowed that, in talking to a child, out of accommodation,

[1] Deut. i. 31.
[2] Ps. cxlv. 3.
[3] *Ibid.*, xcvi. 4.
[4] *Ibid.*, cxlviii. 2-3.

one does not speak in grown up and finished language but in that of children?

God also speaks to children. The Saviour too says, Behold, I and the children whom God hath given me.[1] To an old man who speaks to a child like a child, or, to put it more plainly, like a baby, it might be said, You bare with the ways of your son; you took upon you the way of a babe and adopted his condition. In this sense I wish you to regard Scripture as saying, The Lord thy God did bear with thy ways, as a man will bear with his own son.[2] It appears that they who made the translation fom the Hebrew text, not finding the equivalent term in use with the Greeks, here, as in so many other cases, invented and fashioned the term, τροποφορεῖν, that is, The Lord thy God bare with thy ways, as a man might bear—as in the example I have just given you—with his own son. As then we repent, when God speaks to us in our repentance He says, I repent. And when He threatens us, He makes no display of foreknowledge, but threatens as if He were addressing babes. He does not display His foreknowledge of all things before their occurrence,[3] but, if I may use the term, He acts the part of a babe and pretends not to know the future. At any rate He threatens a nation because of its sins and says, If the nation repent, I too will repent.[4] Didst thou not then, O God, at the time of threatening know whether the nation would repent or would not repent? When Thou didst make promises, didst Thou not, I ask, know whether the man or the nation addressed would remain or would not remain worthy of Thy promises? God makes no claim to know.[5]

---

[1] Isa. viii. 18. [2] Deut. i. 31.
[3] Cp. Sus. 42-3. [4] Jer. xviii. 8.
[5] Or with a different reading, Nay, God but acts the part.

You may find many such human traits in Scripture, as in the passage, Speak unto the children of Israel; it may be that they will hearken and will repent.[1] It is not really in doubt that God says, It may be they will hearken. For God does not doubt so as to say, It may be they will hearken and will repent. But He wishes to make your freedom abundantly clear, and to leave you no right to say, If He foreknew my loss, I must be lost. If He foreknew my salvation I shall certainly be saved. He assumes then no foreknowledge of the future in store for you, so as to preserve your freedom of choice by not anticipating and not foreknowing whether you will repent or not. And to the prophet He says, Speak; it may be thy will repent.[2] You will find a thousand other such statements about God bearing with the ways of men. If you hear of God's anger and of His wrath, do not think that wrath and anger are experienced by God. These are adaptations of the use of language for the correction and improvement of a babe. We too make ugly faces at children, not by reason of our true feelings, but for a purpose. If we preserve upon our countenance the kindly feeling of our soul towards the child, and give expression to the affection we have for it, not distorting ourselves, nor making any change for the child's correction, we ruin it and make it worse. So God is said to feel wrath and declares that He is angry, for your conversion and improvement. As a matter of fact, He feels no wrath and no anger. You however will undergo the consequences of wrath and anger, finding yourself in trouble hard to bear because of wickedness, when you are corrected by what we call the wrath of God.

---

[1] Jer. xxvi. 3.   [2] *Ibid.*

X

Eternal generation. As light ever sheds its radiance, so does the Father continually beget the Son. We too in our measure may have such abiding relationship with God.—(In Jerem. Hom. ix. 4; Lomm. xv. 211–12; B. iii. 70. From the Greek.)

They are turned back to the iniquities of their forefathers,[1] I was saying that the devil was also formerly our father, before God became our father; if indeed the devil be not even now our father, as we will prove possible from the General Epistle of John, in which it is written, Every one that doeth sin is born of the devil.[2] If every one that doeth sin is born of the devil, then as often as we sin, we are as it were born of the devil. Unhappy then is that man who is continuously begotten of the devil; as on the other hand blessed is he who is continuously begotten of God. For I will not say that the righteous man is begotten of God once for all, but that he is continually begotten in every good action, wherein God begets the righteous man. If then I shall make clear to you that in the case of the Saviour the Father did not once beget the Son, and then His Father released Him from this relationship, but that He continually begets Him; I shall also prove the like in the case of the righteous man. Let us see then, What is our Saviour? He is the brightness of His glory.[3] It is not that the brightness of His glory was once for all generated and is now generated no more, but so long as light produces brightness, so long is the brightness of God's glory generated. Our Saviour is the Wisdom of God. Wisdom is the brightness of light everlasting. If then the Saviour is continually being generated, that is the

[1] Jer. xi. 10. [2] 1 John iii. 8. [3] Heb. i. 3.

reason for His saying, Before all the hills He begets me.[1] It is not, Before all the hills He has begotten me, but, Before all the hills He begets me, and the Saviour is continually begotten of the Father. Likewise, if you too have the spirit of sonship, God continually begets you in Him, in every deed, in every thought, and so begotten you come to be a continually begotten son of God in Christ Jesus. To whom is the glory and the majesty for evermore. Amen.

XI

Eternal generation. The relationship between the Father and the Son is an abiding relationship, similar to that which exists between the light and its radiance.— (In *Epist. ad Hebraeos* Fragmentum, Pamphili *Apologia.* iii. Lomm. v. 297; xxiv. 328. From the Latin.)

What else can we regard as the Light Eternal but God the Father? He, inasmuch as He is the Light, never existed without His associated radiance. For a light without its radiance could never be conceived.[2] And if this is true, there never was a time when the Son did not exist. He was not however, as we do say of the Light Eternal, ingenerate; we must not appear to bring in two principles of light. Rather, as the radiance of the Light ingenerate, having that real Light as origin and source, He was born of that Light. But there was not a time when He did not exist.[3]

---

[1] Prov. viii. 25.

[2] Cp. *Eterna ac sempiterna generatio, sicut splendor generatur ex luce.* De Princip. I. ii. 4. The whole chapter is important. See Huet. II. ii. 24.

[3] Bigg, *Platonists*, 167, points out that this famous phrase is really Origen's, not an addition of Rufinus. Its quotation by Pamphilus guarantees this; see too Athanasius, *De Decr. Syn. Nic.* 27.

PART II

THE WORK AND OFFICE OF THE DIVINE WORD

XII

The Son is the instrumental cause in all creation. Even the Holy Spirit exists through Him.—(Comm. in Joann, ii. 10 ; Lomm. i. 108–10 ; Br. i. 69–71 ; B. iv. 64–5. From the Greek.)

All things were made through Him.[1] The instrumental cause never holds the first position but always the second. For example, in the Epistle to the Romans, 'Paul,' it says, 'a servant of Jesus Christ, called to be an apostle, separated unto the gospel of God, which He promised afore through His prophets in the Holy Scriptures concerning His Son, who was born of the seed of David according to the flesh, who was declared to be the Son of God with power, according to the Spirit of holiness, by the resurrection of the dead; even Jesus Christ our Lord, through whom we received grace and apostleship, unto obedience of faith among all the nations for His name's sake.'[2] For God beforehand promised His gospel through the prophets, the prophets acting as ministers and filling the place of the instrumental cause. And again God gave grace and apostleship unto obedience of faith among all the nations to Paul and the others, and He gave this through Christ Jesus the Saviour, through

[1] John i. 3.   [2] Rom. i. 1–5.

His instrumentality. Also in the Epistle to the Hebrews the same Paul says, At the end of the days He hath spoken unto us in His Son, whom He appointed heir of all things, through whom also He made the worlds,[1] teaching us that God has made the worlds through His Son, since in the making of the worlds the only begotten Son was the instrument. Thus in the present passage also, if all things were made through the Word, they were not made by the Word, but by a superior and greater power other than the Word. Who else can this be but the Father?

And as it is true that, All things were made through Him,[2] we must examine whether even the Holy Spirit was made through Him.[3] For I suppose that any one who holds that the Spirit was made and who allows the statement, All things were made through Him, will find it necessary to admit that the Holy Spirit was made through the Word, the Word itself being anterior to the Spirit. But any one who is unwilling to allow that the Holy Spirit was made through Christ, must consequently call the Spirit unbegotten, if he holds to the truth of the statement in this gospel. Besides these two disputants, of whom one allows that the Holy Spirit was made

---

[1] Heb. i. 2. Note the acceptance of the Pauline authorship of this epistle. See *infra* § 1.

[2] John i. 3.

[3] Other important passages on the Holy Spirit are *De Princip.* I. iii and II. vii. In the former Origen remarks that he can nowhere find the Spirit described in Scripture as 'a creature'. The doctrine of the Third Person was of course still somewhat undefined. Cp. Swete, *On the Early History of the Doctrine of the Holy Spirit*, pp. 21-4. *The Holy Spirit in the Ancient Church*, pp. 127-34; also Denis, pp. 117-25. '*Sans doute, la doctrine du Saint-Esprit, soit que l'on considère la nature de cette troisième hypostase, soit que l'on considère ses rapports avec les deux autres, est encore fort incomplète et fort vacillante, quoique beaucoup plus explicite que dans les prédécesseurs d'Origène.*' Cp. too S. Basil, *De Spiritu Sancto*, 73.

through the Word, and the other regards the Spirit as unbegotten, there will be also a third who will maintain that there does not exist any separate entity of the Holy Spirit at all, apart from the Father and the Son, or who perhaps will rather be inclined, if he regards the Son as distinct from the Father, to identify the Spirit with the Father. That there is a distinction of the Spirit from the Son is admittedly made clear in the passage, Whosoever shall speak a word against the Son of man, it shall be forgiven him; but whosoever shall blaspheme against the Holy Spirit shall not have forgiveness, neither in this world, nor in the world to come.[1] We however, who are convinced that there are three persons, the Father and the Son and the Holy Spirit, and who believe that nothing is unbegotten except the Father, accept as more reverent and as true the view that the Holy Spirit is the most honourable of all the things that were made through the Word and first in rank of all that have been made by the Father through Christ. And perhaps this is the reason why the Spirit does not receive the title Son of God, since the Only begotten alone is Son by nature from the beginning. The Son's ministry seems to be necessary to the existence of the Holy Spirit, not for His bare being alone but also for His wisdom and rationality and righteousness and for all the other qualities which we must regard Him as possessing through participation in those characteristics of Christ which we have described. And I suppose the Holy Spirit supplies the material, so to say, of the graces that come from God to those who through Him, and through their share in Him, are called the saints. This material of the graces, as we have termed it, derives its efficacy from God; it is

---

[1] Matt. xii. 32; Mark iii. 29; Luke xii. 10.

administered by Christ; its existence is by virtue of the Holy Spirit. I am moved to take this view by language Paul uses somewhere about gifts; There are diversities of gifts, but the same Spirit. And there are diversities of ministrations, and the same Lord. And there are diversities of workings, and the same God who worketh all things in all.[1]

XIII

The creative activity of the Word. The distinction between 'was' and 'became'. The timeless existence of the Word.—(Comm. *In Joann.* Frag. i; Br. ii. 211–13; B. iv. 483–85. From the Greek.)

Because he regards Him as the Creator of all things, he gives Him the name of The Word.[2] For since in general all creation depends upon word or reason, this and none other was the right term to signify that He was the maker of all things. For, with us, creators who are men have a craft, and a craft is a state of creative activity combined with genuine reason. But the Son of God, being none other than the creator of wisdom and of craft, is fittingly named Word or Reason. He does not make all things through Reason or the Word, being Himself another entity distinct from it; He himself, God the Word, is the maker. Then since this Word, God in His very being and by nature that very thing, the Son of God, for the salvation of men was made man, the Word was named Flesh.

And because some have fallen from right faith and think He only had existence from the time when He was

---

[1] 1 Cor. xii. 4–6.
[2] In later theology the creative office of the Second Person has fallen into abeyance. It survives of course in the clause in the Nicene Creed, 'By whom all things were made'

made man and came forth from the Virgin, most rightly with such in view the Theologian [1] writes, In the beginning was the Word.[2] Using the verbs in their strict sense, he says significantly, ' Became ', of His flesh and, ' was ' of His divinity. It would indeed have been more accurate in regard to God the Word to say, Is. But as he was making clear the permanent existence of the Word, in contrast to His becoming man at a particular time, the Evangelist used, Was, in place of, Is. But in regard to the eternal things we must not interpret the verbs in their strict senses. Sometimes the things they signify have an existence measured by time, as in, What was not previously, was; but sometimes they simply signify existence. In like manner, Is, stands for What now exists; will be, for what will exist. But since the Word of God, being God, is eternal, we are not in His case to understand the verbs with any added significance of time. What they mean does not come under time. From the very words the Theologian uses we can catch the sense. Right at the opening of his book he writes, In the beginning was the Word.[3] Moses too in his account of the creation says, In the beginning God created the heaven and the earth.[4] But John does not say, In the beginning the Word became or was made, but In the beginning was the Word. He was, in the beginning, as the maker of heaven and earth. For if, All things were made by Him,[5] and of this All the heaven and the earth are part, then He is the creator in their coming into being.

Further, since he did not say, In the beginning of

---

[1] This seems used here as a ' distinctive title of St. John '. But cp. Swete's note on p. 1 of his edition of the Apocalypse.
[2] John i. 1.   [3] *Ibid*.
[4] Gen. i. 1.   [5] John i. 3.

something was the Word, the term must be taken in an absolute sense, so that the meaning is, In the beginning of the angels and in the beginning of the archangels was the Word, and in short in the beginning of all created things, seen and unseen, was the Word; of all things He was the beginning and the maker. For in Christ were all things created, in the heavens and upon the earth, things visible and things invisible, whether principalities or powers or thrones or dominions. All things have been created through Him and unto Him. And He is before all things, and in Him all things consist, who is the beginning, the firstborn from the dead.[1] For if all things consist in Him and He is before them, being their beginning because He is their cause, it follows that we must say that He is in the coming to be of all things. Certainly, as He was their creator, He must have been before them and in the very beginning of their existence. Then, since the writer has said, He was in the beginning, he must make clear in what manner and with whom He had to act as maker. Therefore to the clause, In the beginning was the Word, he adds, The Word was with God.[2] For when He came to us, when He was born of a virgin, He was sent by the Father; wherefore also, He tabernacled amongst us,[3] and had the very name, God with us.[4] But when He created, since it was not as a man sent by God that He brought all things into being, He was with God and He was God.[5]

Also the Son of God is called wisdom, having been formed to be the beginning of the ways of God, according to the text in the Proverbs.[6] For the Wisdom

---

[1] Col. i. 16–18.   [2] John i. 1.   [3] *Ibid.*, i. 14.
[4] Isa. vii. 14; viii. 10; Matt. i. 23.
[5] From this point the text differs in different authorities. B. here followed, takes a different text from Br.
[6] Prov. viii. 22.

of God existing with Him whose wisdom He is, had no relation with any other, but being the good pleasure of God He willed that created things should come into being. This Wisdom then resolved to assume the relationship of creator towards the things that were to be, and this is the meaning of the statement that wisdom was created to be the beginning of the ways of God. Upon these ways does God advance, calling all into being, regulating, providing, benefiting, delighting in this wisdom that has been formed. The Word then is said to be the beginning not because it is different in its essence from wisdom but only in aspect and relationship, so that the same existence, which here the Scriptures name according to its intrinsic nature, is in one regard associated with God as wisdom and in another has inclined, to use this term, towards things created, as the creative Word. Nor is it here alone that the Son of God is termed the Word. You can quote similar language not from the New Testament alone but also from the Old. By the Word of the Lord were the heavens made.[1] Also, He sendeth His Word and healeth them.[2] And Luke says, Even as they delivered them unto us, which from the beginning were eyewitnesses and ministers of the Word.[3]

XIV

The Bread and Wine in the last supper, the body and blood of the Lord, are the Word which is the food and drink of souls.—(In Matt. Comm. Series, 85; Lomm. iv. 416–17. From the Latin.)

And as they were eating, Jesus took bread and gave thanks and brake it and gave to His disciples, and said,

---

[1] Ps. xxxiii. 6.   [2] *Ibid.*, cvii. 20.   [3] Luke i. 2.

Take and eat, for this is my body. And He took a cup and gave thanks and gave to them, saying, Drink ye all of it: for this is my blood of the new Covenant, which shall be shed for many unto remission of sins.[1] That bread which God the Word acknowledges to be His body is the word that is the food of souls, the word that proceedeth from God the Word, bread from the Bread of Heaven, which is placed upon the table of which it is written, Thou hast prepared a table in my sight against them that trouble me.[2] And that drink, which God the Word acknowledges to be His blood, is the word that satisfies and nobly inebriates the hearts of those that drink it. It is in the cup of which it is said, Thy cup that inebriates, how excellent it is.[3] And that drink is the product of the true vine, which says, I am the true vine.[4] It is the blood of that cluster which, placed in the wine-press of suffering, produces this drink. So also the bread is the word of Christ, formed of that wheat which falls upon good ground and brings forth much fruit.[5] God the Word did not call that visible bread which He was holding in His hands His body, but the word He called so, in mystical likeness of which that visible bread was to be broken. Nor was it that visible drink that He called his blood, but the word, in mystical likeness of which that drink was to be poured out. What else can the body and blood of God the Word be save the word that sustains and the word that makes glad the heart?

But why did He not say, This is the bread of the new Covenant,[6] as He did say, This is my blood of the new Covenant? Because the bread is the word of righteousness, by eating of which souls are sustained; but the

---

[1] Matt. xxvi. 26-8.
[2] Ps. xxiii. 5, LXX.
[3] *Ibid.*, xxiii. 5, LXX.
[4] John xv. 1.
[5] Matt. xiii. 8.
[6] *Ibid.* xxvi. 28.

drink is the word of the knowledge of Christ, according to the mystery of His birth and passion. Since then the Covenant of God for us lies in the blood of Christ's passion, so that believing that the Son of God was born and suffered according to the flesh we may be saved, though not by righteousness, in which alone, without faith in Christ's passion, salvation could not be—for this reason it is only of the cup that it is said, This is the cup of the new Covenant.[1]

XV

The Word of the Lord which came to the prophets is the same Word which became flesh in Jesus. Christ is the true Judah and we the men of Judah, to whom Jeremiah's warnings were addressed.—(In Jerem. Hom. ix. 1; Lomm. xv. 203–6; B. iii. 63–5. From the Greek.)

On the passage, The word that came to Jeremiah from the Lord, saying, Hear ye the words of this covenant, *so far as,* they are turned back to the iniquities of their forefathers.[2]

As concerns the coming of our Lord Jesus Christ which is recorded in history, His advent in bodily form was universal in its character and one that shed light upon the whole world, when the Word became flesh and

---

[1] For Origen's doctrine of the Eucharist see Bigg, *Christian Platonists*, pp. 219 *sqq*. In general 'The Alexandrines held a real but spiritual and in no sense material Presence of Christ in the Eucharist'. See especially *In Matt.* xi. 14; *In Lev.* Hom. xiii. 3 *sqq. In Num.* Hom. xxiii. 6; Lomm. iii. 105–7; ix. 402–11; x. 284–85; B. vi. 471 *sqq*. vii. 218. Also Huet. II. xiv. 2 and the references to Origen in Waterland *Doctrine of the Eucharist*, chh. vi. and vii. In its general lines Origen's view is fairly clear, but his thought is mystical, with no Latin precision, and no shadow of future controversies resting upon it.

[2] Jer. xi. 1–10.

tabernacled amongst us.[1] There was the true light, even the light which lighteth every man coming into the world. He was in the world, and the world was made by Him, and the world knew Him not. He came unto His own and they that were His own received Him not.[2] It must however be recognized that at earlier times also there was an advent, albeit not in bodily form, in each of the saints. Also, after that visible advent of His, there is a further advent in us. If you wish to have a proof of this, consider the passage, The word that came to Jeremiah from the Lord, saying, Hear, and so on. For what is the word which came from the Lord, be it to Jeremiah, or to Isaiah, or Ezekiel, or to any one else, except it be that which in the beginning was with God?[3] I know no other word of the Lord than this, of which the evangelist said, In the beginning was the Word and the Word was with God and the Word was God.

And this too we should recognize, that for each of those who can most profit by it there is an advent of the Word. For what am I the better, if there has been an advent of the Word in the world, but I do not receive Him? And on the other hand, though there has been as yet no advent in the whole world, but you allow that I share the experience of the prophets, then I have the Word. I would say that Christ came to Moses, to Jeremiah, to Isaiah, to each of the righteous. The words spoken by Him to His disciples, Lo, I am with you all the days, even unto the end of the world,[4] were literally true and came to pass even before His advent. For He was with Moses and with Isaiah and with each of the saints. How could they have spoken

---

[1] John i. 14.
[2] *Ibid.*, i. 9–11.
[3] *Ibid.*, i. 1.
[4] Matt. xxviii. 20.

the word of God, if the Word of God had not made His advent within them? And there is special need that these facts should be recognized by us who belong to the church, for we maintain[1] that there is the same God in the Law and in the Gospel, the same Christ both then and now, for evermore. Some there will be who sever the godhead that was anterior to the advent of our Saviour, according to their conception of it, from the godhead that was preached by Jesus Christ. But we recognize one God, both then and now; one Christ, both then and now. So much is suggested by the phrase, The word that came to Jeremiah from the Lord, saying, etc.

What is it then we also are to hear? Hear ye the words of this covenant, and speak unto the men of Judah and to the inhabitants of Jerusalem.[2] We are the men of Judah, because of Christ. For it is evident that our Lord hath sprung out of Judah.[3] And if I make it evident to you that the name of Judah as used in Scripture refers to Christ, then the men of Judah will not be the Jews who disbelieve in Christ, but ourselves who are believers in Christ. Judah, let thy brethren praise thee. Thy hands are upon the neck of thine enemies.[4] Let them praise thee. It was not the former Judah, the son of Jacob, that his brethren praised. It is the later Judah his brethren shall praise. For it is this Judah that says, I will declare Thy name unto my brethren, in the midst of the congregation will I praise Thee.[5] It is not to the earlier Judah that it is said, Thy hands are upon the neck of thine enemies. What evidence is there that the earlier Judah laid his hands upon the neck of his enemies? The narrative has recorded nothing of the kind about him. But if you consider the advent of the

---

[1] As against the Gnostics. [2] Jer. xi. 1-2.
[3] Heb. vii. 14.   [4] Gen. xlix. 8   [5] Ps. xxii. 22.

Lord Jesus, who overcame the devil and stripped principalities and powers and made an example of them and triumphed upon the tree, you see how in this Judah the prophecy has been fulfilled which says, Thy hands are upon the neck of thine enemies. If that be so and the Word here speaks to the men of Judah, to whom can it speak but to us who believe in Christ, who by reason of the tribe of Judah is Himself called Judah?

XVI

It was the human nature in Jesus, not the Divine Word, which died. And this same human nature was exalted into unity with the Word.—(Comm. in Joann. xxxii. 25; Lomm. ii. 461–64; Br. ii. 198–99; B. iv. 469–70. From the Greek.)

When therefore he was gone out, Jesus saith, Now is the Son of man glorified, and God is glorified in Him. If God is glorified in Him, God shall also glorify Him in Himself, and straightway shall He glorify Him.[1] The beginning of the Son of man being glorified, after the glories of His signs and wonders and the glory of His transfiguration, was the departure of Judas, with the Satan who entered into him, from the place where Jesus was. That is why the Lord said, Now is the Son of man glorified. Also there are the words, I, if I be lifted up from the earth, will draw all men unto myself,[2] spoken by the Saviour as He signified by what manner of death He should glorify God, for He did glorify God even in dying. Accordingly, when the divine purpose that Jesus should die began to come into operation, Judas having after the sop gone out to effect his designs against Jesus,

---

[1] John xiii. 31–2.   [2] *Ibid.*, xii. 32.

the words were spoken, Now is the Son of man glorified. Moreover, since Christ cannot be glorified without the Father being glorified in Him, there is added accordingly to the words, Now is the Son of man glorified, the statement, And God is glorified in Him. Yet the glory arising from His death on behalf of men belonged not to the only-begotten Word, which by nature could not die, nor to the Wisdom or the Truth or the other diviner elements which we name in Jesus, but to His humanity, to the man who was also Son of man, born of the seed of David according to the flesh.[1] For this reason He said in an earlier passage, Now ye seek to kill me, a man that hath told you the truth.[2] And in the place we are discussing He says, Now is the Son of man glorified.

It was this human nature, I believe, that God also highly exalted, after Jesus had become obedient unto death, yea the death of the cross.[3] For the Word which was in the beginning with God,[4] the God-Word, was incapable of being further exalted. But the exaltation of the Son of man, which came to Him after He had glorified God in His death, lay in this, that He was no longer other than the Word but identical with it. For if, He that is joined unto the Lord is one spirit,[5] so that of such a man and of the Spirit it could no longer be said, They are two; how much more must we say that the humanity of Jesus became one with the Word. He who counted not equality with God a thing to be grasped was highly exalted;[6] but the Word remained in His proper exaltation, or perhaps was restored to it, as again, He was with God, the God-Word now being man. In the death of Jesus, who glorified God, the words come true, Having spoiled principalities and powers He made

---

[1] Rom. i. 3. [2] John viii. 40. [3] Phil. ii. 8.
[4] John i. 1. [5] 1 Cor. vi. 17. [6] Phil ii. 6.

a show of them openly triumphing over them in the tree,[1] and also the saying, Having made peace through the blood of His cross, whether things upon earth or things in the heavens.[2] For in all these was the Son of man glorified, God also being glorified in Him.[3]

XVII

On the significance of the term 'Son of Man'.—(*Selecta in Psalmos.* Lomm. xi. 428-30. From the Greek.)

Ye sons of men, how long will ye be slow of heart? Why do ye love vanity and seek after falsehood?[4] etc. The phrase 'sons of men' one of us will regard as a periphrastic term, just as 'sons of the Achaei' is a customary expression with the Greeks. But others, starting from the case of the Saviour who is frequently called Son of man, will wish to investigate the reason for men being called not simply men but frequently by the title 'sons of men'. As regards the Saviour I do not suppose it is merely by way of circumlocution that he is named Son of man. For it is said, He gave him authority to execute judgment because he is Son of man.[5] This then must be recognised as a general principle; that, when the saints are called gods, the term man must be regarded as a

---

[1] Col. ii. 15. R. V. has 'having put off from himself' for A. V. 'having spoiled'.

[2] Col. i. 20.

[3] Other passages referring to the two natures in Christ, and their unification, are *De Prin*; I. ii. II. vi. *C. Cels.* ii. 9; In *Joann.* xix. 2; xx. 11; Frag. xl; In *Ep. ad Rom.* i. 5; In *Lev.* Hom. xii. 5. Lomm. ii. 137-39; 218-20; vi. 22-6; ix. 394; Br. ii. 2-3; 49-50; 254-55; B. vi. 299; 340; 515; vi. 464; vii. 190-1. § vi *supra*. See too Huet. II. ii. It cannot be said that Origen's views on the subject are wholly clear, but he held quite definitely that the Lord had a human soul, distinct from the Logos. In a measure, even for other men, the union of the human soul with the divine Word was possible. *In Num.* Hom. xx. 2; Lomm. x. 248; also § xxxv.

[4] Ps iv. 2.   [5] John v. 27

reproach; but when sinners are named brutes and beasts, it stands for high commendation. As an instance of the former use we have, I said, Ye are gods and all of you sons of the Most High. Nevertheless ye die like men and fall like one of the princes.[1] Also, Whereas there is jealousy and strife, are yet not carnal and walk after the manner of men?[2] For the second use we have, O Lord, thou shalt preserve man and beast.[3]

The first definite person we find named in Scripture ' son of man ' is, speaking at the moment from memory, Daniel. And after him Ezekiel. They were prophets in the captivity. But before the captivity, so far as our researches go in the undisputed books which pass current as inspired, there is no one named by this title. What need is there to refer to the Saviour? The Gospels are full of this expression. It was, as we think, because the men of the captivity were sinners that Daniel alone, to their reproach, because he had preserved the dignity of man's nature, made according to the ' image and like ness ', was addressed as ' son of man '. As much may be said also of Ezekiel. For the name ' man ' was first given to him who was made by God according to His image and likeness, so that he would be man in the true sense. It is also to be considered in regard to the Saviour whether the human element in him was the Son of man, the human element in the image of the invisible God having a human paternity.[4]

---

[1] Ps. lxxxii. 6–7.   [2] 1 Cor. iii. 3.   [3] Ps. xxxvi. 6.

[4] No question as to the Virgin Birth is here implied. Indeed the phrase ' Son of man ' was often interpreted as equivalent to ' Son of Mary '. So Irenæus, *Haeres* III. xix. 3 (*Maria . . . . quae et ipsa erat homo*), and Tertullian, *Adv. Marcion* iv. 10. Origen means that the human element in our Lord's person came from a human source. Cp. § *VI supra.* The article on ' Son of Man ' in *Encyc. Biblica* (IV. col. 4715) regards Origen's authority for the interpretation of this disputed term as considerable.

XVIII

Many of the Saviour's offices are assumed on our account.—
(*Comm. in Joann.* i. 20; Lomm. i. 41-3; Br. i. 24-5;
B. iv. 24-5. From the Greek.)

God is entirely one and single. But our Saviour, because the world is manifold, since God purposed Him to be the propitiation[1] and firstfruits of all creation, becomes many things, becomes perhaps anything, according as the whole creation capable of being set free has need of Him. For this reason He becomes the light of men, when men brought into darkness through evil have need of the light that shineth in darkness and is not apprehended by it;[2] though He would not have become the light of men had men not been in darkness. And we may observe something similar in regard to His being the firstborn of the dead.[3] For if, to make the supposition, the woman had not been deceived and Adam had not fallen, but man created for incorruption had retained his incorruption, the Lord would not have come down to the dust of death;[4] nor would He have died, if there had not been sin, through which for His love to man He had to die. Not having done this, He would not have been the firstborn from the dead. Also we might enquire whether He would ever have become a shepherd, had man not been made comparable to the senseless beasts[5] and brought to resemble them. For if God saves men and beasts,[6] the beasts that He saves He saves through giving them a shepherd, as they are incapable of having a king.

So should we collect the titles of the Son and examine which of them are accessory titles, that would never have

---

[1] Rom. iii. 25. [2] John i. 5. [3] Rev. i. 5.
[4] Ps. xxii. 15. [5] *Ibid.*, xlix. 12. [6] *Ibid.*, xxxvi. 6.

been so numerous, had the saints begun and remained in a state of bliss. Only as Wisdom perhaps would He have still remained; as Word too, and as Life, and certainly as Truth. But the other additional titles, assumed for our sake, would not have been His. And blessed are they who in their need of the Son of God have so far advanced as no longer to require Him as the physician who heals those who are sick, or as shepherd, or as ransom, but only as wisdom, and word and righteousness or in whatever other capacity He comes to those who by reason of their perfection have power to receive His fairest gifts.[1]

XIX

The body of the Lord was a natural human body. This body fasted, felt weariness, eat and drank, received scars, needed sleep. Whatever spiritual meaning such statements may have, they are also true in a literal sense.[2]
—(*In Ep. ad Galatas.* Frag. Lomm. v. 264–70. From the Latin.)

To what we have said above this addition must be made. Christ's body was not something different from the substance of earth, inasmuch as He is the son of David and the son of Abraham. Thus Matthew wrote, The book of the generation of Jesus Christ, the son of David, the son of Abraham.[3] And thus Paul says that

---

[1] This thought of the manifold character of Christ is a favourite one. Cp. Denis, 102-3.

[2] An important passage. It proves that however ready Origen may have been to give a spiritual and mystical interpretation to statements of fact, still he is not prepared to surrender the historic element in Christianity. He directly joins issue with the Docetae, and is on the whole further removed from their position than was his teacher, Clement.

[3] Matt. i. 1.

Christ is of the seed of Abraham and of the seed of David, according to the flesh.[1] So the statement that, When He had fasted forty days and forty nights, He afterward hungered,[2] no doubt shows that even His body, just as is usual with our bodies, could be evacuated and filled. If any one confronts us with the difficulty of explaining the miracle of a forty days fast, that is easily solved by adducing the further instances of Moses and Elijah,[3] who are likewise said to have undergone a period of fasting. The fact too that, tired by the effort of His journey and the heat, He sits to rest upon the well and is athirst,[4]—what does it mean but the exhaustion of the muscles and the drying up of the moist element in His body through the sun's excessive heat? As for His postponing His desire to drink and not drinking, for He was interested in better things, we are not to say that the reason of this was because He felt no thirst.

The fact again that He was often invited to supper, and that He eat and drank in the sight of all, was no piece of deception, no trick to deceive the eyes of onlookers; nor, as some hold, did He do these things in semblance only, especially as He took food and drink in such measure as to incur the blame of some who charged Him with greed. They said His appetite for food and drink was excessive. And if any one is bold enough to maintain that this is so stated because His eating was just a pretence, and the others did not know how it was done, to this answer may be made from our Lord's own words, John the Baptist came neither eating nor drinking, and they say, He hath a devil. The Son of man came eating and drinking, and they say, Behold a

---

[1] Rom. i. 3; Gal. iii. 16. [2] Matt. iv. 2.
[3] Ex. xxxiv. 28; 1 Kings xix. 8. [4] John iv. 6-7.

gluttonous man and a wine bibber.[1] When the Saviour says Himself that the Son of man came eating and drinking, how can any one dare to say that He did not eat and did not drink? That would be plain disbelief in His teaching. Now if He eat and drank, and the elements of wine and food became part of His flesh, they were doubtless dispersed through all the constituent parts of His body and its interconnected members. What is by nature spiritual—such is the opinion of some people regarding his body, a sufficiently crude and ridiculous view to take—cannot possible take in the material substance of wine and food. And if any one in reply puts forward incongruous and unpleasant questions, demanding whether digestion took place in His body, I see nothing inappropriate in assenting; it follows from the nature of the body. If however they demand of us instances in proof of this, we may tell them that their stupid questions have gone far enough. For where is there any mention of such details in regard to the apostles, or other holy men, or even in regard to wicked men and sinners?

Also the question of His circumcision will occasion us no difficulty. We say that, having a human body, He was accordingly circumcised, and His foreskin was buried, perhaps for a season; if otherwise, the point will be considered in another treatise. But this circumcision will place the adverse party in a difficult situation. For how could a spiritual body be circumcised with a metal instrument? From this cause some of their number have unblushingly published books on the foreskin of His circumcision, wherein they attempted to demonstrate that it changed into a spiritual substance. Nor will the situation be less difficult for those who say the body

[1] Matt. xi. 18–19.

of Christ was a psychic body.[1] In regard to the blood and water which flowed from His side, when the soldier pierced it with his spear,[2] the same view must be taken. For those who understand the meaning of the record that the prints of the nails were in His body,[3] the statement is quite plain. His flesh was the flesh of earth, that is of human nature. At any rate it was not such as to escape liability to the infliction of scars. Also if He had not been conscious of many results of human weakness in the very hour of death, why is His soul troubled? Why is He sorrowful for it even unto death?[4]

All this is evident proof that His words, The spirit indeed is willing but the flesh is weak,[5] were no pretence but a human utterance. Evidence as strong is to be found in the fact of His sleeping. It is said that He was in the stern, asleep on the cushion, as Mark records,[6] and was aroused from sleep by a man. This may have a spiritual meaning, but the original truth of the narrative remains, even when you accept the spiritual sense. He may be always curing the blind in the spiritual sense, whenever He brings light to minds darkened by ignorance, still He did also once make whole the physically blind. The dead too He is always raising. Still He did once perform such wonders as the raising of the daughter of the ruler of the synagogue, and of the widow's son, and of Lazarus. And though, when awakened by his disciples He is ever stilling the

---

[1] *Animale corpus*, in the Latin, no doubt represents ψυχικὸν σῶμα in Origen's Greek Cp. 1 Cor. xv. 44. R.V. 'A natural body'.
[2] John xix. 34.
[3] *Ibid.*, xx. 25.
[4] Matt. xxvi. 38 ; John xii. 27.
[5] Matt. xxvi. 41 ; Mark xiv. 38.
[6] Mark iv. 38.

storms and tempests of the church, still it is certain too that those deeds were once performed of which an account is given in the narrative. This is the sound principle for interpreting the meaning of Scripture,[1] nor should we listen to those who say that He was born, not of Mary, but, through Mary.[2] The Apostle, anticipating this view, stated before, When the fulness of the time came, God sent forth His Son, made of a woman, made under the law, that He might redeem them which were under the law.[3] You observe; he did not say, Made through a woman, but, Made of a woman.

XX

The greatness of the Saviour. It extends even to places as remote as Britain. It ascends high as the heavens, it descends low as Hades.—(*In Lucam.* Hom. vi; Lomm. v. 106-7. From the Latin.)

The greatness of our Saviour did not appear at the time when He was born, but now, after being apparently suppressed by His opponents, it has shone out. Consider the greatness of the Lord; the sound of His teaching has gone forth into every land, His words unto the ends of the world.[4] Our Lord Jesus, who is the Power of God, has spread into all the world. He is present with us, according to what is read in the Apostle, When ye are gathered together, and my spirit, with the power of our Lord Jesus Christ.[5] The power of our Lord and

---

[1] Cp. *De Princip.* IV. ii. 5; iii. 4.
[2] This was the view of the Valentinians. They held that the Lord brought His body from heaven and passed through the Virgin as water passes through a channel. Epiph. *Haeres.* xxxi. 7; Iren. III. xvi. 1.
[3] Gal. iv. 4-5.
[4] Ps. xix. 4.
[5] 1 Cor. v. 4.

Saviour is even with those who are cut off in Britain[1] from our world, with the inhabitants of Mauretania, and with all under the sun who have believed in His name. Consider then the greatness of the Saviour, how it is spread all the world over, and of a truth not even yet have I set forth His real greatness. Ascend to the heavens and behold Him, how He has filled the heavenly places, for He has been seen of angels.[2] Descend in thought into the depths, and you shall behold that He has descended even there. For, He that descended is the same also that ascended, that He might fill all things . . . that in the name of Jesus every knee should bow, of things in heaven and things on earth and things under the earth.[3] Contemplate the power of the Lord, how it has filled the world, every place that is in heaven, on earth, under the earth; how it has gone right into heaven and ascended unto the heights. For we read that the Son of God has passed through the heavens.[4] If you see these things, you will likewise realize that, He shall be great,[5] is no passing observation but a word fulfilled in reality. Great is our Lord Jesus, present or absent. To this our gathering and assembly He has given a share of His might. Be it our prayer to the Lord God that each one of us may deserve to receive this. To whom be glory and dominion for ever and ever. Amen.

---

[1] Cp. Bright, *Early English Church History*, p. 5. 'We cannot reasonably doubt that some Christians did pass over from Gaul to our shores during the second century, if not earlier, and planted here and there some settlements of the Church.' Other references to Britain in Origen are to be found in *In Matt. Comm. Ser.* 39; *In Ezech.* Hom. iv. 1; Lomm. iv. 271; xiv. 59; B. viii. 362. For its remoteness, cp. Virgil *Ecl.* i. 66 : '*Et penitus toto divisos orbe Britannos*'.

[2] 1 Tim. iii. 16.
[3] Ephes. iv. 10; Phil. ii. 10.
[4] Heb. iv. 14.
[5] Luke i. 32.

PART III

THE HOLY SCRIPTURES—PRINCIPLES AND EXAMPLES OF EXEGESIS

XXI

Scripture has many interpreters.—(*Selecta in Psalmos*; Lomm. xiii. 82-3. From the Greek.)

Sinners have discoursed folly unto me, not according to thy law.[1] Either he has in mind the old wives' fables, which form the instruction of the Jews, or else the commandments of men and the nonsense of the wise men of this world. For many try their hand at interpreting the divine Scriptures, churchmen, heretics who are outside the church, Jews, and Samaritans, but they do not all speak aright. Rare indeed is he who has the grace of God for this task. Many make profession to speak but their lives are not right, or are even lawless. So whatever they say is folly and nonsense. Sound and strong and saving speech there cannot be in the soul of a sinner.

XXII

All the Holy Scripture is one perfect and harmonious instrument of God.—(*Comm. in Matt.* ii; *Philocal.* vi; Lomm. iii. 3-6; xxv. 49-50; *Philocal.* Ed. Robinson, 49-50. From the Greek.)

On, Blessed are the peacemakers.[2] To the man who, in either of these senses,[3] is a peacemaker nothing in the divine oracles is crooked or perverse. All is plain to those who understand.[4] And since to such a man there

---

[1] Ps. cxix. 85; LXX. [2] Matt. v. 9.
[3] As the preceding passage does not survive, it is uncertain in what exact sense Origen had interpreted the term.
[4] Prov. viii. 8-9.

is nothing crooked or perverse, he consequently perceives abundance of peace in all the Scriptures, even in those which seem to contain discord or contrarieties one with another. There is too a third peacemaker, the man who shows that what to others seems the discord of the Scriptures is no discord, and who makes their harmony and peace evident, be it of the Old with the New ; or of the Law with the Prophets ; or of one passage from the Gospel with another ;[1] or of the Gospels with the Apostolic writings ; or of one Apostolic writing with another. Indeed all the Scriptures are, according to Ecclesiastes, words of the wise, like goads, and like nails well fastened, which are given out of the 'collections' from one shepherd,[2] and nothing in them is in excess. The Word or Reason is the one shepherd of all reasonable beings. To those who have not ears to hear this may have the appearance of discord; in reality all is harmonious.

For as the different strings of the psaltery or lyre, each of which produces a particular sound not apparently similar to the sound of another, are regarded by the unmusical person who does not understand the theory of musical concord as unharmonious by reason of the dissimilarity of their sounds ; even so they who know not how to hear God's harmony in His holy Scriptures think there is discord between the Old and the New, or between the Prophets and the Law, or between the different Gospels, or that the Apostle[3] is out of harmony either

---

[1] There is good authority for this clause. Lommatzsch omits, Robinson includes it.

[2] Eccl. xii. 11 ; R. V. has ' As nails well fastened are *the words* of the masters of assemblies.' By the last term in the original persons must be denoted. See Plumptre *in loc.* But Origen seems to have taken the LXX παρὰ τῶν συνθεμάτων in the sense of ' collections ' or composite works, with the many elements which form the whole of the Scriptures in mind.

[3] i.e., Paul. He is constantly spoken of as ' the Apostle '.

with the Gospel, or with himself, or with the other Apostles. But when the man trained in the music of God arrives, a man of skill in deed and word, and therefore named David, a name which is interpreted ' capable of hand ',[1] he shall produce the sound of God's music, knowing from his art how to strike the strings in time, now the strings of the Law, now harmoniously with them the strings of the Gospel, now the strings of Prophecy, and when occasion demands the Apostolic strings that harmonize with them or similarly with the Gospel. For he knows that all Scripture is the one perfect and attuned instrument of God, producing from its various notes a single sound of salvation for those who are willing to learn, a sound that stills and checks every activity of an evil spirit, as David's music stilled the evil spirit that was choking Saul.[2] So you see the peacemaker in the third sense, the man who follows Scripture, who perceives the peace which pervades it, who imparts this peace to those who seek aright and are sincere in their love of knowledge.[3]

XXIII

All Scripture, down to its minutest details, has purpose and meaning. We find difficulties and stumbling blocks, but these are due to our own limitations.[4]—(*In Jerem.*, Hom. xxxix; *Philocal.* x; Lomm. xv. 418–20; xxv. 59–61; B. iii. 196–98; *Philocal.* Ed. Robinson, 58–9. From the Greek.)

If some time, as you read the Scripture, you stumble over a thought, good in reality yet a stone of stumbling and a rock of offence, lay the blame on yourself. For

---

[1] The Hebrew name means 'Beloved'. It is not clear what is Origen's authority for his interpretation.
[2] 1 Sam. xvi. 14.
[3] Reading $\varphi\iota\lambda o\mu\alpha\theta o\hat{v}\sigma\iota\nu$ with Robinson.
[4] The passage treated is Jer. xliv (li in LXX) 22.

you must not give up the hope that this stone of stumbling and this rock of offence do possess meaning, so that the saying may come to pass, He that believeth shall not be put to shame.[1] First believe, and you shall find under the apparent stumbling block much holy benefit. If we were commanded to speak no idle word, as men who should give account of it in the day of judgment;[2] and if, so far as our power goes, we make it our ambition to cause every word that proceeds out of our mouth to be effective both in us who speak and in those who hear; what are we to think about the prophets but that every word spoken by their mouth was effective? Small wonder if every word spoken by the prophets produced the proper effect of a word. Nay, I hold that every wonderful letter written in the oracles of God has its effects. There is not one jot or one tittle written in Scripture which, for those who know how to use the power of the Scriptures, does not effect its proper work.

It is like the case of herbs; each has its power, whether for health of the body or for some other purpose. But it is not for every one to understand the purpose for which each herb is useful. This belongs to those who have acquired knowledge, the people who spend their time over herbs, so as to see at what time one is to be taken, to what part of the body another is to be applied, in what manner another is to be prepared, so as to be of benefit to the user. In this way the saintly man is a sort of spiritual herbalist, culling from the sacred Scriptures each jot, each chance letter, and discovering the force of the letter and the purpose for which it is of use, and that nothing written is devoid of meaning. If you like to hear a second illustration of this, each member of our body

---

[1] Isa. viii. 14; Rom. ix. 33. [2] Matt. xii. 36.

was made by the divine Craftsman for some function. But it is not for all men to know what is the force and the use of each of the members, down to those quite unimportant. It is physicians who have had experience in dissections who can tell for what end each part, even the smallest, has been made by Providence to be useful. I pray you to think of the Scriptures as in this way all herbs, or as one complete body of the word. And if you are neither a herbalist of the Scriptures, nor a dissector of prophetic language, consider not that aught in Scripture is without purpose, but blame yourself rather than the sacred Scriptures, when you fail to discover the meaning of what is written. This preface I make quite in a general sense, possibly of use in regard to the whole of Scripture, so that they who desire to devote themselves to study may be induced not to let a single letter pass without examination and enquiry.

XXIV

Moses passes. Joshua, that is Jesus, reigns.—(*In Josuam*, Hom. ii. 1; Lomm. xi. 21-3; B. vii. 296-97. From the Latin.)

We must now give an account of the death of Moses. For unless we have understood in what sense Moses dies, we shall be unable to perceive in what sense Joshua, that is Jesus, reigns.[1] If then you bear in mind the overthrow of Jerusalem; the desertion of its altars; the absence of sacrifices, burnt offerings and drink offerings;

---

[1] 'The homilies on Joshua, belonging to the latest period of Origen's life, perhaps offer the most attractive specimen of his popular interpretation. The parallel between the leader of the old Church and the Leader of the new is drawn with great ingenuity and care.' Westcott, art. in *D.C.B.* Our distinction between the names Joshua and Jesus is of course very unfortunate.

the lack of priests; the lack of high priests; the cessation of the Levites' ministry; when you see all these things at an end, say that Moses, the servant of the Lord, has passed away. If you observe that no one comes three times a year to appear before the Lord, or makes offerings in the temple, or kills the Passover, or eats unleavened bread, or offers first-fruits, or dedicates the firstborn—when you see that all these ordinances are disregarded, say that Moses, the servant of the Lord, has passed away. But when you observe the entering in of the heathen to the faith, the building of churches, the altars not sprinkled with the blood of beasts but hallowed by the blood of Christ; when you see priests and Levites making offering not of the blood of bulls and of goats but of the word of God by the grace of the Holy Spirit,[1] then say that Jesus has taken over and holds the leadership of Moses, not Jesus or Joshua the son of Nun, but Jesus the son of God. When you see that Christ our Passover is sacrificed, and that we eat the unleavened bread of sincerity and truth; when you see in the church the fruit of the good ground, thirty-fold, sixty-fold, an hundred-fold—widows, that is, virgins, martyrs; when you see that the seed of Israel is increased by those that are born not of blood, nor of the will of a man, nor of the will of the flesh, but of God;[2] when you see the gathering together of the sons of God who once were scattered abroad; when you see the people of God observing the Sabbath not by abstaining from ordinary intercourse but by abstaining from deeds of sin; when you see all this, say that Moses, the servant of the Lord, has passed away and that Jesus, Son of God, holds the leadership.

[1] Cp. § xiv. It is uncertain whether he has the Eucharist or teaching in mind.
[2] John i. 13.

EXEGESIS

To conclude, in a certain book, though it is not regarded as canonical, there is a symbolical statement of this mystery. It is recorded that two Moses appeared, the one living in the spirit, the other dead in the body.[1] Of which no doubt this was the veiled meaning; that if you set your eyes upon the letter of the law, empty, and devoid of all such significance as we described above, that is Moses dead in the body. But if you can take away the veil of the law and understand that the law is spiritual, that is the Moses who lives in the spirit.

XXV

As Joshua read the Law of Moses to the children of Israel, so does Jesus interpret the Law to the Church.—(*In Josuam*, Hom. ix. 8; Lomm. xi. 95–6; B. vii. 352–53. From the Latin.)

Afterward, we are told, Joshua read all the words of the law, that is the blessings and the curses, according to all that is written in the book of the law. There was not a word of all that Moses commanded which Joshua read not before all the assembly of the children of Israel.[2] Now the explanation of the narrative is quite easy. It tells how the son of Nun read all the words of the law, which Moses wrote, before all the assembly of the children of Israel. But how our Lord Joshua, that is Jesus, does this for his own people, it will not, I think, be waste of time to show.[3] Now it is my belief that,

---

[1] Cf. Joseph. *Ant*. iv. 8, 48. Also Clem. Al. *Strom*. VI. xv. 132.
[2] Josh. viii. 34–5.
[3] From Origen's standpoint the Old Testament only became really intelligible through its spiritual interpretation in Christianity. Jesus 'made the water wine'. *In Joann*. xiii. 62. Cp. *In Lev*. Hom. iv. 7; Lomm. ii. 128–29; ix. 230; Br. i. 324; B. iv. 294–95; vi. 326.

whenever Moses is read to us, and the veil of the letter is removed by the grace of God, and we begin to understand that the law is spiritual, and that, for example, when the law says, Thou shalt not muzzle the ox when he treadeth out the corn,[1] its words refer not to oxen but to Apostles; or again that, when it is said in the law that Abraham had two sons, one by the handmaid and one by the free woman,[2] I am to understand thereby the two covenants and the two peoples—such a law, a law so interpreted, a law which Paul describes as spiritual, does Jesus our Lord read. It is He who repeats this in the ears of all the people, bidding us not follow the letter that killeth, but hold to the Spirit that giveth life.

Joshua therefore, that is Jesus, reads the law to us when He explains to us the hidden things of the law. For we, who belong to the catholic church, do not reject the law of Moses, but we welcome it, provided it is Jesus who reads it to us, so that as He reads we may lay hold of His understanding and interpretation. We must surely believe that he who said, We have the mind of Christ, that we might know the things which are given to us by God; which things also we speak[3]—derived his understanding from that source. So was it with those who said, Was not our heart burning within us, while He opened to us the Scriptures in the way?[4] when beginning from the law of Moses, right on to the prophets, He read to them and unveiled all the passages which had reference to Himself.

---

[1] Deut. xxv. 4; 1 Cor. ix. 9.
[2] Gal. iv. 22.
[3] 1 Cor. ii. 12-13, 16.
[4] Luke xxiv. 32

XXVI

The Law written in the heart is not the law of ordinances but the law of nature. This has affinity with the Gospel. Only in the spirit can the law be kept. The conscience that bears testimony to the law in our hearts is the spirit, co-existing with, but distinct from, the soul.—(Comm. in Ep. ad Rom. ii. 9; Lomm. vi. 105–108. From the Latin.)

For when Gentiles which have no law do by nature the things of the law, these, having no law, are a law unto themselves; in that they show the work of the law written in their hearts, their conscience bearing witness therewith, and their thoughts one with another accusing or else excusing them; in the day when God shall judge the secrets of men, according to my gospel, by Jesus Christ.[1] It is certain that Gentiles which have no law are not said to do by nature the things contained in the law so far as regards Sabbath days or new moons or the sacrifices which are described in the law. For it is not that law which is written in the hearts of the Gentiles. What they can recognize by nature is of this kind; not, for example, to commit murder or adultery, not to steal, not to bear false witness, to honour father and mother, and the like. Possibly also it is written in the hearts of the Gentiles that there is one God, the creator of all. Yet it seems to me that these things which are said to be written in the heart have a special affinity with the laws of the Gospel, where everything goes by the standard of natural equity. For what is so akin to natural feeling as that men should

---

[1] Rom. ii. 14–16.

not do to others what they are unwilling should be done to themselves?[1]

Now the law of nature can be in harmony with the law of Moses according to the spirit, not according to the letter. For what natural sense is there in, for example, the command to circumcise a child on the eighth day,[2] or not to interweave wool with linen,[3] or not to eat anything leavened on the days of unleavened bread?[4] Several times we have raised these difficulties with Jews, and requested them to show us any advantage they possessed, but we know their one habitual answer to be, that this was the decision of the lawgiver. We, who think that all these things must be spiritually understood, believe accordingly that it is not the hearers but the doers of the law who are justified[5]—not of the law according to the letter, which in view of its impossibility can certainly not have a 'doer'—but of the law according to the spirit, by which alone the law can be fulfilled. This therefore is the work of the law which the Apostle says even Gentiles can fulfil by nature.[6] For when they do the things of the law, the law seems to be written by God in their hearts, not in ink, but in the spirit of the living God.[7]

When it says, In their hearts, we are not to think that the law is said to be written on some member of the body which is called the heart. For how could the flesh produce such counsels of wisdom, or retain such stores of memory? Be it remembered that heart is the term

---

[1] Tobit iv. 15; Lightfoot, *Hor. Heb.* (Ed. Pitman) xi. 152. Origen follows Rabbinical and heathen writers, who give the maxim in its negative form. In the Gospel (Matt. vii. 12) it is characteristically positive.

[2] Lev. xii. 3.   [3] Deut. xxii. 11.
[4] Ex. xii. 15, 19.   [5] Rom. ii. 13.
[6] *Ibid.*, ii. 14.   [7] 2 Cor. iii. 2.

usually given to the reasoning faculty of the soul. And the Apostle says that they who have the law written in their hearts enjoy the testimony of a sound conscience. And this seems to compel us to consider what it is the Apostle calls conscience, whether it be some element distinct from the heart and from the soul. For of this conscience it is elsewhere said that it condemns and is not condemned, and judges a man but is not judged, as John says in the words, If our conscience condemn us not, we have boldness towards God.[1] And again Paul himself says in another place, For our glorying is this, the testimony of our conscience.[2]

As then I observe such large freedom in that which ever rejoices and glories in good deeds, and in wrong deeds is not accused, but itself condemns and accuses the very soul to which it is attached, I hold that conscience is this very spirit which is said by the Apostle to co-exist with the soul,[3] as we previously made clear; it is a sort of tutor and governor associated with it to advise it of the better course or to punish and accuse it for its faults. It is of this also that the Apostle says, No man knoweth the things of a man save the spirit of the man which is in him.[4] It must be the very spirit of conscience of which he says, The Spirit itself beareth witness with our spirit.[5] Possibly this is that very spirit which is attached to the souls of the righteous, which have in all things been obedient unto it. Hence it is written, Praise the Lord, ye spirits and souls of the

---

[1] 1 John iii. 21, where 'heart,' not 'conscience', is the term used.
[2] 2 Cor. i. 12.
[3] 1 Thess. v. 23, ' spirit and soul and body '.
[4] 1 Cor. ii. 11.
[5] Rom. viii. 16.

righteous.¹ But if the soul be disobedient to it and obstinate, after death the spirit will be severed and separated from it. I suppose for this reason it is said of the Unjust Steward in the gospel that the Lord shall 'divide'² him and assign him his portion with the unfaithful.³ Perhaps it is the same spirit of which it is written that An incorruptible spirit is in man.⁴ And just as we said previously that it would be severed and separated from the sinful soul, that this might receive its portion with the unfaithful, similarly we may also apply in this sense the saying, Then shall two men be in the field, one shall be taken and one be left. Two women shall be at the mill, one shall be taken and one be left.⁵ So far in regard to the words, Their conscience also bearing witness.

XXVII

There is a Law of Moses. There is also a Law of Nature. In Romans iii. 19, Paul has the latter in mind. This Law is universal, valid for all men, save infants and idiots, perhaps also for angels and heavenly beings.—(Comm. in Ep. ad Rom. iii. 6; Lomm. vi. 189-93. From the Latin.)

Now we know that what things soever the law saith, it speaketh to them that are under the law; that every mouth may be stopped, and all the world may be brought under the judgment of God; because by the works of the law shall no flesh be justified in His sight: for

---

[1] Song of the three children, 64.
[2] Luke xii. 46, 'cut him asunder.'
[3] '*Partem ejus cum infidelibus ponet.*' Probably 'locate a part of him, i.e. his soul, with the unfaithful' was Origen's real meaning.
[4] Job xxxii. 8; Wisdom xii. 1.
[5] Matt. xxiv. 40-41.

through the law cometh the knowledge of sin.[1] At the outset we made the preliminary remark that in this Epistle the Apostle would speak of various laws, the distinction and difference between which must be taken into account in every passage ; otherwise it will perplex the reader's mind. Consequently, in this present passage, where it says, Now we know that what things soever the law saith, it speaketh to them that are under the law, we must carefully investigate which law it is that speaks to them that are under the law, and by its admonitions to them strips away every excuse, so that they cannot find any escape from their sins. Such is the meaning of the words, That every mouth may be stopped and all the world may be brought under the judgment of God.

Now if we determine to understand the passage as referring to the law of Moses,[2] which without question speaks only to those whom it has circumcised and taught from their mother's womb, how can we consistently believe that by this law, which only affects by its precepts one single people, every mouth shall be stopped and all the world be found subject through this law to God? What part or lot can all nations or the whole world be held to have in this law? And how can the knowledge of sin be said to come about through the law of Moses, seeing that many before that law can be shown to have been aware of their sin? Cain, for example, after he had sinned said, Mine iniquity is greater than can be

---

[1] Rom. iii. 19-20.
[2] Modern commentators do not, in the main, agree with the wider interpretation Origen here gives to ὁ νόμος in this passage. They hold that St. Paul has the Jewish law, either the Old Testament or the Pentateuch alone, in mind. Origen's meaning is admirable but it was probably not St. Paul's. See Sanday and Headlam *in loc.*

forgiven.[1] The patriarchs, too, when they had gone down into Egypt to Joseph and were troubled by the charge he pretended to bring against them, said one to another, We are verily guilty concerning our brother, in that we saw the distress of his soul, when he besought us and we would not hear; therefore is this distress come upon us.[2] Job also, who is admitted to have lived before the law, says, Even if I sinned unwillingly, if I covered my transgression or was alarmed by a multitude of people so that I did not publish my offence—[3] We are clearly taught that all these men recognized their sin. It may be gathered then from these examples that the Apostle Paul was not speaking of the law of Moses when he said, The law speaketh to them that are under the law; but that he is speaking of the law of nature, which is written in the hearts of men.

This therefore is the law which, what things soever it saith, speaketh to those who are under the law, And under the law are those who are of sufficient age to know the difference between good and evil. Without law are all to whom the knowledge of this distinction has not yet come. Such a state Paul describes; I was alive apart from law once.[4] By appealing to this law of nature we shall see that the Apostle said quite consistently that every mouth should be stopped and all the world become subject to the judgment of God. No man, either of the Jews of the Gentiles, is without his share in this law which is in men by nature. That is why we can find good reason in the saying, That God might be justified in His words and prevail when He comes into judgment.[5] We might say this for example; If it be

---

[1] Gen. iv. 13; see R. V. margin. [2] Gen. xlii. 21.
[3] Job xxxi. 33-4; LXX. [4] Rom. vii. 9.
[5] Rom. iii. 4; Ps. li. 4.

asked, What has God given to man, and what has man accomplished through the gifts of God?—then God will appear to be judged along with men. And it will be found that God has given to man all the feelings and all the instincts by which he may advance and make his way to virtue; besides He has implanted in him the power of reason, by which he knows what he should do and what avoid. These things we find that God has bestowed upon all men alike. But if after receiving these gifts man, to whom nothing on God's side is lacking, fails to tread in the path of virtue, then man is found to have been by his own defect unequal to the gifts that were given him by God. Rightly then in such a test is God said to prevail and to be justified in His words.

This is what the law of nature says to all who are under law. From its commands infants alone, as I hold, are exempt, in whom as yet there is no power of decision between right and wrong. Also you may consider whether we shall class with them persons who for some reason are without mental capacity. With these exceptions I hold that no one escapes this law. It is even a point for enquiry whether, not men alone, but even angels and every rational creature, of whatever kind, are not under the obligations of this law. If law has been rightly defined by the learned to be that which lays down what should be done and prohibits what should not be done, a law of this kind would certainly seem to have been implanted even in the higher and heavenly orders, for these certainly are under obligation to obey in one case, to decline in another. Had they not been subject to this law, the inspired Scripture would never say of them, The angels which kept not their own principality but left their proper habitation, God hath kept in everlasting bonds under darkness, bound in hell, unto the judgment of the great day.[1] It is clear they had a law. This was not kept, and therefore they undergo what Scripture describes in the foregoing passage. Paul also, when he says, Know ye not that we shall judge angels?[2] clearly recognizes that they whom he describes as summoned to trial are subject to law.

If any one raises objection because we said above that God is liable to judgment together with men, protesting against our seeming to say that even God is under law, hear what wonderful caution on this point is to be found in the Apostle's letter. He does not say that Christ is under law, but that He is the fulfilment of law. As Christ is righteousness, whereby all become righteous; as He is truth, whereby all men stand firm in truth; as He is life, whereby all men live; so is He law, whereby all men are under law. He comes thus to judgment not as one who is under law but as one who is law.[3] Indeed I think that they who are already perfect and who, being joined unto the Lord, are made one spirit with Him, are no longer under law but are themselves law, as in another place the same Apostle says, Law is not made for a righteous man.[4] Thus, what things soever the law saith, it speaketh to them that are under the law, that every mouth may be stopped—in the sense we gave the passage above—that all the world may be 'subject to', or as we read elsewhere 'liable to',[5] the judgment of God. The latter accords better with the Greek texts.

---

[1] Jude 6; see Bigg's note. [2] 1 Cor. vi. 3.
[3] The divine nature, in other words, is not externally but internally limited. It has definite moral characteristics.
[4] 1 Tim. i. 9.
[5] The Latin words used are '*subditus*' and '*obnoxius*'. The latter, like the original Greek ὑπόδικος, is a legal term. It is Rufinus the translator, of course, not Origen, who raises the point.

XXVIII

Paul uses the term 'Law' in many senses. In the Law of Moses there is a literal and a spiritual element. This Law is and always was impossible in the letter. (Comm. in Ep. ad Rom. vi. 12; Lomm. vii. 67-9. From the Latin.)

As in the foregoing passage he has mentioned so many laws,—for he has spoken of the law of God, of the law of the mind, of the law of the spirit of life, and on the other hand has mentioned also the law which is in our members, the law of death, and the law of sin—it is a point of no little investigation to decide about which of these laws he here in this passage says, For what was impossible to the law, in that it was weak through the flesh.[1] I take it however that here too, as we have often remarked in other connections, the Apostle is dividing the law of Moses into two parts; one element in it he names the flesh, another the spirit. The legal obedience which is rendered according to the letter he calls the mind of the flesh, as he speaks of a Jew of this type as, Vainly puffed up by his fleshly mind.[2] But the obedience which is understood in a spiritual sense he terms the spirit, as also in another place he says, The letter killeth, but the spirit giveth life.[3] So in the expressions he uses in this passage, Impossible to the law, and, In that it was weak through the flesh, the meaning according to the letter may be understood.

For indeed that meaning was impossible and weak, if interpreted according to the flesh, that is according to the letter. What was ever so impossible as the keeping of the Sabbath day according to the letter of the law, as we

[1] Rom. viii 3.   [2] Col. ii. 18.   [3] 2 Cor. iii. 6.

have in several connections often before remarked? A man is bidden not to leave his house, not to change his position, not to lift any burden. As the Jews who keep the law according to the flesh recognize that these things are impossible, they invent stupid and absurd interpretations, whereby they may appear to patch up the law's impossibility. What shall I say of the system of sacrifices, which all at once has become wholly impossible? Where there is no temple and no altar, there is obviously no place for offering sacrifices.

In each of these cases the law is, I will not say impossible and weak, but even already and indisputably dead. It was weak before this death, in the days when it attempted, though it did not succeed, to take away sins by the blood of bulls and of goats. It was weak also in the rules about leprosy which it never had the power to explain or to fulfil. In all these and countless other respects the law was thus impossible, and so far as regards its meaning after the flesh it was weak. Therefore, God, sending His own Son in the likeness of sinful flesh, and in view of sin—or as it stands more correctly in the Greek, For sin—condemned sin in the flesh.[1]

XXIX

The outward and inward Gospels.—(*Comm. in Joann.* i. 7–8; Lomm. i. 19–21; Br. i. 10–12; B. iv. 11–13. From the Greek.)

We must not fail to recognize that for those who had some perfection, who were not babes or under tutors and guardians,[2] for whom in a spiritual sense the fulness of the time was come, there was an advent of Christ even

---

[1] Rom. viii. 3.   [2] Gal. iii. 25; iv. 2.

earlier than His bodily advent, spiritual in character. Such were the Patriarchs, and Moses 'the servant',[1] and the Prophets who beheld Christ's glory. And just as, previous to His visible and bodily advent, there was this advent for the perfect; so too now after His coming and its proclamation is there an advent for those who are still babes, under guardians and stewards and not yet arrived at the fulness of the time. With these the forerunners of Christ, even words appropriate to child souls, have made their advent, 'schoolmasters', as they might rightly be called. But the Son Himself, the glorified God-Word, comes not yet, waiting out the preliminary training which is necessary for men of God who are to receive His divinity.[2]

Also it is well to observe that, just as there is a law that contains the shadow of those good things to come,[3] which are made clear by the veritable law when it is preached; so too the Gospel, as it is ordinarily understood by the general reader, teaches a shadow of the mysteries of Christ. But what John calls the eternal Gospel,[4] the spiritual, as it might properly be termed, makes clear and direct presentment to those who understand[5] of all that concerns the very Son of God, both of the mysteries which are presented by His words, and of the realities of which His deeds were the emblems. It will be in keeping with this to believe that, as there is a Jew and a man that has been circumcised in an outward sense, and also one circumcision that is outward, in the flesh,[6] and another

---

[1] Heb. iii. 5.
[2] Cp. § xv for this idea of many comings of Christ.
[3] Heb. x. 1.
[4] Rev. xiv. 6; cp. *Com. in Ep. ad Rom.* i. 4; Lomm. vi. 20.
[5] Prov. viii. 9.
[6] Rom. ii. 28.

that is secret; so is it with Christianity and with Baptism. Thus Paul and Peter, formerly Jews outwardly and circumcised, acquired later from Jesus corresponding qualities in their inward life. Yet for the salvation of the many, and to attain their purpose, they not only admitted in word, but even showed in action, that outwardly they still were Jews.

The same may be said of their Christianity. Just as it is impossible for Paul to be of service to Jews after the flesh unless, when reason directs, he circumcises Timothy and, when there is due cause, shaves his own head and offers sacrifice,[1] and in a word becomes unto the Jews a Jew[2] that he may gain the Jews; even so he whose aim it is to help the many will not find it possible to improve and lead on to better and higher things those who are learning the elementary lessons in the outward Christianity, through the Christianity that it is in secret alone. Hence it is essential that our Christianity should have both a spirit and a body. Where there is need for a man to preach the bodily gospel, and to say among those who are after the flesh that he knows nothing save Jesus Christ and Him crucified,[3] so must he act. But where men are found well qualified through the Spirit and bearing fruit therein, with a passion for the heavenly wisdom, to them some share must be given of the word that ascends from the incarnate life to that which was in the beginning with God.[4]

These remarks in our examination of the Gospel we believe to be not without value, for we are making a sort of attempt to distinguish in their significance the sensible

---

[1] Acts xvi. 3; xxi. 24.
[2] 1 Cor. ix. 20.
[3] *Ibid.*, ii. 2.
[4] John i. 2.

Gospel from the intelligible[1] and spiritual. Indeed our present purpose is the translation of the sensible gospel into the spiritual. For of what use is the exposition of the sensible gospel, unless it be translated into a spiritual one? Of little or none, since even ordinary people feel sure they can learn for themselves the plain meaning from the text. But every difficulty confronts us when we attempt to make our way to the depths of the Gospel's meaning and to track out the truth within it bare of types.

XXX

The admonitions of the Lord are frequently not intended to be interpreted literally. Three instances.—(Comm. in Matt. xv. 2; Lomm. iii. 329–30. From the Greek.)

If anyone wishes to take further examples of the occurrence of the letter that killeth[2] in the New Testament, let him hear for instance how the Saviour said to the Apostles, When I sent you forth without purse and wallet and shoes, lacked ye anything? Then follow the words, And they said, Nothing. Then Jesus said unto them, But now, he that hath a purse, let him take it, and likewise a wallet. And he that hath no sword, let him sell his cloak and buy one.[3] Suppose that a man because Jesus said this, failing to perceive the intention of the words, should sell the cloak you see him wear and buy a murderous sword; he takes the sword; he acts contrary

---

[1] As a rule 'spirit' and 'spiritual' are our nearest equivalents for $νοῦς$ and $νοητός$. Cp. Inge, *Plotinus*, ii. 37-8, especially the note, '$Νοῦς$ for the Christian Platonists is almost equivalent to $λόγος$ and $πνεῦμα$ which tend to flow together in their theology'. But some other term, such as 'intelligible', must be found for $νοητός$ when, as here, it is joined with $πνευματικός$.

[2] 2 Cor. iii. 6.   [3] Luke xxii. 35, 36.

to the intention of Jesus; he misinterprets His word; and he shall perish, perhaps even perish by the sword,[1] though what that sword is the present is not the time to explain.[2]

There are also the words, Salute no man on the way.[3] Suppose a man, failing to examine what Jesus meant by this command, should in his zeal for the apostolic life salute no one on the way, he would appear a churlish fellow to those who observed his conduct. And when the observers refer the cause of his disposition to the word, for sake of which he determined to behave in this fashion, they would be induced to hate the word of God, thinking that it makes those who are in the word fierce and churlish. For this he who saluted no man on the way would have the responsibility; for the sake of the letter he would suffer death; the letter killeth him. Or suppose a man cut out his right eye,[4] saying it caused him to see evil sights, or the right hand of his body, or his right foot after the flesh, he would be in the like case with those who kill because of the letter. For he himself would have kept to the letter, whereas he ought to have risen to the spirit of the utterance. Indeed other teachers of an earlier time have not been afraid to give occasion by their books for some people rashly allowing themselves, on the plea of the Kingdom of Heaven, to be made eunuchs in the third manner.[5] This third manner is similar to the two before.

---

[1] Matt. xxvi. 52.
[2] That is, he could, *more suo*, give it a mystical meaning.
[3] Luke x. 4; cp. *De Prin.* IV. iii. 3.
[4] Matt. v. 29.
[5] i.e. by their own deed. Matt. xix. 12. Origen here and in the preceding section of this book has his own act in view. Westcott in *D.C.B.* describes the passage as 'a most touching confession of his error'. He was an old man when he wrote the *Commentaries on Matthew*. Cp. Euseb. *H.E.* vi. 8; Huet. I. i. 13.

XXXI

How it was that the Baptist did not know Christ and could yet bear testimony to Him. The descent of the dove at the baptism must be spiritually interpreted.—(*In Joann.* Frag. xx; Br. ii. 236–39; B. iv. 499–501. From the Greek.)

And I knew him not.[1] I who teach you, he says, did not say these things by the light of nature or by the ordinary understanding of men. For I knew Him not; but it was through the revelation of the Holy Spirit and of the Father that I bore testimony concerning Him. For I was sent to bear witness of the Light[2] and I received the beginning of my knowledge of Him to whom I bore witness at the time when I was sent. Also one may attempt to explain the passage in question in another way. It is possible that in one respect he, John, understood, and that in another he did not know. So if he does say about the Saviour, I knew Him not, there is no contradiction in his statement to the witness that he gave. It is evident from the passage that formerly he was in ignorance, but that now through God's revelation to him he knew Him. This is quite clear from the words which immediately follow. For John himself says afterwards that he beheld the Spirit in the form of a dove descending upon the Lord. And I knew Him not, he says, but He that sent me to baptize with water, He said unto me, Upon whom thou shalt see the Spirit descending, He is my Son.[3] And I saw and bare witness. If then, even before the descent of the Spirit, he did know Him as Lamb and Man and the Prophet and the Christ and the true Light, still he lacked the

[1] John i. 31. [2] *Ibid.*, i. 8. [3] *Ibid.*, i. 32–3.

knowledge of the Son of God, and that it is He who baptizeth in the Holy Spirit. This knowledge he had on seeing the sign that was given.

This point explained, one may enquire in what sense John says he beheld the Spirit. For it is not right to suppose that the Spirit, which has an immaterial existence, was seen by the eyes of sense. Together with this point, so as to deal with the subject as a whole, we will examine expressions of a like character in prophecy. For many of the Prophets, and in a word many holy men, have recorded after seeing appearances and visions that they beheld them. Now since in other connections as well there are two distinct divisions of seeing and beholding, namely sense perception and intellectual apprehension, it is impossible that holy men should have seen by sense perception either God or, in a single term, the Trinity, or anything that, though inferior to the Trinity, has intelligible or spiritual existence. It remains that they beheld their visions spiritually, not according to their actual nature, but in proportion to their own powers of seeing by means of a corresponding object. So no doubt, though the Holy Spirit has no figure or shape or form of any kind, John receives the idea of a dove ; and, though the Holy Spirit never moves from place to place, he sees its descent from heaven upon Jesus as He is baptized. And what follows shows that in none of these cases does the apprehension come through sense perception. Upon whom thou shalt see, it says, the Spirit descending and remaining on Him.[1] The descent of anything, provided it be a body, we can see even by sense perception. But it is not by sight but by intelligible apprehension that

---

[1] John i. 33.

what descends is seen to remain on him on whom it has descended.[1] Sense perception has no power to apprehend that a thing remains, so as to guarantee this act of vision. As another proof one may remark how the other Evangelists state the descent of the Spirit upon the Son to have been seen by John; He saw the heavens opened or rent asunder.[2] We cannot see such an opening or rending of the heavens by sense perception; such perception is not even possible in the case of the denser bodies, water and air, I mean; let us say of the aether also, if that is anything distinct from the heavens. All that passes through continuous substances, provided they are not solid, goes right through them without any other force providing an opening and passage for it. What passes through makes the opening, which reunites after the passage of the passing body. You cannot see a dividing of water unless you introduce a more solid body. If so, an opening of the heavens would not come under sight. The Holy Spirit that descended thence is not a body. So this also was beheld by the Baptist in a spiritual sense.

The fact is also to be noticed that the Holy Spirit remained on Jesus alone. For if it had descended and remained on any other as well, it would not have been a sign to distinguish Him who baptized in the Holy Spirit. And this may also be proved thus: the Holy Spirit dwells in unstained and pure souls, never enduring to be where there is sin. For a holy spirit of discipline will flee deceit and will start away from thoughts that are without understanding.[3] And David in some sin makes request to God, saying, Take not Thy holy spirit from

---

[1] The text is uncertain here.
[2] Matt. iii. 16; Mark i. 10; Luke iii. 21.
[3] Wisd. i. 5.

me.[1] Since then Jesus alone did no sin nor had He guile in His mouth[2]—for only of Him was it said, Who knew no sin[3]—naturally the Spirit descending on Him remained.[4] All this, the descending, I mean, of the Spirit from heaven, and its remaining on Him, was written for a higher purpose. It has no significance of fact but spiritual truth, as has been already said. The Holy Spirit is inseparable from the Son. The Son has not a position in space, neither has the Father, so that the Holy Spirit could move from place to place and pass from the Father to the Son. As a principle, what relates to the godhead we should interpret spiritually, even though it be expressed in human language, for instance standing, sitting, going up, and whatever similar terms are used in Scripture of the godhead.

XXXII

Paul is our authority for the spiritual exegesis of the Old Testament.—(In Exod. Hom. v. 1 ; Lomm. ix. 48-50 ; B. vi. 183-85. From the Latin.)

Paul the Apostle, the teacher of the Gentiles in faith and truth,[5] imparted to the church, which he gathered together from the Gentiles, the principle on which it ought to estimate the books of the law, which had been received from others and to the church were hitherto unknown and wholly strange. He feared lest, receiving an instruction not of its own and being ignorant of the principle of such instruction, the church might run risk in

---

[1] Ps. li. 11.
[2] Isa. liii. 9 ; 1 Pet. ii. 22.
[3] 2 Cor. v. 21.
[4] John i. 33.
[5] 1 Tim. ii. 7.

using a strange Testament.[1] On this account he himself in some passages gives us examples of the meaning, so that we too may adopt a like method elsewhere. We must not believe that we have become disciples of the Jews because we are at one with them in reading the Old Testament. This is the point then in which he insists that the disciples of Christ differ from the disciples of the synagogue; the law, through the misunderstanding of which they failed to welcome Christ, we by our spiritual interpretation prove to have been a precious gift for the teaching of the church. The only meaning the Jews recognized was this; that the children of Israel set out from Egypt, and their first journey was from Rameses; journeying thence they came to Succoth; journeying from Succoth they came to Etham, at the encampment by the sea. Next the cloud went there in front of them, and the rock followed, of which they drank. They also crossed through the Red Sea, and came into the wilderness of Sinai.

Now let us examine the nature of the rule of interpretation which Paul imparts to us from this passage. Writing to the Corinthians he says in a certain place;[2] We know that our fathers were all under the cloud (and all passed through the sea; [3]) and were all baptized unto Moses in the cloud and in the sea; and did all eat the same spiritual meat; and did all drink the same spiritual drink: for they drank of a spiritual rock that followed them: and the rock was Christ. You observe how greatly the sense Paul gives us differs from the narrative of the text. What the Jews think of as crossing the sea

---

[1] '*Instrumentum*' is the translator's term. It is common in Tertullian. *E. G., Apol.* 18; *Adv. Marcion*, iv. 1.
[2] 1 Cor. x. 1-4.
[3] B. omits.

Paul calls baptism ; what they regard as the cloud Paul terms the Holy Spirit. In a similar sense must be interpreted the teaching of the Lord in the Gospels, when he says, Except a man be born of water and of the Holy Spirit, he cannot enter into the kingdom of God.[1] The manna again, which the Jews regarded as food for the belly and satisfaction for the appetite, Paul terms spiritual meat. And not Paul alone but the Lord as well says of this in the Gospel, Your fathers did eat the manna in the wilderness and they died. But he that shall eat of the bread which I give him shall not die for ever. And after this he says, I am the bread, which came down out of heaven.[2] Next Paul makes a clear statement about the rock that followed them and says, That rock was Christ.

What then are we to do who have received from Paul, a master of the Church, such principles of interpretation ? Does it not seem right to keep a rule of this kind, as given to us, by observing a like standard in other cases ? Or, as some desire, are we to desert what the great and noble Apostle[3] has told us and turn again to Jewish fables ? For myself, were I to interpret this passage otherwise than as Paul approves, I should think it a surrender to the enemies of Christ, exactly what the prophet says, Woe unto him that giveth his neighbour drink with a violent overthrow.[4] Let us cultivate then these seeds of spiritual interpretation, which we have received from the blessed Apostle Paul, just so far as the Lord through your prayers shall be pleased to enlighten us.[5]

---

[1] John iii. 5.   [2] *Ibid.*, vi. 49-51.
[3] '*Tantus ac talis Apostolus*'. Cp. his mention of the '*Solita magnificentia*' of Paul in *In Ep. ad Rom.* x. 14. Lomm. vii. 420.
[4] Hab. ii. 15. LXX.
[5] Origen often refers to the literalism of Jewish exegesis and to the sanction Paul gives to allegory. Cp. '*Si quis haec secundum litteram solum audire vult et intelligere, magis cum Judaeis quam-*

XXXIII

Paul is the trusted servant who has had, not full vision, but passing glimpses in the royal palace of divine truth. Revelation is real but partial. (Comm. in Ep. ad Rom. v. i; Lomm. vi. 322-24. From the Latin.)

There is another point to which I think attention should be drawn at once. It seems to me that the Apostle Paul, especially in the passages with which we are now dealing,[1] uses often the language that would befit a faithful and wise servant who was taken by his lord, some mighty king, into the royal treasure-house and shown the different spacious chambers, with their various puzzling approaches, one of them as he would be shown intended for entrance, another for exit. Sometimes too several entrances would lead to a central chamber, in the way we see large houses frequently built on earth. To this faithful servant, as he is taken round, there would also be shown the storehouse of the royal silver, another for the gold, also for precious stones, for pearls, for different necklaces, one place too for the royal purple, another for the crowns. Besides he would be shown the queen's bedsteads, situated in several different apartments. But all these would not be fully displayed to him, with doors thrown wide open, but

---

cum Christianis debet habere auditorium. Si autem vult Christianus esse et Pauli discipulus, audiat eum dicentem quia lex spiritualis est ' *In Gen.* Hom. vi. 1; Lomm. viii. 181 ; B. vi. 66. Literalism in exegesis was of course also found within the Church. See Redepenning i. 302 ; also *supra*, p. xxxii.

[1] Rom. v. 12 *sqq*.

only with doors ajar, so that he could recognize indeed his lord's treasures and the wealth of the king, but not obtain clear and complete information of these various objects.

And afterwards this servant, who has been so trusted that his lord the king has made him acquainted with the vast extent of his possessions, would be sent to assemble an army for the king, to hold a levy and inspect the troops. By reason of his fidelity, in order to obtain more men for service and to assemble a more numerous army for the king, he will find it necessary to publish in part what he has seen. Yet also, by reason of his wisdom, knowing that it is necessary to hide the king's secret, he will rather make use of hints than of full descriptions. There will be no hiding of the king's power, yet the details of the arrangement and decoration of the palace and its plan will remain undivulged.

This, as I said, is what the Apostle Paul seems to me to do in this passage. Not only because, as he himself says,[1] it is in part he knows, in part he understands, but also in our interest, since we are unable to take in even the things he knows in part, he restrains his language and gives us in one or two words just a glance or look into the chamber of every mystery. Now he will enter by one door and go out by another. Now he will come in on one side and hasten away to another chamber. If you look for him, you will not find that he has gone out by the same way as he came in.[2]

---

[1] 1 Cor. xiii. 9–12.
[2] Origen's comment on this characteristic passage of St. Paul shows real insight. The many ideas, the abrupt changes, the hints of thoughts not developed, the lack of order and control, are all in keeping with Origen's suggestive and appropriate figure.

XXXIV

The comments of Heracleon on our Lord's conversation with the woman of Samaria are sometimes commendable, sometimes mistaken. (Comm. in Joann. xiii. 10; Lomm. ii. 18–19; Br. i. 256–57; B. iv. 234–35. From the Greek.)

Let us also consider the comments of Heracleon[1] on the passage. He says that earlier life and its glory were feeble and temporary and defective. It was, he says, a life of the world. And he thinks he can bring proof of its being a life of the world from the statement that the cattle of Jacob drank of it.[2] Now if he meant that the knowledge which is in part[3] is feeble, temporary and defective, whether it be knowledge derived from Scripture as compared with the unspeakable words which it is not lawful for a man to utter,[4] or whether it be all the knowledge that we now have in a mirror, in a riddle,[5] which vanishes away when perfection is come, then we should not have criticized his view. But if he takes this line in order to discredit what is old,[6] he would be open

---

[1] Herecleon was a Valentinian Gnostic, according to Clement of Alexandria (*Strom.* IV. ix. 71), the most esteemed member (δοκιμώτατος) of the school. Origen quotes him frequently, usually criticizing his expositions. 'Minute care runs through his commentary on St. John . . . but his allegorical interpretations are of the usual sort, neither better nor worse than others'. So Gwatkin, *Early Church History*, ii. 46. Cp. also A. E. Brooke, *The Fragments of Heracleon* in Texts and Studies i. 4; De Faye, *Gnostiques et Gnosticisme* 53–80 and Salmon in $D.C.B.$

[2] John iv. 12.
[3] 1 Cor. xiii. 9.
[4] 2 Cor. xii. 4.
[5] 1 Cor. xiii. 12.
[6] i.e. The Old Testament. This was definitely rejected by Marcion and his followers, and only accepted by the other Gnostic schools with the reservation that the God of the Old Testament, the creator or demiurge, was distinct from, and inferior to, the supreme Deity, who was revealed by Christ.

to criticism. He says that the water the Saviour gives proceeds from the Spirit and its power. In this he makes no error. On the words, Shall never thirst,[1] his interpretation runs word for word thus; 'The life of the Lord is eternal, never subject to corruption, as is the former life drawn from the well, but abiding. For the grace and the gift of our Saviour can never be taken away; they are never exhausted, never corrupted, in him who has share of them.'

As to his statement that the former life was subject to corruption, if he had meant the life according to the letter, seeking himself and finding the life according to the spirit, which comes by the removal of the veil,[2] his view would have been quite sound. But if he is bringing a general charge of corruption against what is old, clearly he does this because of his failure to see that those earlier good things did contain the shadow of things to come.[3] There is something attractive in his interpretation of 'springing up', as implying that those who partake richly of what is given from above,[4] themselves in turn pour forth what has been given to them unto the eternal life of others. Moreover he praises the woman of Samaria for having shown an unquestioning faith, in keeping with her nature, raising no questions on what the Lord said to her. Now if he had meant to approve of the woman's deliberate choice, without any suggestion that hers was a higher nature,[5] we too should have agreed with him. But if he is referring the cause of her agreement with the Lord to natural character, such agreement not being given to all, then we must refute his argument. I do not understand

---

[1] John iv. 14.   [2] 2 Cor. iii. 16.
[3] Heb. x. 1.   [4] 2 Pet. i. 11.
[5] Another reference to the Gnostic theory of distinct natures.

how Heracleon, giving an interpretation not justified
by the text, says of the words, Give me this water,[1] that
the woman, after being stung for a while by the Word,
afterwards hated the very place of that living water, as
it had been called. Further also, commenting on, Give
me this water, that I thirst not neither come hither to
draw, he states that the woman in saying this makes
clear the laborious, hardly obtainable and unwholesome
character of that water. What evidence can he give that
Jacob's water was unwholesome?

XXXV

*The Song of Songs is a dramatic love poem. Herein the
relations of the Beloved to her Lover are symbolic of the
relations of the Church to Christ and of the individual
soul to the Divine Word.*—(*In Cant. Cantic.* i. Lomm.
xiv. 327-32 ; B. viii. 89-92. From the Latin.)

Let him kiss me with the kisses of his mouth.[2] We
should bear in mind, as we have already observed in the
introduction, that this book has the character of a
marriage poem and is written in the form of a drama.
And a drama, we have stated, means the introduction of
certain characters, who speak their parts, while others at
intervals join them, others retire, others come in, and
thus the whole action lies in the changes of the
characters. This then will be the scheme of the whole
book, and on this principle we shall apply to it interpretation, treating it as a story, to the best of our
ability. But the spiritual meaning is equally to be

---

[1] John iv. 15.   [2] *In Cant. Cantic.* i. 2.

determined by the principle indicated in the introduction. This relates to the Church's attitude to Christ, under the names of the Beloved and the Lover; or to the soul's union with the Word of God. Here then, viewing the poem as a story, we have before us a certain woman beloved, who has received from her noble lover most valuable gifts, described as her wedding gifts or dowry.[1] As however long time passes and the lover delays, we see her agitated by the longing for his love, distracted as she lies at home, doing anything and everything so as at last to secure the sight of her lover and the delight of his kisses. Since she sees that neither can her passion be put off, nor can she obtain her desires, she betakes herself to prayer and appeals to God, knowing Him to be the father of her lover. Let us observe her then, lifting holy hands without anger or dispute, in elaborate attire joined with modesty and restraint, arrayed in the most costly ornaments appropriate to the adornment of a noble woman beloved. But she feels the surging longing for her lover. She is distraught through the inward wound of love, and, as we have said, she pours out her prayer to God and says of her lover, Let him kiss me with the kisses of his mouth. Such is the meaning the poem contains, if we interpret it as a story written in the form of a drama.

Let us see however whether an inward interpretation can in the following manner be appropriately applied to it. Suppose the Church, longing for union with Christ. Regard the Church as the assembly of all the saints. Suppose this Church, all it members represented by a single character, speaking and saying, All things are

---

[1] Gifts received by the bride from her lover, like wedding gifts, ἔεδνα, in Homer.

mine ; I possess in full measure the gifts which I have received before marriage by way of wedding gifts or dowry. For long time, during my preparations for union with the King's son, the first born of all creation,[1] His holy angels have attended me and ministered unto me, bringing to me the law, as a wedding gift. For the law is said to have been ordained through angels by the hand of a mediator.[2] The prophets also have ministered unto me. They too have not only said all things to give me evidence and information about the Son of God, unto whom by the offering of these pledges—so they are called—and wedding gifts they sought to betroth me. They have also, in order to kindle in me the passion and longing for Him, made announcement to me in prophetic voices of His coming, and filled with the Holy Spirit have foretold His countless virtues and His immeasureable deeds. They have portrayed His appearance, His beauty, His gentleness, so that from all they said I could scarce endure the fire of my passion for Him. But since the age is now well nigh at its end, and still His presence is not allowed me, but I only behold His ministers ascending and descending to me, therefore to Thee, the Father of my lover, I pour out my prayer and make entreaty that at last, having pity upon our love, Thou wilt send Him, so that now He may speak to me no longer through His ministers, the angels and prophets alone, but that He Himself may come and kiss me with the kisses of His mouth—pour, that is, the words of His mouth into my mouth—and I may hear Him as He speaks and watch Him as He teaches. For these are the kisses of Christ, which He bestowed upon the Church, when at His coming Christ Himself, dwelling in the

---

[1] Col. i. 15.   [2] Gal. iii. 19.

flesh, preached unto her the words of faith and love and peace. This was the promise in Isaiah, who, sent in advance of the beloved, had said, Not an ambassador or an angel, but the Lord Himself shall save us.[1]

As a third interpretation, let us bring in the soul, whose every desire it is to be joined in fellowship with the Word of God and to enter into the mysteries of His wisdom and knowledge, as into the chamber of a heavenly bridegroom. Unto this soul His gifts by way of dowry have been already given. For just as the dowry of the church was the books of the law and of the prophets, so to the soul the law of nature, the reasonable mind, the freedom of the will, must be accounted as marriage gifts. Regard the teaching of her earliest training as coming down to her from guides and teachers, bearing these gifts for her dowry. But since she does not find in them the full and complete satisfaction of her longing and her love, she prays that her clear and virgin mind may have the light of the illumination and the intercourse of the very Word of God. For when the mind is filled with divine knowledge and understanding through no agency of man or of angel, then may the mind believe that it receives the very kisses of the Word of God. For these and similar kisses suppose the soul to say in prayer to God, Let Him kiss me with the kisses of His mouth. For so long as the soul was unable to receive the full and substantial teaching of the very Word of God, she had the kisses of his friends, knowledge, that is, from the lips of teachers. But when she begins of her own accord to see things hidden, to disentangle intricacies, to solve what is complicated, to expound parables and riddles and the words of the wise upon

---

[1] Isa. xxxiii. 22.

correct lines of interpretation, then may the soul believe she has now received the very kisses of her lover, that is, of the Word of God. Kisses, the writer says, in the plural, that we may understand that the bringing of each particular hidden meaning into light is a kiss of the Word of God bestowed upon the perfect soul. Possibly it was upon this principle the prophetic and perfect mind used to say, I opened my mouth and drew in my breath.[1]

By the mouth of the lover we understand to be meant the power whereby He enlightens the mind. Addressing as it were some word of love to her, supposing she be worthy to receive the visitation of such excellence, He explains to her all unknown and hidden things. This is the truer, closer, holier kiss, which is said to be given by the lover, the Word of God, to His beloved, the pure and perfect soul. Of this reality the kiss, which at the hour of the Mysteries we give one to another in church, is a symbol.[2] Whenever then we make enquiry in our heart as to divine doctrines and interpretations, and discover truth without teachers, so often may we believe that kisses are given unto us by our lover, the Word of God. And when, seeking for some point in the divine meaning, we fail to discover it, then may we take up the spirit of this petition and ask God for the coming of His Word and say, Let Him kiss me with the kisses of His mouth. And our Father knows the capacity of each soul, and understands at what time, to which soul, and which kiss of His Word He should give, in the way of course of understanding and of instruction.

---

[1] Ps. cxix. 131.
[2] Cf. *In Ep. ad Rom.* x. 33 ; Lomm. vii. 438-39 ; also references in Tertullian and in Clement ; Warren, *Liturgy of the Ante-Nicene Church*, 131.

XXXVI

Shadows (In Cant. Cantic. iii. Lomm. xv. 13-16; B. viii. 181-84. From the Latin.)

In connection with the mention of this shadow under which the Church declares she has desired to sit,[1] I do not deem it out of place that we should put before you such passages as we can discover in the divine Scriptures, so that the nature of the shadow of this apple tree may be more fully and spiritually recognized.[2] Jeremiah says in the Lamentations, Christ, the Lord, the spirit of our countenance, was included in our corruptions, unto whom we said, Under His shadow we shall live among the nations.[3] Thus you see how at the prompting of the Holy Spirit the prophet asserts that it is upon the nations that life is bestowed from the shadow of Christ, and how to us it is not His shadow that gives life.[4] Also at the conception of His body it is said to Mary, The Holy Spirit shall come upon thee and the power of the Most High shall overshadow thee.[5] If then at His conception there was the overshadowing of the Most High, His shadow will appropriately give life to the nations. Appropriately too His beloved, the Church, desires to sit under the shadow of the apple tree, in order clearly that she may be partaker of the life that is in His shadow. As for the other trees of the forest,

---

[1] *Cant. Cantic.* ii. 3.
[2] This is a characteristic passage. Origen collects from Scripture numerous references to shades and shadows, and leaves the reader to harmonize them. The shadow may be the reflection and outline of the reality; or it may be the protecting shelter from heat. Scriptural and Platonic associations are, as often, blended.
[3] Lam. iv. 20.
[4] He may mean the Church has the reality, not the shadow only, though this does not suit what follows.
[5] Luc. i. 35.

their shadow is such that he who sits beneath it seems to sit in the region of the shadow of death.[1]

And further, to make the passage we have in hand clearer and clearer still, let us ask in what sense the apostle asserts that the law has the shadow of good things to come, and speaks of all that is written about holy days and sabbaths and new moons—the directions, I mean, which were carried out in the letter—as the shadow of good things to come;[2] also in what sense he declares that all the ritual of the ancients was a pattern and shadow of heavenly things. Certainly, if that is the case, all who were under the law and possessed the shadow of a still truer law, are represented as sitting under the shadow of the law. But we have no connection with this shadow, for we are not under the law but under grace.[3] Yet though we are not under the shadow which was caused by the letter of the law, still we are under a better shadow. For we live under the shadow of Christ among the nations. There is a certain advance in passing from the shadow of the law to the shadow of Christ. Because Christ is the life, the truth and the way, we are first brought under the shadow of the way, also under the shadow of the life, also under the shadow of the truth, so that we may know in part, in a mirror and in a riddle, in order that later on, if we advance by this way, which is Christ, we may be able to arrive at knowing face to face the things which we had first beheld as in a shadow and in a riddle.[4] No man will be able to reach what is true and perfect, unless he has first had a desire and longing to sit in this shadow. Job too says, All the life of men upon earth is a shadow;[5] I suppose

---

[1] Isa. ix. 2.
[2] Heb. x. 1.
[3] Rom. vi. 14.
[4] 1 Cor. xiii. 12.
[5] Job vii. 1–2 ; xiv. 2.

because the soul in this life is overshadowed by the veil of this solid body.

All then who are in this life must be under a sort of shadow. And some there are who sit in the region of the shadow of death, they, that is, who do not believe in Christ. But the Church declares with confidence, I sat down under the shadow of my beloved with great delight; though truly there was a time when a man could sit under the shadow of the law and be protected from the severity of the glare and heat. But that time passed away. Now we must come to the shadow of the apple tree. However much the shadows of which a man may avail himself vary, still it seems that every soul, so long as it is in this present life, finds some shadow necessary, I suppose because of the heat of the sun, at the rising of which straightway the seed, which has not struck its roots deep, withers and perishes.[1] The shadow of the law did indeed slightly avert this heat; but the shadow of Christ, under which we now live among the nations, faith, that is, in His incarnation, will wholly turn aside and extinguish it. For he who was wont to scorch those who walked under the shadow of the law, at the time of Christ's death was seen to fall like lightning from heaven, though still the period of his shadow is running out its course in the ending of the age. For, as we remarked, after the consummation of the age we shall behold the truth, not in a mirror nor in a riddle, but face to face. A like character too I find in the passage, Under the shadow of thy wings will I rejoice.[2] Also, later on in this book, the beloved says, My beloved is mine and I am his; he feedeth his flock

---

[1] Matt. xiii. 5-6.   [2] Ps. lvii. 1.

among the lilies, until the day be cool and the shadows flee away.[1] By this he teaches us that a time will come when all shadows shall be taken away and truth shall alone be left.

XXXVII

On the Song of the Well in the book of Numbers. The literal sense has not much value, but the well may be mystically interpreted as the source of spiritual truth. (In Num. Hom. xii. 1; Lomm. x. 125–30; B. vii. 93–97. From the Latin.)

There has been read to us from the book of Numbers the lesson of the well and of the song which Israel sang at the well. We see that it abounds, as is usual, or even beyond what is usual, in hidden meanings. It says, There is a well. This is the well whereof the Lord said unto Moses, Gather the people together and I will give them water to drink.[2] Yet I do not consider that the literal historical sense has in these words much claim. What is the sense of the Lord giving special orders unto Moses to gather the people, so that he may give them water from the well to drink? As if the people would not even of their own accord assemble at the well to drink. Why then is the prophet so specially bidden by his own insistence and effort to gather the people to draw water from the well? Thus does the worthlessness of the letter send us on to the treasure of the spiritual meaning.

On this account I think it is appropriate to collect mystic sayings about wells, so that from a comparison of several passages any obscure point in the text now before

---

[1] *Cant. Cantic.* ii. 16-17.   [2] Num. xxi. 16.

us may become clear.[1] Now the Spirit of God says by Solomon in the Proverbs, Drink waters out of thine own cisterns, and from the spring of thine own wells, and let not thy waters be dispersed abroad beyond thy spring—although in other copies we have read, And let thy waters be dispersed abroad beyond thy spring.[2] Thy waters are to be for thyself alone and no stranger is to share them. Each one of us then, according to this description, has a well in his own nature. Nay, we will say more ; each one of us has not one well but many wells, not one cistern of water but many cisterns. For it did not say, Drink waters out of thine own cistern, but, Out of thine own cisterns ; not, From the spring of thy well, but, From the spring of thy wells. We read too that the patriarchs had wells ;[3] Abraham had, and Isaac had. I suppose Jacob had one too.

Making a start with these wells, run through all Scripture, making note of the wells, and come right through to the Gospels. There you will find the well on which our Saviour sat and rested after the toil of His journey, on the occasion when, as the woman of Samaria came and wished to draw water from the well, the force of the well or of the wells in Scripture is explained, and a comparison is made of the different waters, and there also the secrets of divine mystery are revealed.[4] For it is said that if a man drinks of the water which that earthly well contained, he will thirst again ; whereas he who drinks of the water which Jesus gives, in him there shall be a fountain of water springing up unto eternal life.

---

[1] His customary method. See *supra*, p. xix.
[2] Prov. v. 15-16. The variation is in the LXX. The passage originally had a very different meaning from that which Origen gives to it.
[3] Gen. xxvi.
[4] John iv. 6 *sqq.*

Also in another passage in the Gospel there is mention no longer of a fountain or of a well, but of something more. He that believeth, it says, in Him, out of his belly, as the Scripture saith, shall flow rivers of living water.[1] You see then that he that believeth in Him has within him not only a well but even wells, and not only springs but even rivers, springs and rivers which not only refresh this mortal life but even give a life that is eternal. In accordance then with the passage in the Proverbs which we have quoted, wherever wells and a spring are mentioned together, we must believe that the Word of God is intended. It is a well if it conceals some deep mystery. It is a spring if it flows forth in plenty for the people. Nor is it a useless question to ask how we can explain the plural number as used of the wells and the singular as used of the spring—for Wisdom says in the Proverbs, Drink waters from the spring of thine own wells.[2] Let us consider then what are the wells which he speaks of as having one spring. I think the knowledge of the Father ingenerate may be understood as one well, and the apprehending of the only-begotten Son should be understood as a second well. For the Son is different from the Father, and He that is the Father is not also the Son, as He says Himself in the Gospel, It is another that beareth witness of me, even the Father.[3] And again I think a third well may be seen in the knowledge of the Holy Spirit. For He too is different from the Father and from the Son, as it is said of Him no less clearly in the Gospel. The Father shall send you another Comforter, even the Spirit of truth.[4] It is then this distinction of three persons in Father, Son and Holy Spirit which is suggested

---

[1] John vii. 38.
[2] Prov. v. 15. LXX.
[3] John viii. 18.
[4] *Ibid.* xiv. 16–17.

by the plural number of the wells. Yet of these three wells there is one spring. For the substance and nature of the Trinity is one. In this way the distinction in holy Scripture which lies in the words, From the spring of thy wells,[1] will be found not without meaning. Careful precision is given to its mystic language, so that what is said in plural of the Persons may be in keeping with the Substance in the singular.[2]

Also we may find wells of another kind. There is a knowledge of things, about which the man who was filled with the wisdom of God used to say, For himself gave me an unerring knowledge of the things that are, to know the constitution of the world and the operation of the elements; the beginning and ends and middle of times; the alternation, variation and succession of seasons; the circuit of years and the position of stars; the natures of living creatures and the ragings of wild beasts; the violences of winds and the thoughts of men; the diversities of plants and the virtues of roots.[3] See you what wells there be in the knowledge of things? The knowledge of plants, for instance, is a well, and possibly the nature of each plant has a well of its own. There is a well too in the knowledge of living creatures, and possibly each kind of living creature has its own well. There is a well again in the scheme of the seasons, in its alternations and variations. Since every one of these contains a science deep and profound, they are rightly in a figure termed wells.

And so long as the mystery of Christ was hidden from the ages and the generations, the science of these things

---

[1] Pro. v. 15.
[2] How much of this interpretation comes from Origen, how much from Rufinus, it is of course impossible to say.
[3] Wisd. vii. 17-20.

was rightly described as wells. But when, as Paul says, God revealed them to believers through His spirit,[1] these things are all made to be springs and rivers, so that the knowledge of them is not so much now contained in secret, as poured forth for the multitude, giving refreshment and satisfaction to believers. Therefore, I believe, the Saviour used to say to his disciples that he who believes in Him and drinks the water of His teaching, in him shall be no more a well or a spring but rivers of living water.[2] For just as that one well, which is the Word of God, becomes wells and springs and rivers innumerable, so too the soul of man, which is made in the image of God, can obtain and give forth from itself wells and springs and rivers. Still it is true that the wells in our soul have need of the digger, for they must be cleansed, and all that is earthly must be cleared away from them, that those channels of rational thought which God has formed in the soul may send forth streams pure and undefiled. For so long as the earth covers up the channels of the water and clogs the outflow of the stream, the flow of pure water cannot break forth. This, for instance, explains the saying that the servants of Abraham dug wells but the Philistines stopped them and filled them up with earth.[3] Isaac also who had inherited his father's property dug the wells again and removed the Philistines' earth, which they through jealousy had thrown into the waters. Another point we notice in Genesis, from which book we recognize this narrative to be taken, that while Abraham was alive the Philistines did not dare to fill up the wells or to throw earth into them. But when he had departed from this life, at once the Philistines grew strong and made designs

---

[1] 1 Cor. ii. 10.   [2] John vii. 38.   [3] Gen. xxvi. 15.

upon his wells. But they are soon renewed by Isaac and return to their proper order.

Besides this, the servant of Abraham, when Isaac is going to betroth or marry a wife, finds Rebecca at the well.[1] Rebecca means Patience, and she does not become the wife of Isaac anywhere except at the well. In the same way Jacob, when he came to Mesopotamia, having orders from his father not to take a wife of another race or of foreign blood, finds Rachel in his turn also at the well.[2] And Moses meets Zipporah at the well.[3] If you have understood the significance and character of the wives of holy men, do you too, if you wish to win Patience as your bride, or Wisdom, or the other Virtues of the soul, and to say, as it is said about Wisdom, Her did I love, her did I seek to make my wife,[4] come often, come without fail, to those wells, and there shall you find such a bride as these. For it is by the living waters, by the streams, that is, of the living Word, that all the virtues of the soul assuredly dwell. There are many wells which we speak of as within the soul. And there are many others, which may be recognized in particular passages and meanings of Scripture.

Yet that well is beyond others notable and exceptional about which in the present passage the Scripture says, that not certain ordinary men dug it, but the princes, and others even more exalted, whom it terms kings.[5] For this reason a Psalm is sung to God at this particular well. Therefore is it written, Go, saith he, to the well. This is the well of which the Lord said to Moses, Gather the people together and I will give them water from the well,

---

[1] Gen. xxiv. [2] *Ibid.* xxix.
[3] Exod. ii. [4] Wisd. vii. 10.
[5] Num. xxi. 18.

saith the Lord. Moses is bidden to gather the people, that they may assemble at the well and drink water. Now we have often shown that Moses must be understood as the law. It is then the law of God which summons thee to resort to the well. To what well but that of which we have spoken before, even Jesus Christ, the Son of God, existent in His own person, yet with the Father and the Spirit named as the one holy spring of Deity ? To this well, then, that is to the faith of Christ, the law summons us. For He said Himself, Moses wrote of me.[1] For what purpose does He summon us ? That we may drink water and sing unto Him a song. That is, with the heart we are to believe unto righteousness, and with the mouth we are to make confession unto salvation.[2]

---

[1] John. v. 46.   [2] Rom. x. 10.

PART IV

THE HOLY SCRIPTURES—PROBLEMS AND CRITICISM

XXXVIII

Alike in Nature and in Scripture God's workmanship is only partially understood. For the present, in each case, we must accept difficulties.—(*Selecta in Psalmos.* Also *Philocal.* ii. Lomm. xi. 375–77 ; xxv. 38–9 ; *Philocal.* Ed. Robinson 39–40. From the Greek.)

If, The words of the Lord are pure words, as silver tried by fire, tested in earth, purified seven times,[1] and if the Holy Spirit deliberately, with all exactitude, has prompted them through the ministers of the word, you will surely not fail to observe the exact proportion in which the wisdom of God extends to all inspired Scripture, right to the most casual letter. That perhaps is the reason why the Saviour said, One jot and one tittle shall in no wise pass away from the law till all things be accomplished.[2] We know how, in its work of creation, the divine skill is not only displayed in the heavens, and in sun and moon and stars, as it pervades the whole of their mass, but also on earth it operates in the same way in any common substance, so that the bodies of the tiniest animals have not been neglected by the Creator. Far more is this true of the souls that exist in them, each soul receiving some special property, the saving element

---

[1] Ps. xii. 6.   [2] Matt. v. 18.

in the irrational.¹ It is so with the plants of the soil; in each is an element of design, affecting its roots and leaves and the fruit it can bear and the characteristics of its qualities. Now we take the same view of all the Scriptures that proceed from the inspiration of the Holy Spirit. A sacred Providence has bestowed through books a more than human wisdom upon the race of men and has planted the saving oracles, the traces of wisdom, one might say in every letter, so far as this is possible. He who has once accepted these Scriptures as the work of Him who created the world, must be convinced that whatever difficulties in regard to creation confront those who strive to understand its system, will occur also in regard to the Scriptures.² There are things in creation hard to discover, or even undiscoverable for the nature of man. We are not in consequence to condemn the Creator of the universe; not, for instance, because we cannot discover the reason for the creation of scorpions or of other venomous beasts. The right thing then for a man who feels the weakness of our race, and who knows it is impossible for us to understand the reasons of God's design even when most minutely examined, is to ascribe the knowledge of these things to God, who will later on, if we be judged worthy, reveal to us the matters about which we are now reverently in doubt. So too in regard to the divine Scriptures we must recognize that many things contained in them are difficult to explain.

As for those ³ who announce that, after revolting from the Creator of the world, they have recourse to a God of their own making, they ought to discover a

---

¹ Cp. the λόγοι σπερματικοί of the Stoics.
² Bishop Butler, as is well known, quotes this passage in the Introduction to the *Analogy of Religion*.
³ The Gnostics.

solution of the difficulties with which we confront them, or else to persuade their own conscience, after such shocking audacity, to put a stop to its impiety, equally in regard to their own views on the disputed subjects, and with regard to the difficulties with which they are challenged. For if the difficulties we raise remain just the same, even if they abandon the idea of God, how much more reverent would it have been to retain the conception of God, known as the Creator from His handiwork, and to avoid godless and impious utterances with regard to a deity so great.[1]

XXXIX

There are eleven Psalms of Moses. The title of Psalm xc (lxxxix), which ascribes it to Moses, applies also to the ten Psalms which follow. Psalm ci (c) is by David. (Selecta in Psalmos. Lomm. xi. 352-54. From the Greek.)

Now I used to think that in the book of Psalms there was one which had for its title, A Prayer of Moses the Man of God.[2] But later on, having my interest in some of the oracles of God aroused through Jullus, the patriarch, and through one of those who were termed wise men among the Jews,[3] I heard that through the whole book of the Psalms, beginning with the first and second,

---

[1] The heretics, that is to say, since they must admit the unsolved problems in nature with which the orthodox confront them, should restrain their bold assertions and suspend judgment in regard to the similar problems in Scripture.

[2] This is the title of Ps. xc.

[3] Origen often considered the views of Hebrew interpreters: cp. *Magister quidam qui ex Hebraeis crediderat. In Num* Hom. xiii. 5; *Audivi quondam a quodam Hebraeo hunc locum exponente. In Ezech.* Hom. iv. 8; Lomm. x. 151; xiv. 68; B. vii. 114; viii. 369.

those Psalms which in the Hebrew have no title, or which have a title but not the name of the writer, belong to the author whose name stands at the head of the last preceding Psalm that has a title. Speaking on these matters he used at first to assert that thirteen Psalms belong to Moses. But, from what I heard [1] . . . their number is eleven.

Later I enquired of one they account a wise man and was told that the number is eleven, of which the 89th begins, Lord, thou hast been our refuge from one generation to another.[2] The next, called with us the 90th, begins, He that dwelleth in the secret place of the Most High; also, so he said, a Psalm of Moses. So too the Psalm that has a title but not the writer's name—I mean the 91st, entitled, A Psalm, a Song for the Sabbath Day —he said was by Moses; it begins, It is a good thing to give thanks unto the Lord, and to sing praise unto thy name, O Most High. The Psalm we call the 92nd was also without a title, which begins, The Lord reigneth; He is apparelled with majesty. This too he said was by Moses. So also the 93rd, which begins, O Lord, the God to whom vengeance belongeth; and the 94th, which begins, O come let us sing unto the Lord; and the 95th, which begins, O sing unto the Lord a new song, sing unto the Lord all the whole earth; and the 96th, which begins, The Lord reigneth, the earth shall rejoice. Likewise the 97th, of which the title is only, A Psalm. For the words, Of David, which stand in some copies, were neither written in the Hebrew nor in the other versions. It begins, O sing unto the Lord a new song, for He hath done marvellous things. The 98th, was also ascribed to the same

---

[1] There is a lacuna in the MS. here.
[2] This of course is our Ps. xc. Origen follows the numeration of the LXX. The later English versions follow the Hebrew.

writer, which begins, The Lord reigneth, let the peoples rage. Also the 99th, entitled A Psalm of thanksgiving, which begins, Make a joyful noise unto the Lord, all ye lands. After these eleven the title of the next, both in the Hebrew and by general admission, is, A Psalm of David. So Psalm 100[1] does not fall within those by Moses.

XL

The order of the Psalms is not chronological. Possibly numbers are assigned to the Psalms corresponding to the significance of their contents. Or the whole collection may have been put together without any plan.—(Selecta in Psalmos. Lomm. xi. 370–71. From the Greek.)

It is agreed that the greater part of the Psalms which follow the 50th were composed considerably earlier than the 50th. And the 50th Psalm itself was composed earlier than the date of the 3rd, which gives the words of David when he fled from the face of Absalom his son, and was later than his confession of sin in the 50th. For what reason then are they arranged in such an order?

Some one might say that each of the numerals has a certain force, which must be estimated according to the principle of number.[2] It is for example a fact that for certain reasons seven is an honoured number in the divine Scripture. The Sabbath is awarded its privilege as the seventh day. Pentecost comes after seven times seven. Among the months the seventh counts; among years the seventh year. By the multiplication of seven in reckoning years we have the Jubilee, which comes round with seven sevens of years. In the opposite sense to this two is

---

[1] i.e. our ci.
[2] Like Philo (cp. *De Creat. Mundi*, 3) and the Pythagoreans, Origen had a great belief in the mystic properties of number. See *supra*, p. xl *sqq*.

regarded as an unclean number. It was said to Noah, Thou shalt take into the ark the clean animals seven by seven, the unclean two by two.[1] The single number has for excellent reasons great prominence, be it the single unit, or the single ten, or the single hundred. It is so with three and five and seven, and with the other numbers in like manner. On this theory it is held that to each number the Psalms have appropriate adaptation. Thus David's confession is in keeping with the number fifty, because of the law of the fiftieth year, in which provision is made for the remission of debts. Consequently the order of the Psalms does not go according to any sequence of time but according to the force of the numbers.

But another man would say that the book has nothing elaborate of this kind in it, but is a simple collection into one whole of Songs and Psalms and other writings from diverse sources, either because Ezra[2] had these records made after the other Scriptures, or because the wise men of old among the Hebrews collected the current Psalms, each as he might remember, and then caused their publication in any order, selection being made upon the ground of their plain meaning.

XLI

On the Songs of Ascents (Pss. cxx–cxxxiv). (Selecta in Psalmos. Lomm. xiii. 107. From the Greek.)

Only they who ascend in life and in word are at home in 'The Ascents' and in the mystical hints of them contained in these Psalms. We suppose

The first Song of Ascents (Ps. cxx, *Ad Dominum*)

---

[1] Gen. vii.
[2] For the tradition which connects Ezra with the formation of the Canon, see II (iv) Esdras xiv and Ryle, *Canon of the O. T.*, Excursus A.

was recited among the people whenever the enemy was expected:

The second (cxxi, *Levavi oculos*) when they were making preparations and needing allies:

The third (cxxii, *Lætatus sum*) after they had fought with the enemy and got the better of them:

The fourth (cxxiii, *Ad te levavi oculos meos*) when they were hoping for victory at the end:

The fifth (cxxiv, *Nisi quia Dominus*) after success:

The sixth (cxxv, *Qui confidunt*) when they were returning:

The seventh (cxxvi, *In convertendo*) when they had returned:

The eighth (cxxvii, *Nisi Dominus*) while they were constructing the temple:

The ninth (cxxviii, *Beati omnes*) after they had attained peace, giving a description of the happy man, because they had received back their friends and were happy with them:

The tenth (cxxix, *Sæpe expugnaverunt*) as they were enjoying deep peace. They say that they had been many times at war, but that the enemy had never overpowered them:

The eleventh (cxxx, *De profundis*) when they had now leisure for the things of God and comprehended their depths:

The twelfth (cxxxi, *Domine, non est*) as not being elated by their knowledge:

The thirteenth (cxxxii, *Memento, Domine*) as a prayer for the restoration of the Anointed:

The fourteenth (cxxxiii, *Ecce, quam bonum*) for the restoration of the church:

The fifteenth (cxxxiv, *Ecce nunc*) on their duty of

hastening to the house of God, standing therein, and blessing Him, raising their hands unto the sanctuary, that they also may be blessed of the Lord.

XLII

It cannot have been literally true that David had grown old without ever seeing a righteous man in want. He is speaking however of the age of the soul, which like the body has its stages of growth. (Selecta in Psalmos, Hom. iv. 3; Lomm. xii. 211-14. From the Latin.)

I have been young and now am old; yet have I not seen the righteous forsaken, nor his seed begging their bread. All the day long he dealeth graciously and lendeth, and his seed shall be blessed.[1] They who maintain that these words of the divine Scripture are to be taken in their plain sense, as a statement of fact, will no doubt assert that in the passage David states that, having passed the age of his youth and being now come even to the time of his old age, he had never seen the righteous man so forsaken as to be short of bread. And what do we make of Paul the Apostle, who in recounting and describing the lives of the prophets speaks of them as destitute, afflicted, wandering in goatskins, in holes of the rocks and in caverns?[2] Describing his own lot too he often speaks of being in hunger and in thirst.[3] As we learn from the narrative of Scripture that the righteous man often does suffer such things, how can we suppose that David makes this statement in its plain meaning?[4]

But let us see if there be not perchance other ages of

---

[1] Ps. xxxvii. 25-6.   [2] Heb. xi. 37-8.   [3] 2 Cor. xi. 27.
[4] Undoubtedly David, or the writer whoever he was, did so. The passage is of interest, as showing that Origen does not always meet the difficulties with which he deals.

our inward man, corresponding to our outward and bodily age. Thus it is sometimes said to men of already full age that they are children, to others that they are old men, to others that they are youths, and clearly these terms cannot properly be used of their bodily age. Besides, though many before Abraham had lived six hundred, five hundred, at least three hundred years, of not one of them is it said that he was, An old man and full of days,[1] except of Abraham alone. Whereby we must understand that the description did not apply to the age of his body but to the maturity of his inward man. Hence we also should desire to be called presbyters and elders, not for our bodily age or for our position, but by reason of the full grown intelligence of our inward man and the steadfastness of an established character. In this sense Abraham was called an elder, full grown, in a good old age. There is then an age of childhood according to the inward man; there is an age of youth; there is an age that is old. This accords with the Apostle's saying, When I was a child, I spake as a child, I understood as a child, I thought as a child. But now that I am become a man I have put away childish things.[2] I take it these things are said by the Apostle not in regard to the age of his body. He means that when he first believed he was a child, new born, craving for rational and uncontaminated milk;[3] then he understood the Scriptures as a child, he regarded the Gospel as a child, he thought as a child. But afterwards, increasing in years after the example of Christ, of Whom it is said, He advanced in age and in wisdom and in favour with God and man,[4] Paul put away childish things. So he said, When I became a man I put away childish things. We

[1] Gen. xxv. 8.
[2] 1 Cor. xiii. 11.
[3] 1 Pet. ii. 2.
[4] Luc. ii. 52.

must understand David to say, I have been young and now am old, as meaning, Whereas I was a child according to the inner man, now I am old. Had he not grown old, he would not be a prophet. Prophecy is for old men. Even if occasionally you see a young man prophesy, you would not hesitate to say of him that he is a prophet because after the inward man he is old. Jeremiah for example on hearing the words, Before I formed thee in the belly, I knew thee, and before thou camest forth out of the womb, I sanctified thee, and I have appointed thee a prophet unto the nations, answered, I am young, I cannot speak. But He who gave him grace not to be a child, but to be old according to the inward man, said unto him, Say not I am young.[1]

Otherwise, unless the passage is so understood, what will be the sense of saying to a child, whose age is young and untaught, Say not I am young, that is to say, Say not what is true ? Young then he was according to his bodily age. But since the Lord had placed His words in his lips, words whereby he should root out, and pull down, and destroy, and build again, and plant, and this force in his words, illuminating and sanctifying the prophet's soul, did not suffer it to be the soul of a child, it is therefore said to him with good reason, Say not, I am young. In the same sense these words of David, I have been young and now am old and yet have I not seen the righteous forsaken nor his seed begging their bread, must be understood according to the preceding account of the youth and the old age of the inward man. Otherwise, as concerns the outward man, we must hold that the righteous man is so far forsaken by God, when sickness of body comes to him, when trouble arises, or poverty, or the various calamities of this life.

[1] Jer. i. 5-7.

XLIII

The Church recognizes four Gospels only. The Heresies have many Gospels.—(*In Lucam*, Hom. i; Lomm. v. 86–7. From the Latin.)

You must know that not four Gospels alone but very many were written,[1] from which these that we possess were selected and entrusted to the churches. This we may learn direct from the introduction of Luke, which is worded thus; Forasmuch as many have taken in hand to draw up a narrative.[2] The phrase he uses, Taken in hand, contains a suggested charge against those who, without the grace of the Holy Spirit, have rushed into the composition of Gospels. Matthew, Mark, John and Luke did not 'take in hand' to write, but they wrote Gospels because they were filled with the Holy Spirit. So it is that many have taken in hand to draw up a narrative concerning those matters which are most certainly known amongst us. The church has four Gospels;[3] the heresies many, of which one is written, According to the Egyptians, another, According to the Twelve Apostles. Basilides also was bold enough to write a Gospel and to call it by his own name. Many have 'taken in hand' to write; many too have 'taken in hand to draw up a narrative.' Only the four Gospels have been approved as sources of doctrine, having the authority of our Lord and Saviour. I know a certain Gospel which is called that According to Thomas, another According

---

[1] What remains of this literature is best seen collected in E. Preuschen's *Antilegomena*.

[2] Luke i. 1.

[3] Cp. the well-known passage in Irenæus, III. xi. 8 where it is urged that, as there are four points of the compass and four winds, so there must be four Gospels, neither more nor less.

to Matthias. Also we have read several others, lest our information should seem at fault, so as to deal with those who fancy they know something if they are acquainted with these books. In all these we give approval to nothing but what the church approves ; that it to say, only the four Gospels are to be received. So much I say because of the opening words of the lesson, Many have taken in hand to draw up a narrative concerning those matters which are fully established among us.

XLIV

The date of our Lord's arrival in Capernaum. Can we reconcile John's Gospel with the Synoptics on this point? On discrepancies in the Gospels.—(Comm. in Joann. x. 3 ; Lomm. i. 277-79 ; Br. i. 183-85 ; B. iv. 172-73. From the Greek.)

We must make it clear that the truth of these statements lies hidden in their spiritual significance, for many finding no solution of the discrepancy have abandoned their confidence in the Gospels. They hold them not to be true, neither written by divine inspiration nor composed from reliable records. For it is in each of these two ways their composition is asserted to have been achieved. Those who accept the four Gospels, and who hold that their apparent discrepancy is not to be reconciled through the higher interpretation,[1] must inform us, in addition to the problems we have mentioned in regard to the forty days of the Temptation, for which no place can be found in John, at what time did the Lord come to Capernaum ? If it was after the six days that

[1] Cp. p. xxviii, note.

followed His baptism,[1]—the miracle at the marriage in Cana of Galilee taking place on the sixth day,—it is evident that neither had He been tempted, nor did He go to Nazareth, nor was John yet under arrest. Then, after Capernaum, where He stayed not many days,[2] the Passover of the Jews being at hand, He went up to Jerusalem, when He drives the sheep and the oxen out of the temple and pours out the small coin of the money-changers.[3] Apparently in Jerusalem Nicodemus, the ruler of the Pharisees, came to Him by night, and heard the words that we may take from the Gospel.[4] After this Jesus came and His disciples to the country of Judaea and He stayed there with them and baptized. At this time John too was baptizing at Aenon near to Salim, for there was much water there and they came to him and were baptized. For John was not yet cast into prison. At that time also there was a dispute of John's disciples with the Jews about purifying, and they came to John, saying about the Saviour, Behold, He baptizes and all men come to Him.[5] They heard from the Baptist words which we can take verbatim from the passage itself.

Now if, when we enquire the time of Christ's first visit to Capernaum, they keep to the text of Matthew and the other two Gospels, and say the time was after the temptation, when He left Nazareth and came and dwelt in Capernaum by the sea, how will they maintain the truth

---

[1] Origen calculates the Lord's baptism as the first day; 'the morrow' (John i. 35) as the second; 'the morrow' (John i. 43) is the third; the marriage, on 'the third day' (John ii. 1) after, is thus on the sixth day from the baptism, reckoning inclusively. No room is left for the Temptation.
[2] John ii. 12.
[3] *Ibid.*, 13–15.
[4] John iii. 1 *sqq.*
[5] *Ibid.*, 26.

both of the statement in Matthew and in Mark that He retired to Galilee because He had heard of John's arrest,[1] and of the statement in John,—which stands after other works of Jesus, in addition to His stay in Capernaum, after His going up to Jerusalem, after His return thence to Judaea,—that John was not yet cast into prison but was baptizing at Aenon near to Salim ?[2] And in many other instances, if a man carefully examines the Gospels with discrepancies of the narrative in view, which we shall endeavour in each case to make clear so far as possible, bewilderment will fall upon him, and either, abandoning all attempt to give the Gospels their real authority, he will arbitrarily adhere to one of them, not having courage to reject entirely his faith in our Lord ; or else he must accept the four with the admission that their truth lies not in their outward and visible features.

XLV

In Matthew's account of the Lord's conversation with the young ruler it is probable that the words ' Thou shalt love thy neighbour as thyself' are an addition to the original text. The critical reasons for this view. (Comm. in Matt. xv. 13–14 ; Lomm. iii. 354–58. From the Greek.)

Since too we have the Apostle's words, Thou shalt not kill, Thou shalt not commit adultery, Thou shalt not steal, and if there be any other commandment, it is summed up in this word, namely, Thou shalt love thy neighbour as thyself ;[3] and since he who has fulfilled every commandment is perfect ; it is evident that he is

---

[1] Matt. iv. 13 ; Mark i. 14 ; Luke iv. 14, 31.
[2] John iii. 23.
[3] Rom. xiii. 9.

perfect who has fulfilled the commandment, Thou shalt love thy neighbour as thyself.

But if such a man is perfect, one would then ask, How it is that, after the young man has said, All these things have I observed from my youth up: what lack I yet?[1] the Saviour answered—assenting to his statement, All these things have I observed, but implying that he who had observed all these things was not perfect—If thou wouldst be perfect, go, sell that thou hast, and give to the poor, and thou shalt have treasure in heaven, and come, follow me.[2] Now consider whether one way of meeting the problem before us be not this. Probably the words, Thou shalt love thy neighbour as thyself, may be suspected not to have formed part of the Saviour's utterance at that time, but to have been added by someone who did not grasp the exact significance of the passage. Our suspicion that the words, Thou shalt love thy neighbour as thyself, are here an addition, is confirmed by the account of the incident in Mark and in Luke. Neither of these has added to the commandments mentioned in this place by Jesus the words, Thou shalt love thy neighbour as thyself.[3] He who is disposed to insist that the commandment, Thou shalt love thy neighbour as thyself, is here an inappropriate amplification, will also point out that, supposing the same facts to be recorded in the three Gospels in different words, Jesus would not have said, One thing thou lackest,[4] or, yet wantest thou one thing,[5] to a man who claimed to have

---

[1] Matt. xix. 20.
[2] *Ibid.*, 21.
[3] Mark x. 17 *sqq.*; Luke xviii. 18 *sqq.* Origen's point is quite valid. All the MSS. of Mark and Luke omit the words he suspects. From Matthew's text they are only lacking in one Syriac MS.
[4] Mark x. 21.
[5] Luke xviii. 22.

fulfilled the commandment, Thou shalt love thy neighbour as thyself. Specially has this force in view of the words of the Apostle, Thou shalt not kill, etc. And if there be any other commandment, it is summed up in this word, namely, Thou shalt love thy neighbour as thyself.[1]

Moreover as, according to Mark, Jesus beholding this rich man who said, All these things have I observed from my youth, loved him, it seems that He did agree that the ruler had kept all he claimed to have fulfilled. He read his disposition and saw that he was a man who claimed with a good conscience to have fulfilled the commandments named. Had the words, Thou shalt love thy neighbour as thyself, been also spoken in addition to the other commandments, Mark and Luke would not have omitted this comprehensive and most excellent commandment. Unless indeed any one will maintain that the passages have indeed a resemblance but that they do not refer to the same incident. And how could Jesus say, as to one not yet perfect, If thou wilt be perfect, go, sell that thou hast, and give to the poor,[2] and so on, to a man who claimed, in addition to the rest, to have fulfilled the commandment, Thou shalt love thy neighbour as thyself?

Of course if there had not been in many other details diversity in our copies, so that the texts of Matthew do not all agree, and the other Gospels are in like case, a man would have appeared irreverent who suggested that the commandment, Thou shalt love thy neighbour as thyself, was in this passage an addition and was never really mentioned by the Saviour to the rich man. But it is a recognized fact that there is much diversity in our copies,

---

[1] Rom. xiii. 9.   [2] Matt. xix. 21.

whether by the carelessness of certain scribes, or by some culpable rashness in the correction of the text, or by some people making arbitrary additions or omissions in their corrections. As regards the copies of the Old Testament we did discover through God's aid a method of curing diversity.[1] We employed as a standard the other versions. Where a point was uncertain in the Septuagint through diversity in the copies, we made our decision from the other versions. What agreed with them we retained. Words not occurring in the Hebrew we marked with an obelus, not daring wholly to remove them. Some words we added, marking them with asterisks, to show that we had inserted them from the other versions in conformity with the Hebrew text, though they were not found in the Septuagint. He who wishes may pass over these words. But if anyone dislikes my method, he must do as he pleases about accepting such words or the reverse.

Whoever prefers not to regard the commandment, Thou shalt love thy neighbour as thyself, as an addition in this passage, believing that it really was mentioned after the others by the Lord, will say that our Saviour wished gently and directly to show the rich man that he was not correct in stating that he had kept also the commandment, Thou shalt love thy neighbour as thyself.[2] So He says to him, If thou wilt be perfect, go, sell that thou hast, and give to the poor. For in that way he would prove the truth of his claim to have kept the commandment, Thou shalt love thy neighbour as thyself.

---

[1] The reference is to the Hexapla. Cp. *Ad Africanum*, 4; Lomm. xvii. 25. Eus. *H. E.* vi. 16.

[2] It is quite characteristic of Origen to give a tolerably good argument against the view he evidently holds himself.

XLVI

The statement of the Lord that Jerusalem had killed the prophets has little support from the Old Testament. We must therefore suppose it was based upon evidence afforded by the Apocryphal books of the Jews. But in making use of such secondary sources great discrimination is necessary. (In Matt. Comm. Series, 28; Lomm. iv. 237-40. From the Latin.)

It is worth while to enquire what induced the Saviour, speaking in the presence of hearers in whose number were Scribes and Pharisees who boasted of their accurate knowledge of the contents of the Law and the Prophets, to state that Jerusalem killed the prophets and stoned those who were sent unto her,[1] although no such narrative is actually contained in the prophecy of the ancient Scriptures which used to be read in their synagogues. We read indeed that Jeremiah was put into a muddy pit,[2] not however that he was killed in Jerusalem. And neither of Isaiah, nor of Ezekiel, nor of any of the prophets, do we read that he suffered any such fate, so far as my memory tells me. Making search in the second book of the Chronicles, where many things are written concerning prophets of eminence, I find that Asa in his anger did indeed put into prison Ananias, the prophet who brought charges against him, but that he did nothing more to him.[3] Ahab too ordered Micaiah who prophesied against him to go into the prison house and to eat the bread of affliction,[4] but he did not also kill him. Only one prophet, Zachariah, the son of Jehoiada the priest, who accused the people, do we read to have been stoned.[5]

---

[1] Matt. xxiii. 37. [2] Jer. xxxviii. 6. [3] 2 Chron. xvi. 10.
[4] *Ibid.* xviii. 26. [5] *Ibid.* xxiv. 21.

Thus we do not find that prophets were killed in Jerusalem, or that those sent unto Jerusalem were stoned, except as I have said. Consequently we have to consider whether it may not be right to use the Apocryphal books which circulate among the Jews as evidence for the saying of Christ, and not of Christ only, but also of His disciples, Stephen the Martyr, and Paul the Apostle. For Stephen speaks thus; O stiffnecked and uncircumcised in heart and ears, ye do always resist the Holy Spirit: as your fathers did, so do ye. Which of the prophets did not your fathers persecute? And they killed them which shewed before of the coming of the Righteous One : of whom ye have now become the betrayers and murderers.[1] And after that, They cas thim out of the city. And they stoned Stephen calling and saying.[2] . . . . Also Paul in the first Epistle to the Thessalonians says this about killing the prophets; Ye became imitators of the churches of God which are in Judaea in Christ Jesus: for ye also suffered the same things of your own countrymen, even as they did of the Jews: who both killed the Lord Jesus and the prophets, and drove out us and please not God.[3] And to the Hebrews he writes; They were stoned, they were sawn asunder, they were tempted, they were slain with the sword. They went about in sheepskins, in goatskins ; being destitute, afflicted, evil entreated (of whom the world was not worthy) wandering in deserts and mountains and caves and the holes of the earth.[4]

Now it is in the unpublished Scriptures that it is stated Isaiah was sawn asunder,[5] and Zachariah slain and

---

[1] Acts vii. 51-2.   [2] *Ibid.*, 58-9.
[3] 1 Thess. ii. 14-15.   [4] Heb. xi. 37-8.
[5] For the apocryphal *Ascension of Isaiah* which survives in an Ethiopic version, see Charles, article on Apocalyptic Literature in *Encyc. Bib.* §§ 42-7. Cp. Justin Mart. *Dial. C. Try.* 120.

Ezekiel. It was Elijah, I think, who went about in sheepskins and goatskins, for he wandered in the desert and on the mountains. Suppose some one does disallow the Epistle to the Hebrews, as not written by Paul,[1] and also rejects the apocryphal history of Isaiah; still what can he make of the words used by Stephen, or by Paul to the Thessalonians, about the slaying of the prophets, and even of the words of Lord Himself? Or how can he disallow what Paul said to Timothy in the words; As Jannes and Membres withstood Moses, so do these also withstand the truth.[2] We do not know of any record in books accountèd canonical of Jannes and Membres withstanding Moses. And if anyone also considers what is found in the first Epistle to the Corinthians; What eye hath not seen nor ear heard,[3] will he still be able to disallow all such evidence?

All this we have said in discussing the passage in hand, though we are not unaware that of the apocryphal statements many are the fabrications of certain evil persons who speak their iniquities against the Most High.[4] The Hypythians make use of some of these fabrications; the followers of Basilides of others. There is thus need for careful examination. We must not accept all apocryphal stories which are circulated under the names of holy men on the authority of the Jews, who possibly have fabricated stories and supported false teaching for the purpose of overthrowing the truth of the Scriptures that belong to us. Nor must we reject all the apocryphal statements which help to prove our Scriptures true. Thus it needs a great man to understand and fulfil what is written; Prove all things; hold fast that which

---

[1] See § 1.
[2] 2 Tim. iii. 8. See Bernard, *in loc*.
[3] 1 Cor. ii. 9.
[4] Ps. lxxiii. 8. LXX.

is good.¹ However, for the sake of those who have not the ability of the good money-changer to distinguish one word from another, whether they shall be regarded as true or counterfeit, and who are also unable to keep watch over themselves so as to retain the truth in their hearts and yet avoid all appearance of evil, let no one employ in support of his religious views books which are outside the list of the canonical Scriptures.²

XLVII

The statement that there was darkness over all the land at the time of the Crucifixion is attacked. Some believers reply that it was due to an eclipse. But could an eclipse have occurred at that time? Or they say it was miraculous. But such an occurrence would have been mentioned by the heathen chroniclers. Most probably it was local darkness caused by dense clouds which obscured the sun. (*In Matt. Comm. Series*, 134; Lomm. v. 51-6. From the Latin.)

Now from the sixth hour there was darkness over all the land until the ninth hour.³ In reference to this passage some make attack upon the truth of the Gospel. How, say they, can the statement of the text be true, in which it is said that there was darkness over all the land from the sixth hour till the ninth, an occurrence of which history has no record? The reply is made that an eclipse took place at the time, with all the usual accompaniments of an eclipse. Now an eclipse from the very first has

---

[1] 1 Thess. v. 21.
[2] For Origen's Canon see Eus. *H. E*, vi. 25; Ryle, *Canon of O. T.* 214; Westcott, *Canon of N. T.* 3rd Ed. 326 *sqq*. Also Harnack, *Bible Reading in the Early Church*, E. T. 68 *sqq*.
[3] Matt. xxvii. 45.

always occurred at its proper time. But an eclipse of the sun, which regularly happens in accordance with the normal lapse of certain periods, occurs at no other time than when the sun and the moon are in conjunction, when the moon, going on its orbit beneath the sun, interrupts its rays, passing in front of it, and by its passage cutting off the sun's light. But at the time when Christ suffered it is obvious that there was no conjunction of the moon with the sun, for it was the time of the Passover,[1] which is kept by custom when the moon is receiving the full illumination of the sun and is visible all the night. So how could there be an eclipse of the sun when the moon was full and had the sun's full light?

Now some of the believers, in their desire to provide a reply to these objections, finding themselves in a difficulty through the arguments of those who maintain the view described, have stated their case as follows: If no fresh miracle had occurred at the time of Christ's passion, but everything had followed its normal course, this eclipse of the sun might be believed to have been a normal eclipse. But since it is agreed that certain other miracles which occurred at that time were not normal occurrences but strange and marvellous—for the veil of the temple was rent in twain from the top to the bottom; and the earth did quake, and the rocks were rent; and the tombs were opened, and many bodies of the saints that had fallen asleep were raised[2]—it is evident that this eclipse as well, in close conformity with the other miracles, was a strange event, quite out of the normal order. Again in reply to this the sons of this world,

---

[1] As the Hebrew month began with the new moon, the 14th Nisan would always have the moon full.
[2] Matt. xxvii. 51-2.

who in their generation are wiser than the sons of light,[1] argue as follows ; Suppose that eclipse, not very long ago, under the rule of the Romans, did occur out of the normal order, so that there was darkness over all the land unto the ninth hour, how comes it that no one among the Greeks, no one among the barbarians, has left a contemporaneous account of so marvellous an event, not even any one of those who have put together Chronicles and recorded unusual events anywhere occurring ; but it is only your authors who have mentioned it ? Phlegon[2] indeed in his Chronicles did state that an eclipse occurred in the reign of Tiberius Caesar, but he did not inform us that it occurred when the moon was full.

Consider whether this be not a strong objection, of force to impress any man of good sense, who gives assent not to what some people say nor to what others write, but who listens to everything with reason and good judgment. It is true that for any of the faithful who believes indeed but does not believe with reason and good judgment, it is not a very difficult matter to be so strong in faith that even if those who seek to destroy our faith do bring a thousand charges against the trustworthiness of the Gospels, still he is entirely unmoved by their arguments. For while pretending to believe the Gospel Scriptures such opponents take advantage of some disputed point or other, difficult, or it may be even insoluble, and in their antagonism to Scripture endeavour to remove faith in Christ and in His Gospels from our soul. They cite astonishing occurrences and endeavour to assign miracles accomplished by the power of God to

---

[1] Luke xvi. 8.
[2] C. 130 A.D. His short work, the *Mirabilia*, is extant ; also fragments of his *Olympiades sive Chronica*.

the normal procedure of the world. I have therefore deemed it a good thing, while welcoming the right intention of those who wish to be steadfast in the faith, to discover, so far as ability is given me by God, explanations of the charges of the critics, in support of the truth of the Gospel. So may the faithful be protected in their faith not alone by simple faith but also by the knowledge of its grounds.[1]

We say then that Matthew and Mark have not stated that an eclipse occurred at that time. Neither did Luke according to very many copies, which have, And it was about the sixth hour, and a darkness came over the whole land until the ninth hour; and the sun was darkened. In some copies however the words, And the sun was darkened, do not occur, but, There was darkness over all the land, the sun being eclipsed.[2] Possibly some one in the desire to make the statement more plain made bold to place, The sun being eclipsed, in the place of, And the sun was darkened, believing that the darkness could not have happened except by reason of an eclipse. Yet I rather believe that the secret enemies of the church of Christ have altered this phrase, making the darkness occur by reason of ' The sun being eclipsed ', so that the Gospels might be attacked with some show of reason, through the devices of those who wished to attack them. It is my own opinion that, just as the other signs which occurred during our Lord's passion occurred only in Jerusalem, so the darkness was only over all the land of Judaea until the ninth hour. The events of which I say that they occurred only in Jerusalem are the rending of the

---

[1] Cp. § lxviii.
[2] Luke xxiii. 44-5. The MS. authority is fairly evenly divided between the two readings. R. V. adopts τοῦ ἡλίου ἐκλείποντος and so favours the eclipse.

veil of the temple, the quaking of the earth, the rocks being rent, the graves opened. The rocks were not rent outside Judaea, nor were other graves opened except those that were in Jerusalem or, possibly, in the land of Judaea. There was no earthquake at that time except in Jerusalem. Of no other place is it recorded that all the fabric of the earth at that time quaked, so as to make the event perceptible, say, in Ethiopia or in India or in Scythia. Had this been the case it would without doubt be found in the narratives of those who have recorded in chronicles other remarkable occurrences.

Just then as the statement, The earth did quake, is taken as referring to the ground in Jerusalem, or, if anyone likes to give it a wider meaning, to the land of Judaea; so too you must understand the words, There was darkness from the sixth hour until the ninth hour over all the land, to mean that there was darkness over all the land of Judaea, or at any rate over Jerusalem, alone. He who so interprets the passage is not to be blamed for his interpretation. He wishes not to fall into ridicule with the wise of this world, through his attempt to prove the greatness of the miracle; nor to arouse incredulity among the wise rather than belief. Against this some one says: If the darkness at that time over all the land of Judaea or over Jerusalem did not occur because of an eclipse, but from some other cause, tell us what the cause was. This is our answer to the questioner; First that the evangelists do not so much as mention the sun[1] in this passage—only that there was darkness over all the land. If then there was darkness over all the land without the sun being mentioned, it is without doubt natural to suppose that dense clouds, not

[1] An overstatement. Even the reading he prefers in Luke xxiii. 45, runs, καὶ ἐσκοτίσθη ὁ ἥλιος.

one but several, of wide extent, collected above the land of Judaea and Jerusalem so as to obscure the rays of the sun. Hence the profound darkness from the sixth hour to the ninth. How that darkness occurred in this place, we have explained, and possibly the darkness that could be felt for three days in Egypt also arose in the same manner,[1] not from an eclipse but either because thick clouds had congregated together, or because the atmosphere was at that time specially opaque over the Egyptians alone.

XLVIII

Man is liable to temptation; God is not. Therefore John's Gospel, speaking of the Lord as God, omits the temptation. The other three describe Him as man and include it. We too must one day pass beyond temptation and share the divine life. (*In Lucam* Hom. xxix; Lomm. v. 196-98. From the Latin.)

In carefully examining the meaning of Scripture I think I discover the reason why John gives no account of the Lord's temptation. Only Matthew, Luke and Mark give it. For John, who had begun his Gospel with God, saying, In the beginning was the Word and the Word was with God and the Word was God,[2] and who was unable to insert any succession of the divine generation but had only declared that He was from God and with God, simply adds, And the Word became flesh.[3] Further because God of whom of he is speaking cannot be tempted, he consequently includes no mention of His temptation by the devil. But since in Matthew's Gospel the book of

---

[1] Ex. x. 21. [2] John i. 1.
[3] John i. 14. Origen means that in regard to our Lord's divine origin John had nothing to state which corresponded to the human genealogies in Matt. and Luke.

the generation of Jesus Christ is recorded of Him, and in Luke His generation is detailed, and in Mark He is the man who is tempted; on this account there is a record of His appropriate reply, Man doth not live by bread alone.[1] Therefore if the Son of God, Himself God, was made man for you and is tempted, you, a man by nature, have no right to be aggrieved if you happen to be tempted. And if in temptation you imitate Him who was tempted for you and overcome every temptation, your hope then lies with Him who was once a man but has now ceased to be a man. For if He who once was man, after He had been tempted and the devil departed from Him till the time of His death, on arising from the dead shall die no more, whereas every man is subject to death; he consequently who dies no more is no longer man but God. And if He who once was man is God, you too must be like Him, for we shall be like Him and we shall see Him as He is.[2] You too must become a god in Christ Jesus, to whom be the glory and the dominion for ever and ever. Amen.

XLIX

The Epistle to the Romans is the most difficult of the Epistles of Paul. It is also the most advanced spiritually. For Paul did develop spiritually and when he wrote to the Romans had advanced beyond the stage at which he had arrived when he wrote to the Corinthians or to the Philippians. (In Ep. ad Rom. Praefatio. Lomm. vi. 1–5. From the Latin.)

This Epistle to the Romans is accounted more difficult to understand than the other Epistles of the Apostle Paul, which arises in my judgment from two reasons. One of

---

[1] Matt. iv. 4; Luke iv. 4; Deut. viii. 3.   [2] 1 John iii. 2.

these is the fact that he uses language which at times is involved and wanting in precision. The other is that in this Epistle he raises many problems, and especially those on which the heretics usually rely in their attempts to show that the reason of each of our actions must be assigned not to intention, but to some natural peculiarity. From a few texts in this Epistle they attempt to overthrow the meaning of the whole of Scripture, which teaches that freedom of will was bestowed upon man by God. For this reason we must first ask the help of God, who teacheth man knowledge,[1] who gives through the Spirit the word of wisdom,[2] and who lighteth every man that cometh into the world,[3] that He may be pleased to make us worthy to understand parables and secret utterances, the words of the wise and their dark sayings.[4]

So shall we come at length to the opening of our exposition of the Epistle of Paul to the Romans, making the preliminary remark, that in this Epistle, as is usually observed by scholars, the Apostle appears to have reached a higher degree of perfection than in the rest. Even when writing the first Epistle to the Corinthians he had made great advance, yet there is some degree of uncertainty about himself in his words when he says, But I buffet my body and bring it into bondage, lest by any means after that I have preached to others I myself should be rejected.[5] Also in writing to the Philippians he makes it clear that so far there is in him only a lower degree of that perfection which he afterwards attained, for he speaks of being conformed to the death of Christ, If by any means he may attain unto the resurrection from the dead. He would not say, If by any means, if he regarded the matter as already beyond doubt. Also, in a later passage

[1] Ps. xciv. 10.   [2] 1 Cor. xii. 8.   [3] John i. 9.
[4] Prov. i. 6.   [5] 1 Cor. ix. 27.

of the same Epistle, he shows the like uncertainty, when he says, Not that I have already obtained or am already made perfect, but I press on if so be that I may apprehend that in which also I was apprehended of Christ. Brethren, I count not myself yet to have apprehended.[1] And if any one regards this as said through self-abasement, let him consider in a later passage in what large terms he describes his own advance ; But one thing, he says, I do, forgetting the things which are behind and stretching forward to the things which are before, I press on toward the goal unto the prize of the high calling of God in Christ Jesus. And after this he says, Let us therefore as many as be perfect be thus minded.[2]

In this he shows that perfection is of two kinds. One is that which consists in the full attainment of excellence, by which standard he says he is not perfect. The other is when a man advances so far that he cannot fall or look back, of which he spoke in the words, Let us therefore, as many as be perfect, be thus minded. Is there any evidence to show that he was more perfect when he wrote the second Epistle to the Corinthians than when he wrote the first ? Certainly there is, in the words we find written there, in which he says, We are pressed on every side, yet not straitened ; we are perplexed, yet not unto despair ; pursued, yet not forsaken ; smitten down, yet not destroyed ; always bearing about in the body the dying of Jesus, that the life also of Jesus may be manifested in

---

[1] Phil. iii. 11–13. It is not clear whether Origen had other grounds, beyond those he found in the stage of Paul's spiritual development, for placing Romans after Philippians. In the Muratorian Fragment the Epistle to the Philippians stands before the Epistle to the Romans. In Marcion's ten admitted Epistles of Paul Romans stood fourth, Philippians ninth. Cp. Tert. *c. Marcionem.* v.

[2] Phil. iii. 13–15.

our body.[1] In a man who was ever bearing about in his body the dying of Jesus there could not possibly arise the lust of the flesh against the spirit.[2] The flesh was subject to the spirit, as being dead after the likeness of the death of Christ. If any one tells us that this appears improbable, because the interval between the first Epistle and the second seems not long, he may derive clearer understanding specially from the fact that in the first Epistle the man who had been defiled by the sin of incest was cast out and handed over to Satan for the destruction of the flesh, that his spirit might be saved in the day of the Lord;[3] whereas in the second he brings him back and associates him with the church's members.[4] This he certainly would not do if he had not with the passing of time observed in him the worthy fruits of repentance, and observed also that the flesh had undergone that destruction which the Apostle had mentioned, being dead, that is, to sin and vice that it might live at last to God. As then the interval was sufficient for the incestuous sinner to receive the salvation of his spirit through the commendable destruction of the flesh, surely we must regard the Apostle's advance in attaining to perfection as far more rapid still.

Such was his advance at that earlier stage. To what further heights and elevation he had moved when he wrote to the Romans, we may gather from the words of that very Epistle, in which he says, Who shall separate us from the love of Christ? Shall tribulation, or anguish, or persecution, or famine, or nakedness, or peril, or sword? Even as it is written, For thy sake we are killed all the day long; we are accounted as sheep for the slaughter. Nay in all these things we are more that

---

[1] 2 Cor. iv. 8-10. [2] Gal. v. 17.
[3] 1 Cor. v. 5. [4] 2 Cor. ii. 8.

conquerors through Him that loved us. For I am persuaded that neither death, nor life, nor angels, nor principalities, nor powers, nor things present, nor things to come, nor might, nor height, nor depth, nor any other creature, shall be able to separate us from the love of God, which is in Christ Jesus our Lord.[1] I say the truth in Christ, I lie not, my conscience bearing witness with me in the Holy Ghost. Can we say that he spoke with the same elevation of mind when he said, I buffet my body and bring it into bondage, lest by any means after that I have preached to others I myself should be rejected,[2] as he does in saying, In all these things we are more than conquerors, and, I am persuaded that neither death, nor life, nor angels, nor principalities nor the other powers he names, can separate us from the love of God?

L

The style and authorship of the Epistle to the Hebrews. (*In Epist. ad Hebraeos.* Fragmentum. Euseb., *H. E.* vi. 25. Lomm. v. 301-2. From the Greek.)

The style of the language in the Epistle entitled, To the Hebrews, does not manifest the Apostle's lack of literary training. For that he had no literary skill, that is skill in writing, he himself allowed. But the Epistle in the composition of its phrases has a Hellenic ring, as every one who is a good judge of differences of style would agree. Further, the thought of the Epistle is wonderful, not inferior to the writings of admitted apostolicity. This also any one who is accustomed to read such writings would allow to be true.

To this later on he adds :

I would express my opinion that the thought is the Apostle's, but that the style and composition are due to

---

[1] Rom. viii. 35 ; ix. 1. [2] 1 Cor. ix. 27.

some one who remembered the Apostle's teaching and wrote a running commentary on his teacher's words. If any church holds this Epistle to be Paul's, let it have all satisfaction in this view. Not without reason did the men of an earlier day hand it down as Paul's. But what is the truth as to the actual writer of the Epistle, God knows. As for the tradition that has reached us, some say that Clement, who was Bishop of the Romans, wrote the Epistle. Others, that it was Luke, the writer of the Gospel and the Acts.[1]

LI

Eternal life. The word eternal, αἰών, αἰώνιος, is sometimes used of what has an end, sometimes of what is unending. (Comm. in Ep. ad Rom. vi. 5. Lomm. vii. 22–3. From the Latin.)

In regard to eternal life, although we have frequently dealt with the subject in other places, still we may also in our present discussion briefly make the observation that 'eternity' is sometimes employed in Scripture for that which knows no end, sometimes however for what has no end in the present world but has in the world to come.[2] Sometimes the duration of a certain period, or even the life of a single man, is called eternity, as in the

---

[1] In Alexandria this Epistle was generally attributed to Paul and quoted as his. See Clem. Alex. ap. Euseb. *H.E.* vi. 14. Clement heard this view from some Elder, possibly Pantaenus. Origen's view varied. He speaks of being ready to prove that the Epistle is Paul's, *Ad Afric.* 9; also of Paul's Epistles as being fourteen in number. *In Josuam* Hom. vii. 1. Lomm. xi. 63; xvii. 31; B. vii. 328. Contrast his language here. For the history of opinion on this still uncertain point see Westcott's edition, Introduction, XI, and § 2 in the article *Hebrews (Epistle)* by Robertson Smith and von Soden in *Encyc. Bib.*

[2] For Origen's interpretation of αἰών, αἰώνιος, see Bigg, *Platonists*, 231 n. Also Huet ii. 11, 26.

direction in the law about the Hebrew slave; If, it says, he love his wife and children and desires for their sakes to remain in slavery, thou shalt bore, so it runs, his ear with an awl at the door post and he shall be thy slave for ever.[1] Here without doubt he uses the term eternal, ' for ever ', for the period of a man's life. And again it says in Ecclesiastes, One generation goeth, and another generation cometh; and the earth abideth for ever.[2] Here eternal, ' for ever ', denotes the period of the present world. But when he speaks of life eternal, attention must be directed to what the Saviour himself said; This is life eternal, that they should know Thee the only true God, and Him whom Thou didst send, even Jesus Christ.[3] And again, I am the way, and the truth, and the life.[4] In another passage the Apostle says himself, We shall be caught up in the clouds to meet Christ in the air and so shall we ever be with the Lord.[5] As therefore to be ever with the Lord has no end, so too we must believe that life eternal has no end.

LII

Spirit, soul, body. In Scripture the term spirit has various meanings. (Selecta in Psalmos. Lomm. xii. 129. From the Greek.)

Into thy hands I commend my spirit,[6] etc. The soul he treats as an opponent. As for the body, the saints made little account of it. Fearing to be wounded by

---

[1] Ex. xxi. 5-6. LXX has εἰς τὸν αἰῶνα.
[2] Eccl. i. 4.
[3] John xvii. 3.
[4] *Ibid.* xiv. 6.
[5] 1 Thess. iv. 17. But the Greek is πάντοτε, not εἰς τὸν αἰῶνα.
[6] Ps. xxxi. 5.

deceivers he commends his spirit to God, speaking of His providential powers as His 'hands.' The Saviour too, when nailed to the cross, made use of this saying. Spirit is a term Scripture sometimes uses for the mind, as when insisting that a virgin should be holy, In spirit and in body.[1] Sometimes it employs the term for the soul or life, for instance in James, As the body apart from the spirit is dead.[2] And sometimes for the consciousness which is associated with life, as in the words, No one knoweth the things of a man save the spirit that dwelleth in him.[3] The passage before us may be understood in the three senses. He speaks of having been ransomed by God from his enemies as though he had been taken captive.[4]

---

[1] 1 Cor. vii. 34.
[2] James ii. 26.
[3] 1 Cor. ii. 11.
[4] On the term ' Spirit ' see § ii *supra*.

PART V

THE CHRISTIAN CHURCH

LIII

Moses and Paul agree in teaching the importance of order. There is true order in the Church when ecclesiastical position corresponds with spiritual qualification.—(In Num. Hom. ii. 1; Lomm. x. 18-20; B. vii. 9-10. From the Latin.)

Moses says, Let each man, according to his order and according to his ensign and according to the house of his kinsfolk, take his place in the camp.[1] And Paul says, Let all things be done decently and in order.[2] Think you not it is the one Spirit of God which speaks both in Moses and in Paul?[3] Moses commands places to be taken in the camp in order. Paul directs all things to be done in the church in order. Moses, who was the officer of the Law, commands order to be observed in the camp. Paul, as the servant of the Gospel, desires to have Christian orderliness not in actions only but even in dress. Therefore he says, The women too in orderly apparel.[4]

This leads me to think that they not only wish order to be maintained in the discharge of duties and in dress, but that they intend it also to be understood that there

---

[1] Num. ii. 1-2. [2] 1 Cor. xiv. 40.
[3] Agreement between Moses and Paul is a great point with Origen. It is sometimes secured by strained and unconvincing arguments. E.g. *Sel. in Gen.* Lomm. viii. 71.
[4] 1 Tim. ii. 9.

is a certain order in regard to the soul, as to which it is said that every man should take his place in his own order. This order is shown principally by the fruit of good works; also as well by the greatness of a man's ideas. For it often occurs that a man who has low and poor ideas, and has a taste for the things of earth, will occupy some elevated position in the priesthood or the professor's chair; while he who is spiritual and free from earthly interests, with the power to prove all things and himself to be judged of no man, takes his place in some lower service, or is even relegated to the common crowd. But this is to show contempt for the statutes of the Law and of the Gospel and to do nothing in order. Nay, each one of us, if he be concerned over food and drink, if he give all his interest to things of the world, assigning one hour or two out of the whole day to God, just coming to the church for prayer, giving a passing attention to the word of God, but devoting his main interest to the concerns of the world and of his appetite—such a man does not fulfil the command which says that a man shall take his place in his order, or that which says that all things are to be done in order. For the order laid down by Christ is to seek first the kingdom of God and His righteousness,[1] and to believe that these other things shall be allotted to us by God as of secondary importance.

Let a man then take his place in his order. Do you think that they who fill the priestly office and boast of their order of priesthood take their place according to their true order, or do all that is fitting for this order? Do you think likewise that the deacons take their place according to the order of their ministry? Whence comes it that we so often hear men grow abusive and declare, Look you, a fine bishop. Or, A fine presbyter. Or, A

[1] Matt. vi. 33.

fine deacon. Are not these things said when either a priest or a minister of God is observed to go contrary in some matter to his order, or to violate in some way the priestly or Levitical order? What am I to say of virgins? Or of celibates? Or of all who make open profession of religious life? If something they do is immodest or aggressive or insolent, does not Moses straightway accuse them and say, Let a man take his place in his order. Let each then know his order, and understand what beseems the order he occupies. Let him have such balance in his actions and even in his speech, such moderation in his bearing and in his attire, as are agreeable with the standard of his order, lest he hear it said to him by God, Because of you my name is blasphemed among the Gentiles.[1]

LIV

The blessing given by the Lord to Peter does not hold good for Peter exclusively, since all who share Peter's qualities have share also in his blessing. (Comm. in Matt. xii. 10–11; Lomm. iii. 146–50. From the Greek.)

Possibly if, like Peter,[2] we say the words which Simon Peter used in his answer, Thou art the Christ, the Son of the living God,[3] not because flesh and blood have

---

[1] Rom. ii. 24 and Ezek. xxxvi. 21.
[2] Other passages referring to Peter are *In Joann.* xxxii. 5–9. He is ' More honourable than the other apostles '. *In Exod.* Hom. v. 4. He is ' *magnum illud ecclesiae fundamentum et petra solidissima.* ' Lomm. ii. 393–408; ix. 55; Br. ii. 157–66; B. iv. 433–41; vi. 188. But Origen's most deliberate reference to Peter's position is in this passage. See Bigg, *Platonists*, 215; Westcott in *D.C.B.* Salmon, *Infallibility of the Church*, Lecture xviii, and especially pp. 329–31, where Origen's influence on Augustine's view is mentioned.
[3] Matt. xvi. 16.

revealed it unto us, but because light from the Father in heaven has shone in our hearts, then we too become what Peter was. We are blessed as he was, because the causes of his blessedness apply also in our case, since flesh and blood have not revealed unto us that Jesus is the Christ, the Son of the living God, but the Father in heaven, who speaks from heaven itself, that we may have our citizenship in heaven.[1] He has given to us a revelation which uplifts to the heavens those who remove every veil from their hearts [2] and receive the spirit of the wisdom of God and of revelation.[3] And if we also, saying like Peter, Thou art the Christ, the Son of the living God, not because flesh and blood have revealed it unto us, but because light from the Father in heaven has shone in our heart, become Peter,[4] to us also it would be said by the Word, Thou art Peter, and so on. For every disciple of Christ is a rock, and from Christ they drank who were of the spiritual rock that followed them,[5] and upon every such rock is built every word of the church and its corresponding manner of life. For in each of the perfect, who possess the gathered number of words and deeds and thoughts which constitute blessedness, there exists the church which is being built by God.

But if you consider that it is upon that one man Peter alone that all the church is built by God, what would you say about John, the son of thunder, or about each of the other Apostles? Besides, can we dare to say that against Peter especially the gates of Hades shall not prevail, but that they will prevail against the other Apostles and against the perfect? Is not the reference

---

[1] Phil. iii. 20. [2] 2 Cor. iii. 16. [3] Eph. i. 17.
[4] Cp. *De Oratione*, xiv. 6. εἴ τις εὑρεθείη Παῦλος ἢ Πέτρος.
[5] 1 Cor. x. 4.

to them all? and is not the saying in question, Gates of Hades shall not prevail against it, and the saying, Upon this rock I will build my church,[1] within the power of each of them? Is it to Peter alone that the keys of the kingdom of heaven are given by the Lord? Shall none other of the blessed receive them? But if the words, I will give unto thee the keys of the kingdom of heaven, are common to the others as well, why not also the earlier and the later saying recorded as addressed to Peter?

In this passage the words, Whatsoever thou shalt bind on earth shall be bound in heaven, and what follows, do appear to have been addressed to Peter, but in the Gospel according to John it is to His disciples that the Saviour, after giving them the Holy Spirit by breathing on them, says, Receive ye the Holy Spirit, and what follows.[2] Many will say unto the Saviour, Thou art the Christ, the Son of the living God, but it will not be true of all that so address Him that they have not learned this through the revelation of flesh and blood, but because the Father in heaven has Himself withdrawn the veil that lay upon their heart, so that afterwards beholding as in a glass with unveiled face the glory of the Lord,[3] they might speak in the spirit of God and say of Him, Jesus is Lord,[4] and say to Him, Thou art the Christ, the Son of the living God. Whoever says this unto Him, not because flesh and blood have revealed it but the Father in heaven, shall receive the promise made, as the letter of the Gospel says, to the historic Peter, but as the Spirit teaches, made to every one who becomes such as Peter was. All the imitators of Christ bear Peter's name of Rock, for the spiritual Rock follows all

---

[1] Matt. xvi. 18-19.
[2] John xx. 22.
[3] 2 Cor. iii. 18.
[4] 1 Cor. xii. 3.

that are in salvation,[1] that of it they may drink spiritual drink. These bear the rock name, as Christ was called the Rock. Being members of Christ they were called by His name, Christians; being members of the Rock they are Peters.

From this you may take occasion to say that the righteous bear the name of Christ their righteousness, and the wise of Christ their wisdom. So by reference to His other names you will make names for the saints. To all such might be said the words of the Saviour, Thou art Peter, and what follows down to, Shall not prevail against it.[2]

What is this 'It?' Is it the rock upon which Christ builds his church? Or is it the church? The expression is doubtful. Or is it the rock and the church, as one and the same thing? That, I think, is true. For neither against the rock on which Christ builds His church, nor against the church, shall the gates of Hades prevail, so that not even the way of a serpent upon the rock,[3] as the text in the Proverbs says, should be found there. If against any one the gates of Hades do prevail, such a man would neither be a rock upon which Christ builds His church, nor the church built by Christ upon the rock. For the rock is inaccessible to a serpent, and stronger than the gates of Hades which oppose it, so that by reason of its strength the gates of Hades do not prevail against it. And the church, as the building of Christ, who like the wise man built His house upon the rock,[4] is immune from the gates of Hades, which prevail against every man who is outside the rock and the church, but against it have no power.

[1] 1 Cor. x. 4.
[2] Matt. xvi. 18.
[3] Prov. xxx. 19.
[4] Matt. vii. 24.

LV

Our Lord spoke of the faithful and wise servant. But it is rarely that fidelity and wisdom are found united. And yet both qualities are needed alike in those who administer the church's finances and in those who dispense the Church's truth. (In Matt. Comm. Series, 61; Lomm. iv. 347-50. From the Latin.)

For the present we must understand in their ordinary sense the words, Who is the faithful and wise servant?[1] It is as though some, by virtue of what is ordinarily understood as faith, were faithful but not wise or quick in mind: while others were quick and wise according to the meaning of the term 'wise' here, but not altogether men of faith. Now if anyone will pass in review the great body of those who desire to be Christians, he will find many who are faithful and put into practice their zeal for faith, but who are not also wise. Hence the sons of this world are wiser in their generation than they.[2] Still, they know that, God chose the foolish things of the world that He might put to shame them that are wise.[3] Again he will see others who are regarded as believers, quick indeed and wise, but of only moderate faith; if not unfaithful, still deficiently faithful, for they despise the foolish things of the world which God hath chosen. But it is very rarely that the faithful man and the wise man coincide as one and the same person, so as through both these qualities to give his fellow servants food in due season. For to give food in due season a man must have wisdom. And if he is not to deprive others of food in time of scarcity, he will need faith and fidelity.[4]

[1] Matt. xxiv. 45. [2] Luke xvi. 8. [3] 1 Cor. i. 27.
[4] In the original the one term $\pi i \sigma \tau \iota \varsigma$, Fides, covers our two ideas of belief and trustworthiness.

Also in view of the sins which do occur in men who seem to be believers in Christ, and most commonly in those who are administrators of the church's funds, it is not out of place to remind ourselves that even in the simple sense of the term many of us have need to be faithful as well as wise in administering the revenues of the church. We must be faithful, so that we may not devour what belongs to the widows, that we may remember the poor, and may not take opportunity from that which is written, The Lord ordained that they which proclaim the Gospel should live of the Gospel,[1] to seek for more than simple food and necessary clothing. We must not keep more for ourselves than we give to our hungry or thirsty brother, or to the naked, or to those who in the cares of this life are oppressed by want. And we must be wise, so that we may assist every man according to his deserts, remembering the saying, Blessed is he that considereth the poor and needy.[2] We must not give from the church's stores by any single rule, so as merely to keep the principle of not devouring what belongs to the poor or robbing them. Rather we must be wise to understand the causes of poverty, and the merits of each particular case; how a man was brought up; how much he requires; what is the reason of his poverty.[3] Thus we must not take the same measures in the case of those who from childhood have been brought up in hard and narrow circumstances and in the case of those who after being reared in affluence and luxury have subsequently come to low estate. We must not make the same grants to men as to women; or the same to men

---

[1] 1 Cor. ix. 14.   [2] Ps. xli. 1. LXX.
[3] The early and indeed the later church was not always so wise in its treatment of poverty. Cp. the opening portion of Clem. Al. *Quis Dives Salvetur*.

of many years and to men in their prime; or the same to men in their prime but delicate and consequently unable to earn a living and to those who at least in part can maintain themselves. Enquiry must be made whether they have many sons, not indifferent, but of full capacity, and yet not providing adequate support. Not to say more, the man who desires to administer well the revenues of the church needs much wisdom, that being found a faithful and wise administrator even in these matters, he may attain to blessedness.

Possibly too it is also on account of the large number of Christians who do not sufficiently occupy themselves with the quest for the word, and who yet with this defect are promoted to high office, that we have the greater need to listen to the words, 'Who is that faithful and wise servant whom his lord hath set over his household to give them food in due season? They must not, in their desire to display their wisdom, squander rational and spiritual food upon their fellow servants without distinction'[1] whoever they may be, persons quite unfit, and often far more in need of such teaching as will improve their character and give order to their life, than of the teaching which guides unto wisdom and illuminates with the light of knowledge those whose intelligence is capable of sustaining the radiance of this kind of light. Nor must they shrink from setting forth deeper truths for the benefit of those who can give intelligent attention, lest by the poverty of their exposition they incur the contempt of clever people, whose cleverness is a natural gift, or who possibly gain a repute for intellect by their constant practice of worldly wisdom. Difficult therefore it is to

---

[1] 'Cast not your pearls before swine' was constantly quoted in this sense. Cp. *De Prin.* III. i. 17 (Latin); C. Cels. v. 29; Clem. Al. *Strom.* II. ii. 7; also the references in p. xlv, *supra*.

be both in one, wise alike and faithful, but impossible it is not. The Lord did not bless a man who could never exist when He said, Blessed is that servant whom his master, when he cometh, shall find so doing. Verily I say unto you he will set him over all that he hath.[1]

LVI

The spirit of 'Corban' in the Church. (Comm. in Matt. xi. 9; Lomm. iii. 90-91. From the Greek.)

The elders used to quote to the people a tradition to the effect that whoever should say to his father or to his mother that what he has to give to any of them is Corban, or a gift, is no longer liable to his father or mother for the supply of the necessities of life.[2] This tradition the Saviour criticizes as unsound and opposed to the commandment of God. For if God says, Honour thy father and thy mother, while tradition said, He who dedicates to God as Corban what might be given to his parents, is not bound to honour his father or his mother by a gift; it is clear that the commandment of God about honour to parents is nullified by the tradition of Pharisees and Scribes, which declares that he who has once dedicated to God what parents receive, is no longer bound to honour his father and mother. It was through their covetousness that the Pharisees gave such teaching, that on the pretext of the poor they might take what would have been given to a man's parents. The Gospel is evidence of their covetousness when it says, The Pharisees, who were covetous, heard these things and they scoffed at him.[3]

---

[1] Matt. xxiv. 46-7.   [2] Matt. xv. 5; Mark vii. 11.
[3] Luke xvi. 14.

So too if one of those who with us are named elders, or who hold any sort of authority over the people, prefers in the name of the community to give to the poor rather than to the relatives of the givers, if these happen to be short of necessaries and the givers have not power to do both, rightly would he be called a brother of those who nullified the word of God through their Pharisees' tradition and were criticized as hypocrites by the Saviour. There is grave warning against a man in the name of the poor being himself a willing recipient and supposing that the godliness of others is a way of gain,[1] and not alone in this passage but also in what is written of the traitor Judas. He in appearance was a protector of the interests of the poor and said with indignation, This ointment might have been sold for three hundred pence and given to the poor; but in reality, He was a thief and had the bag and took away what was put therein.[2] So if any one now has the church's bag and says it is for the poor, as Judas did, but takes away what is put therein, he would cast in his lot with Judas who did these things. Like a gangrene[3] they eat their way into his soul, and therefore the devil put it in his heart to betray the Saviour. Afterwards, when he had received the fiery dart of this suggestion, the devil himself entered into his soul, and filled him full.[4] And perhaps when the Apostle says, The love of money is a root of all evils,[5] it is because of this love in Judas that he says it, for it is a root of all the evils that tell against Jesus.

---

[1] 1 Tim. vi. 5.
[2] Matt. xxvi. 9; Mark xiv. 5; John xii. 5-6.
[3] 2 Tim. ii. 17.
[4] Luke xxii. 3; John xiii. 2; Eph. vi. 16.
[5] 1 Tim. vi. 10.

LVII

Contrast Isaiah's offer to be God's messenger with the reluctance of Moses and Jonah. Office in the Church should not be sought. Its purpose is service, not honour or position. (In Isaiam, Hom. vi. 1; Lomm. xiii. 271–75; B viii. 268–70. From the Latin.)

When Isaiah saw the Lord of Hosts sitting upon a throne, high and lifted up; when he saw also the seraphim standing round about Him, and when he received forgiveness of sins through the fire which was brought from the altar and purged his lips by its touch, he tells us that he heard the voice of God not commanding but arousing him and saying, Whom shall I send and who will go unto this people? Then he says that he answered the Lord, Behold, here am I, send me.[1] Being occupied with this passage and examining what is written, I find Moses did one thing, Isaiah another. For Moses, when he was chosen to lead the people out of the land of Egypt, says, Secure some one else to send.[2] He seems even to oppose God. Whereas Isaiah, not chosen, but hearing the words, Whom shall I send and who will go? says, Here am I, send me. So is it worth while to compare spiritual things with spiritual, and to ask which of the two did better; Moses, who after being chosen refused; or Isaiah who, without even being chosen, offered himself to be sent unto the people. I do not think any one observing the difference of procedure, which appears in the two cases, could say that Moses acted as Isaiah did. I have ventured to make comparison between two holy and

---

[1] Isa. vi. 8.
[2] Ex. iv. 13. LXX. has προχέιρισαι δυνάμενον ἄλλον, ὃν ἀποστελεῖς.

blessed men; to point out a distinction, and to assert that Moses acted with more humility than Isaiah. I suppose Moses had in mind the great responsibility of taking command of the people to lead them out of the land of Egypt, and of opposing the incantations and curses of the Egyptians. Therefore he says, Secure some one else to send. But the other, without waiting to hear what he might be bidden to say, or whether he was chosen, says, Here am I, send me. On this account, because without knowing what he would be bidden to say, or whether he was chosen, he said, Here am I, send me, he is bidden to say things which he had no desire to say. For was it not an undesirable task the moment he was bidden to prophesy to commence his words with curses; Ye shall hear with the ear and not understand, and seeing ye shall behold and not perceive, for the heart of this people is waxed fat,[1] and so on? Perhaps—if indeed I ought to speak so boldly—he received the reward of his rashness and boldness in being bidden to utter prophecies which he disliked.

As we have compared Isaiah and Moses, let us make another similar comparison of Isaiah and Jonah. The latter is sent to foretell to the men of Nineveh its fall after three days, and he is reluctant to set out and become the unwilling cause of calamity to the city.[2] But Isaiah, without waiting to hear what he was bidden to say, answers, Here am, I send me. It is a good thing not to rush eagerly to those honours, high positions, and ministries of the church which are from God, but to imitate Moses and with him to say, Secure some one else to send. He who wishes to be saved takes no steps to high position in the church, and, if appointed, takes office for

[1] Isa. vi. 9-10.   [2] Jonah i.

the church's service. If we are to use also the words of the Gospel, The princes of the Gentiles have lordship over them, and they that have authority over them are called officers. But it shall not be so with you. For your princes do not exercise lordship among you, but whoever of you wishes to be greater shall be least of all; he who wishes to be first shall be last of all.[1] He then who is called to a Bishop's office is not called to a prince's position but to the service of the whole church. If you seek scripture evidence for believing that in the church he who rules is servant of all, our Lord and Saviour Himself may convince you, who in the midst of His disciples showed His nature and true greatness not by reclining at table but by ministering. For after He had laid aside his garments, He took a towel and girded Himself and poured out water into a basin and began to wash the disciples' feet and to wipe them with the towel with which He was girded. Teaching us what character our leaders, as servants, ought to possess, He says, Ye call me Master and Lord, and ye say well, for so I am. If I then your Lord and Master have washed your feet, ye also ought to wash one another's feet.[2]

Thus the prince of the church is called to service, that he may be able by such service to attain the throne of heaven, as it is written, Ye shall sit upon thrones judging the twelve tribes of Israel.[3] And listen to Paul, wonderful man that he was, declaring himself the servant of all believers. For I am the least, he says, of the apostles; I am not worthy to be called an apostle, because I persecuted the church of God.[4] Further, if this seems only to show his humility and not his service, hear him

---

[1] Luc. xxii. 25–6.
[2] John xiii. 13–14.
[3] Matt. xix. 28.
[4] 1 Cor. xv. 9.

say, We were babes in the midst of you, as when a nurse cherisheth her children, when we might have been burdensome as apostles of Christ.[1] We then should be followers of the lowly words and deeds of the Lord Himself and of His apostles, and do as Moses did, so that if a man be called to leadership he will say, Secure some one else to send. To God he says, I am not worthy, neither yesterday nor the day before. I am feeble of speech and slow of tongue.[2] And because he spoke humbly to God—feeble of speech and slow of tongue—he hears God answer, Who hath made man's mouth? or who made a man deaf or dumb or seeing or blind? Is it not I, the Lord God? Trust in God, sanctify thyself unto Him. Feeble of voice, slow of tongue, commit thyself still to the Word of God. Later thou shalt say, I opened my mouth and drew in my breath.[3] So far on Isaiah's words, Here am I, send me.

LVIII

The chiefs are punished for the sins of the people. Who would desire the responsibilities of high office? Even guardian angels are judged for their neglect of the souls committed to their charge.—(*In Num.* Hom. xx. 4; Lomm. x. 255-57; B. vii. 196-98. From the Latin.)

And the anger of the Lord was kindled against Israel, and the Lord said unto Moses, Take all the chiefs of the people and expose them unto the Lord over against the sun, and the anger of the Lord shall be turned away from Israel.[4] It is possible that in discussing this passage we may give offence to some persons, but, even

---

[1] 1 Thess. ii. 6-7.
[2] Ex. iv. 10.
[3] Ps. cxix. 131.
[4] Num. xxv. 3-4.

if we do, our obedience and service must be given to the words of the Lord rather than to the favour of men. Israel sinned, and the Lord told Moses to take all the chiefs and to expose them unto the Lord over against the sun. The people sins, and the chiefs are exposed over against the sun. They are led forth for investigation, so that they may be tested by the light.

See what is the lot of the leaders of the people; they are not only put on trial for their own offences, they are also compelled to give account for the sins of the people. Perhaps it is their fault that the people offends. Perhaps they did not teach, they did not warn, they did not take the trouble to convict those who had been the first to do wrong, so as to prevent the spread of the malady to others. The performance of these duties is laid upon leaders and teachers. If through their inaction, through their lack of care for the multitude, the people sins, it is they who are exposed, they who are led forth to judgment. Moses, that is the Law of God, charges them with indolence and slackness; upon them shall the anger of the Lord be turned, and it shall cease from the people. If men thought of these things, they would never desire or intrigue for the leadership of the people.[1] Enough for me to be tried for my own offences; enough for me to give account for myself and for my sins. What occasion is there for me to be exposed for the sins of the people as well? To be exposed over against the sun, before which nothing can be hidden, nothing kept dark?

But perhaps there is also some hidden and secret meaning in the passage, with further teaching for us than the common interpretation seems to possess. Possibly this passage also has reference to those princes

---

[1] He has office in the Church in mind.

of the people of whom we spoke a little earlier. For the angels shall come to judgment together with us, and stand for us before the sun of righteousness; perhaps some responsibility for our sins lies with them; perhaps they failed to pay sufficient care and attention to us, so as to call us back from the disease of our sins. Unless there had been some defect in them, which seemed to deserve blame on our account, the language of Scripture would never say to the angel of this or of that church, Thou hast—for instance—some who hold the teaching of Balaam; or, Thou hast left thy first love, or thy patience, or something else of the same kind, as we mentioned above, on account of which in the Apocalypse the angels of each church are blamed.[1] For if, let us say, the angel who has received me, marked with the sign, from God, looks for a reward for my good deeds, it is certain he will also look for censure for those deeds of mine which are not good. That is why they are said to be exposed over against the sun, doubtless to make it clear whether it was through my disobedience, or through the angel's carelessness, that sins were committed which led to my devotion to Baal-phegor, or to some other idol, according to the character of my sin. Now if my chief, I mean the angel assigned to me, did not fail but counselled me to right action, and spoke in my heart, as he did through conscience calling me back from sin; whereas I, despising his advice and scorning the restraint of conscience, rushed headlong into sin, for me there will be the double penalty, both for despising my adviser and for offending in my deed. Nor should you feel any surprise if we say that angels come to judgment together with men, since Scripture says, The Lord will enter into

---

[1] Rev. ii, iii.

judgment with the elders of His people and the princes thereof.¹ Thus the princes are exposed, and, if the fault be in them, God's anger ceases from the people. We should have the keener vigilance over our actions, now that we know that not ourselves alone shall stand before God's judgment seat for our deeds, but that the angels, as our chiefs and guides, shall also be brought into judgment on our account. Therefore it is that the Scripture says, Obey them that have the rule over you, and submit yourselves in all things. For they watch as those who shall give account for your souls.²

LIX

Are we, the true Judah, to be rejected as Israel was? The Church has increased in numbers but her standard of faith has fallen below its level in the days of persecution. (In Jerem. Hom. iv. 2–3 ; Lomm. xv. 140–41 ; B. iii. 24–6. From the Greek.)

As they received the bill of divorcement, they were consequently utterly abandoned.³ For where are their prophets now? Where are now their tokens? Have they any manifestation of God? Have they any religious rites? any temple? any sacrifices? They have been driven out of their place. Thus did he give to Israel her bill of divorcement.

Then we, we who are Judah—Judah because the Saviour arose from the tribe of Judah, For it is evident

---

[1] Isa. iii. 14. References to guardian angels are frequent ; *De Prin.* I. viii ; II. x. 7 ; *In Matt.* xiii. 5, 27-8 ; Lomm. iii. 219, 259–63. Clem. Al *Ecl. Proph.* 41, 48 ; also the Latin hymn, published in 1628, ' De Angelo Custode '. Trench, *Sacred Latin Poetry,* p. 241.
[2] Heb. xiii. 17.
[3] Jer. iii. 8.

that our Lord hath sprung out of Judah[1]—we turned unto the Lord, and our last state (God grant it has not come already) seems to bear resemblance to their last state if it be not even worse. For that our condition at the end of this age will be similar, is clear from the words of our Saviour in the Gospel, where He says, Because iniquity shall be multiplied, the love of the many shall wax cold. But he that shall endure to the end, the same shall be saved.[2] Also, He that is to come shall do signs and wonders so as to lead astray, if possible, even the elect.[3] Such shall be our condition that the Saviour says with regard to His coming, hinting that perhaps out of so many churches no man of faith would be found, Howbeit when the Son of man cometh, shall He find faith on the earth [4] ? And verily if we judge the situation by the truth and not by numbers, if we judge it by intention and not by the sight of the assembled crowds, we shall see that now we are not men of faith.

But once there were men of faith, when noble martyrdom was common,[5] when after accompanying the martyrs we used to come from the cemeteries to assemble at our places of meeting, and the whole church attended in no downcast mood, and the catechumens were instructed about the martyrs' testimony, and about the deaths of those who confessed the truth even unto death, yet were not alarmed or rebellious against the living God. Then we know men did see marvellous and wonderful tokens. Then there were men of faith, few, but of real faith, who trod the strait and narrow way that leadeth unto life. But now, when we have become many

---

[1] Heb. vii. 14.   [2] Matt. xxiv. 12-13.
[3] Matt. xxiv. 24.   [4] Luc. xviii. 8.
[5] These homilies were probably delivered after the close of the persecution of Maximin, C. 245 A.D. Westcott in *D.C.B.*

in number, since it is not possible for there to be many chosen,—for Jesus makes no mistake when He says, Many are called but few chosen,[1]—out of the multitude of those that profess religion few indeed are they who attain to the lot of God's chosen and to the estate of bliss.

LX

The children of Judah could not wholly expel the Jebusites from Jerusalem. So do tares as well as wheat remain within the Church. (*In Josuam.* Hom. xxi. 1 ; Lomm. xi. 181–83 ; B. vii. 427–29. From the Latin.)

The children of Judah wished to drive out or to destroy the Jebusites from Jerusalem and they were not able. Wherefore the Jebusites dwelt with the children of Judah in Jerusalem unto this day.[2] Starting with the letter, we should like to ask those who believe that these words can retain their meaning according to the letter, what is the sense of the phrase, Unto this day. This expression Scripture always employs to denote the duration of the world. Thus it says, Turn not aside from following the Lord unto this day,[3] that is, so long as the world lasts. Let the literalist then show me in what sense the Jebusite 'so long as the world lasts' does dwell with the children of Judah in Jerusalem. Why, not even the children of Judah themselves dwell in Jerusalem. Neither consequently can it possibly be true that the Jebusites dwell with the children of Judah in Jerusalem, since even they do not dwell there.

---

[1] Matt. xxii. 14.   [2] Josh. xv. 63.
[3] 1 Sam. xii. 20, but the phrase in question does not occur there. In xii. 2, it could not have the sense Origen gives it. For once his memory misled him. Cp. § li.

We however must take these things in a spiritual sense, connecting them with the parable in the Gospel which says of the tares, Allow both to grow, lest haply while ye seek to uproot the tares, ye uproot also the wheat with them.[1] As in the Gospel the tares are suffered to grow together with the wheat, in like fashion here also in Jerusalem, that is, in the church, there are some Jebusites, persons who live a debased and unsatisfactory life, who in faith, in deeds, in all their conversation, have gone astray. For it is impossible for the church to be entirely purified while it is on earth, so that no wicked person or sinner should be known to remain in it, but all within it should be holy and blessed, people in whom not so much as a spot of sin can be found. As it is said of the tares, Lest haply while ye root up the tares, ye root up also the wheat with them; so may it be said of these in whom there are things questionable or hidden sins. For we are not saying that persons who are clearly and unmistakeably guilty should not be driven out from the church. Hear then the Scripture state that the sons of Judah were not able to exterminate the Jebusites, but they dwelt with them in Jerusalem unto this day. I beseech you who are faithful to guard your life and conversation, that ye may in no matter either yourselves suffer offence or cause offence to others. Take the greatest pains, the greatest caution, that no unclean person enter this holy assembly of yours, that no Jebusite dwell therein with you. You see then how the Scripture says that the children of Judah were not able to drive out the Jebusites from Jerusalem. Now Jebusite means 'Treading under foot'.[2] Since then we cannot expel

---

[1] Matt. xiii. 29-30.
[2] It denotes a place trodden down, e.g. the threshing floor of Araunah the Jebusite.

those who tread us under foot, at least let us expel those whom we can, whose sins are evident. We cannot expel any one from the church when there is no evident sin, Lest haply uprooting the tares we uproot also the wheat with them.

LXI

What is a heretic? A heretic is one who holds erroneous opinions about the Father, about the Son, about the Spirit, about human nature, about the resurrection, or about the freedom of the will. (In Epist. ad Titum. Lomm. v. 284–90. From the Latin.)

To the best of our ability, so far as we can be clear upon the point, let us explain what is meant by a heretic.[1] Every one who acknowledges that he believes in Christ, and yet declares that there is one God of the Law and of the Prophets and another God of the Gospels, and declares that the Father of our Lord Jesus Christ is not the God who is announced by the Law and the Prophets, but some other, whom no one knows and no one has heard of—men of this type we describe as heretics, however various, however different, however mythical, be the fictions on which they build their theories. Such are the followers of Marcion, of Valentinus, of Basilides, also those who call themselves Tethiani. Apelles too, though he does not wholly deny that the Law and the Prophets are of God, bears still the

---

[1] The reader who wishes for fuller information on the various forms of heresy mentioned in this section may consult the articles in *D.C.B.*; the chapters on Gnosticism in Gwatkin's *Early Church History* and in Bigg's *Origins of Christianity*; also the valuable work of De Faye, *Gnostiques et Gnosticisme*. The present passage comes from the *Apologia* of Pamphilus and therefore may be trusted to give us Origen's views without modification.

mark of a heretic, inasmuch as he asserts that this Lord who produced the world fabricated it for the glory of another ingenerate and good God. This ingenerate God, in the fulness of the ages, sent Jesus Christ to set the world in order, being requested by the God who had made the world that He would send His own son for the improvement of His own world.

Now if it were only the man whose opinions about God the Father are at variance with the requirements of the rule of religion who must be accounted a heretic, the foregoing account would clearly be sufficient. But our conviction must be identically the same with regard to him who has any erroneous views about our Lord Jesus Christ, whether he follow those who say He was born of Joseph and Mary, as do the Ebionites and the Valentinians; or whether he follow those who deny that He is the Firstborn, the God of all creation, the Word, the Wisdom which is the beginning of the ways of God, established before aught else was made, brought forth before all the hills.[1] Such say that He was only a man.[2] Or a heretic may follow those who allow indeed that He was God, but not that He took upon Him human nature, a soul, that is, and a body of earth. These, on the pretext of giving greater glory to Jesus the Lord, declare that all His actions were in appearance rather than in reality.[3] They do not acknowledge that He was born of a virgin, but say that He appeared in Judaea as a man of thirty years.[4] Others believe indeed that He was born of a virgin, but maintain that the virgin rather imagined that she had given Him birth, though she had

---

[1] Prov. viii. 22–6.
[2] Cp. the references to the Philanthropists in *H.E.* v. 28.
[3] The Docetae.
[4] So Marcion held. Tert., *C. Marcionem* iv. 7.

not in reality done so. The mystery of the attributed birth was, as they declare, hidden even from the virgin. Such people must be kept right away from the church. Sufferers from the malady of Abstraction[1] they set up doctrines by which they entice many disciples to their sect. Those too who say the Lord Jesus was a man foreknown and foredetermined, who before His coming in the flesh had no personal and independent existence, but when born as a man had only the Godhead of the Father within him—they also may not without risk be associated with the church's membership. To the same class belong those who, with more superstition than religion, not wishing to appear to say there are two Gods, nor yet to deny the divinity of the Saviour, maintain that the Father and the Son have one and the same personal being. That is to say, there is one underlying person or hypostasis, though it is given two names for different purposes; one personality, $ὑπόστασις$, under the two titles. These are called in Latin, Patripassians.[2]

Any too who say that there is one Holy Spirit who was in the Prophets, another who was in the Apostles of our Lord Jesus Christ, are guilty of exactly the same impious offence as they who, to the best of their power, sever and divide the nature of the Godhead by asserting that there is one God of the Law and another of the Gospels.

[1] The Latin text has *Philarchiæ morbo languentes*, with a variant *Philargyriæ*. *Philarchia* probably denotes the common Gnostic tendency to refer all to abstract agencies, aeons and the like, while facts and concrete realities are discounted or ignored. For Greek philosphy from Plato onwards matter was the enemy of spirit Christianity made it the organ and medium of spirit. There could be a body of Christ in several senses.

[2] Sabellius so taught, and the doctrine was often known as Sabellianism. As far back as Justin (*Apol.* i. 63) there were teachers who said the Son was the Father. The view was an extreme form of Monarchianism.

Those also who maintain that human souls are not all of one and the same nature or substance, but that the natures of souls are different, must be classed among those heresies which utter wickedness against the Most High [1] and accuse Him of injustice and wrong. There are as well some who endeavour to deprive the soul of its power of free choice.[2] They must be regarded as bringing by their disastrous doctrine a plague upon our common human life, upon virtue, upon restraint. They tell us it rests not with the will of man to do or to say or to think anything that is good. As a result the mind of man will be brought to despise or neglect the judgment of God. Also, as a part of the church's rule, there must be right faith in regard to the punishment of sinners, and in regard to those who will receive by the just decree of God the rewards of their good conversation and life in His kingdom.[3]

Whoever attempts to alter or overthrow any item that we have above described, sins like a man astray and is self-condemned, according to the Apostle's opinion. We too must obey his command and so estimate such a man. The true churchman, in addition to the other features already mentioned, is marked by his faith in the resurrection of the dead. On this point the holy Apostle Paul states that whoever denies the resurrection of the dead must deny consistently the resurrection of Christ. Also in the church's rule account must be taken of the devil and all his army, of the way they stir hostility and opposition against all men and especially against

---

[1] Ps. lxxiii. 8. LXX.
[2] Gnosticism was generally opposed to human freedom. Compare e.g. its theory of three distinct classes or 'natures'. Origen is emphatic in his assertion of moral freedom. Cp. *De Princip.* III. i ; the earlier portion of the *De Oratione*, and Denis, 249 *sqq.*
[3] On punishment in Origen see Bigg, *Platonists*, 227 *sqq.*

believers in our Lord Jesus Christ.[1] They have not the power through such hostility and opposition to lay upon us any compulsion to sin, still they can influence and delude to their ruin those who do not with all diligence fortify their hearts beforehand. And among the principles of the church we must maintain that no man is given over to destruction by God, but each of those who perish perishes by his own indifference and guilt; having freedom of choice he had the power and the duty to choose what is good. Even of the devil himself we must hold this view. He is recorded to have offered resistance in the face of the Lord Almighty and to have abandoned his proper position, wherein he had been without stain. Certainly he could have remained to the end in the position in which he had been from the beginning, if he had so desired. I think to the best of our power we have given a description and account of the nature and character of the heretic; also of the substance and details of his teaching and views, erroneous as we regard them; also of the purity of the church's rule.

LXII

Have the heretics faith? Their faith is a false faith, just as there is a false restraint and a false wisdom. (Comm. in Ep. ad Rom x. 5; Lomm. vii. 384–86. From the Latin.)

But some one may ask, Are even the heretics to be thought to act from faith, because they act according to their convictions? Or, since the faith they hold is evil,

---

[1] But some freedom of speculation was allowed here. Cp. *De Princip.* Præfatio, 6. '*De diabolo quoque et angelis ejus contrariisque virtutibus ecclesiastica praedicatio docuit quoniam sint quidem haec, quae autem sint vel quomodo sint, non satis clare exposuit.*

must we say that every act they do is sin, because it is not done from faith? For my part, I think their confidence[1] has the name of faith rather than its reality. Just as false prophets are sometimes by a misleading title called prophets, or false knowledge is called knowledge, or false wisdom is improperly termed wisdom, so too the confidence of the heretics is called by the misleading name of faith. Hence we must consider whether perhaps any good deed which seems to be accomplished among them may not be turned into sin, as not being done from faith. So was it said of a certain man, Let his prayer be turned into sin.[2] Sometimes too we find a restraint that is not of faith. It is the restraint of those who give heed to seducing spirits and doctrines of devils; speaking lies in hypocrisy; seared in their own conscience as with a hot iron; forbidding to marry and commanding to abstain from meats, which God created.[3] Thus also there is a false faith, that of those who have made shipwreck concerning the faith.[4]

There is also a false wisdom, that of this world, and of the rulers of this world, which shall come to naught.[5] So do the pirates act. It is their practice to light a beacon in the darkness of the night at sea, in the shallow places or where there are hidden rocks, so as to lure mariners, in their hope of finding refuge in port, to shipwreck and destruction. Even so this beacon light of false wisdom or false faith is lit by the princes of this world, or by the spirits of this lower air, not to provide

---

[1] The Latin word used is *credulitas*. In *De Princip*. IV. i. 2 this stands as the equivalent of the Greek πειθώ, which was possibly Origen's word in this passage.
[2] Ps. cix. 7.
[3] 1 Tim. iv. 1–3.
[4] 1 Tim. i. 19.
[5] 1 Cor. ii. 6.

an escape, but to bring ruin upon men who voyage over the waves of this world and the sea of life. It was of these pirates, I suspect, that Job used to say, The arrows of his pirates have come over me.[1] No doubt for this reason the Apostle Paul also says that Satan himself fashioneth himself into an angel of light.[2] Voyaging then over the waters of our life we must not trust to every beacon, not, that is, to every wisdom. As the Apostle counsels, we must prove the spirits that be of God.[3] We must therefore pray without ceasing for the help of God, and hope that He will deliver us out of the snare of the hunter, so that we too may say, Our soul is escaped as a bird out of the snare of the fowlers; the snare is broken and we are escaped. Our help is in the Name of the Lord, who made heaven and earth.[4]

---

[1] Job vi. 4. The arrows of the Almighty are within me. There is nothing in LXX. to justify Origen's version.
[2] 2 Cor. xi. 14.
[3] 1 John iv. 1.
[4] Ps. cxxiv. 7-8.

PART VI

THE TEACHER AND HIS TASK

LXIII

The Christian Scribe gathers things old and new into his store.—(Comm. in Matt. x. 15 ; Lomm. iii. 39-42. From the Greek.)

Since, Every scribe who hath been made a disciple to the kingdom of heaven is like unto a man that is a householder, which bringeth forth out of his treasure things new and old,[1] it is evident, by what is termed a conversion of the proposition, that every one who does not bring forth from his treasure things new and old, is not a scribe who hath been made a disciple unto the kingdom of heaven. Therefore should we endeavour by every means to gather together in our heart, through giving heed to reading, to exhortation, to teaching,[2] and by meditation day and night in the law of the Lord,[3] not only the new oracles of the Gospels and of the Apostles and their revelation, but also the old oracles of the Law that had a shadow of the good things to come,[4] and of the Prophets who prophesied in agreement with the Law. Such a store shall we collect if we both read and know and, remembering what we read, make seasonable comparison of spiritual things with spiritual things,[5] not comparing what is not comparable but things fit for comparison, which

---

[1] Matt. xiii. 52. [2] 1 Tim. iv. 13.
[3] Ps. i. 2. [4] Heb. x. 1.
[5] 1 Cor. ii. 13 ; cp. §§ xxxvi, xxxvii, and p. xix *supra*.

have a certain similarity both of language used in the same sense, and of ideas, and of doctrine, so that at the mouth of two or three or more witnesses from Scripture we may establish and confirm every word of God.[1] By these means we must confute those who, to the best of their ability, make division in the Godhead and sever the new from the old. Very far are they from resembling the householder who brings forth from his treasure things new and old.

Now since he who is made like another is distinct from him to whom he is made like, the scribe who hath been made a disciple to the kingdom of heaven will be the man who is made like, while the householder, who brings forth from his treasure things new and old, will be another person and distinct from him. And he who is being made like to him desires as imitating him to do the same thing. Surely then the man that is a householder is Jesus Himself, who brings forth from His treasure at the season of instruction things new, that is things of the spirit, which are ever renewed by Him in the inward man[2] of the righteous, who themselves are ever renewed day by day; and things old, graven in the letter on stone and on the stony hearts of the old man that by comparison of the letter and by presentation of the spirit He may enrich the scribe who has been made a disciple to the kingdom of heaven and make him like unto Himself. At last the disciple[3] will become as his master, imitating first the imitator of Christ and after him Christ Himself, according to the saying of Paul, Be imitators of me as I also am of Christ.[4] Also in a more

---

[1] Deut. xvii. 6 ; 2 Cor. xiii. 1. [2] 2 Cor. iv. 16.
[3] That is the pupil of the scribe. There are three grades : Christ, the teacher, the teacher's pupils.
[4] 1 Cor. xi.1.

simple sense Jesus the householder is able to bring forth from His treasure new things, that is the Gospel teaching, and old things, the comparison of sayings taken from the Law and the Prophets, of which examples may be found in the Gospels. In regard to these things, old and new, we must hear also the spiritual law which says in Leviticus, And ye shall eat the old store long kept and ye shall bring forth the old from before the new. And I will set my tabernacle among you.[1] For we eat with blessing the old things, the words of Prophecy, and store long kept, the sayings of the Law. And when the new things of the Gospel come, living according to the Gospel, we bring forth the old things of the letter in the character of things that are new,[2] and God sets His tabernacle amongst us, fulfilling the promise He made, I will dwell and walk among them.

LXIV

There is a wrong spirit and there is a right spirit in which we may ask questions about the ways of God. (Comm. in Ep. ad Rom. vii. 17 ; Lomm. vii. 171-73. From the Latin.)

O man, who art thou that repliest against God ? Shall the thing formed say to Him that formed it, why didst thou make me thus ? Hath not the potter a right over the clay from the same lump to make one part a vessel unto honour and another unto dishonour ?[3] Also we read in the Gospels that they who impudently and without faith asked of the Lord by what authority He did

---

[1] Lev. xxvi. 10-11.
[2] That is, give a spiritual or Christian interpretation to the Old Testament.
[3] Rom. ix. 20-21.

His works, and who gave Him that authority,[1] were not even considered to deserve an answer. So in the present passage we see that the Apostle was roused against impudent enquiries and that he put to confusion by his answer the effrontery of the questioner. For he says, O man, who art thou that repliest against God?[2] For man is in God's hands what the clay is in the potter's. It is like the case of the wicked servant; if his master happen to decide that some piece of work ought for sufficient reasons and some good purpose to be done, he shirks fulfilling his master's orders and begins to argue and question with his master; Why do you order this to be done? Who will be the better? Who needs it? To such an impudent servant what reply will be so suitable as to say, Who art thou to make answer to thy master? This is my pleasure. This is the master's will.

Yet I do not think, if a faithful and wise servant were to ask questions because he wished to understand and to admire the wisdom of his master, that to such an one the words, Who art thou? would be said. For instance, when Daniel the prophet wished to know the will of God, for which he was called a 'man of desirablenesses,'[3] it was not said to him, Who art thou? but an angel was sent to explain to him all the providences and judgments of God. We therefore, if we wish to know anything about the secret and hidden things of God, if we are men of desirablenesses and not men of contentions, must search with faith and with humility for those judgments of God which are deeply hidden in the divine writings. That is why the Lord used to say, Search the Scriptures.[4]

---

[1] Matt. xxi. 23.   [2] Rom. ix. 20.
[3] Dan. ix. 23. So Driver renders the Hebrew. Theodotion's version has $ἀνήρ\ ἐπιθυμιῶν$; LXX $ἐλεηνός$.
[4] John v. 39, R. V. Marg.

He knew such secrects were not discovered by those who, with their minds full of other affairs, are hearers or readers for the casual moment, but only by those who with a direct and single heart, with the yoke of toil, with long hours of waking, search deeply into the divine Scriptures—of whom I well know that I am not one. Whoever does seek in that way, he shall find.

LXV

Quiet requisite tor literary work. The interruption of his commentaries on the Gospel according to John. (Comm. in Joann. vi. 1–2 ; Lomm. i. 173–76; Br. i. 108–10 ; B. iv. 106–8. From the Greek.)

Every house that is to have all possible stability in its construction is built in still and quiet weather, so that nothing may prevent it receiving the rigidity necessary to give it strength and fitness to withstand the impetus of a flood[1] or the onrush of a river and all those accompaniments of a tempest, which are wont to show up rotten buildings and to make plain what structures are built with due and proper skill. More especially such a structure of thought as may contain the principles of truth, a sermon for example or a book, is best built at a time when, God giving good aid in its construction to him who purposes so excellent a work, the soul rests calm in the enjoyment of the peace which passeth all understanding,[2] free from all disturbance, like the sea without a wave.

It was in clear recognition of this that the servants of the prophetic spirit and the ministers of the Gospel message seem to me to have regarded themselves as

[1] Luke vi. 48.   [2] Phil. iv. 7.

THE TEACHER'S TASK

deserving to receive the peace that is in secret from Him who ever gives it to those deserve it, who said, Peace I leave with you; My peace I give unto you; not as the world giveth peace do I give peace.[1] Consider whether there be not a hint of this in the history of David and Solomon in regard to the temple. For David, waging the wars of the Lord and withstanding many enemies, his own and Israel's, when he desired to build a temple for God, is prevented by God, who said to him through Nathan, Thou shalt not build me an house, for thou art a man of blood.[2] But Solomon, who saw God in a dream and received wisdom in a dream—for the reality was to be kept for Him who said, Behold, a greater than Solomon is here[3]—living in a peace so deep that every man had rest under his vine and under his fig tree,[4] and taking himself his name from the peace of his times, for Solomon means, The man of peace,[5] through peace had freedom to build the famous temple for God. Also in the time of Ezra, when truth had victory over wine and the hostile king and women, the temple was rebuilt for God.[6]

These remarks we have made to you, revered Ambrosius, by way of explanation, for when we purposed, in accordance with your respected advice, to build in literary form the Gospel tower, we sat down and counted the cost,[7] whether we had the means of completion, lest we should be ridiculed and blamed by the spectators as men who laid a foundation but had not power to carry through their work. On adding up the cost we did not find that the resources for completing the building were

---

[1] John xiv. 27.   [2] 1 Chron. xxii. 8; 1 Kings v. 3.
[3] Matt. xii. 42.   [4] Micah iv. 4.
[5] 1 Chron. xxii. 9.   [6] 1 Esdras iii, iv.   [7] Luke xiv. 28.

available, but we have had confidence in God, who maketh rich in all utterance and in all knowledge,[1] that He would enrich us who were endeavouring to keep the laws of the spirit. We hoped that, progressing in our building through the supplies He affords, we should advance our work even to the parapet of the structure, which prevents the man who has gone up to the roof of the word[2] or subject from falling. It is only from structures that lack a parapet that such falls occur, by reason of the incompleteness of the buildings, which are responsible for loss of life and accidents to the indwellers.

So far as the end of the fifth volume, in spite of the adverse influences of the bad weather in Alexandria,[3] we dictated what it was given to us to say, Jesus rebuking the winds and waves of the sea.[4] Even with the sixth volume we had made some progress when we were removed from Egypt. God who led out his people from that country gave us deliverance. Thereupon, as our enemy by his recent edict, an edict veritably adverse to the Gospel, made a most bitter attack upon us, and raised against us all the winds of wickedness in Egypt, reason bade me halt and face the storm and so preserve my independence, lest unhappy reflections should prevail to introduce disturbed weather even into my soul, rather than at the wrong time, before my mind had gained

---

[1] 1 Cor. i. 5.
[2] He is thinking of the higher or spiritual interpretation of Scripture. Rashly employed it had dangers.
[3] This bad weather was due to the hostility of Demetrius, bishop of Alexandria. Origen had been ordained presbyter by other bishops, Theoctistus and Alexander, in Palestine. This was one, though probably not the only, cause of Demetrius' opposition. *Supra*, p. xv.
[4] Matt. viii. 26.

THE TEACHER'S TASK

calm, advance with the remainder of my book. The absence too of my usual amanuenses[1] hindered the continuation of our dictations. But now that the many fiery darts[2] aimed at us are quenched by God and rendered blunt[3] and our soul, grown accustomed to changed circumstances, is endeavouring with the aid of the heavenly word to bear more lightly the attacks made upon it, we desire to continue our dictation without more delay, possessed as it were of a measure of calm. We pray that God may be with us, whispering His instruction in the recesses of our soul, so that the structure of our exposition of the Gospel according to John may attain completion. May God hearken to my prayer, so that I may be able to proceed with the body of the entire treatise without the interruption of any further circumstances calculated to occasion a break of any kind in the course of my writing.

Be assured that it is with the greatest eagerness that I make this second commencement of the sixth volume, in consequence of the non-arrival, for some reason, of the portion I had already dictated in Alexandria. I thought it better, to avoid letting more time slip by without making further progress in this work, at once to commence on what is left, and not, through waiting for the previously dictated portion, recovery of which is quite uncertain, to lose the considerable profit of the intervening days. Let this introduction be sufficient. And now let us proceed with the text.

---

[1] ταχυγράφοι, as in *H.E.* vi. 23. They were more than seven in number. The cost was borne by Ambrosius.
[2] Eph. vi. 16.
[3] Demetrius excommunicated him, but his old friends stood firm, and the sentence did not have much immediate result.

LXVI

Our Lord cast out of the temple those who sold, not those who bought. In spiritual things we should be buyers, not sellers. The Christian teacher must not sell for money the doves of spiritual truth.—(*In Lucam* xxxviii ; Lomm. v. 231–32. From the Latin.)

After this come the words, He entered into the temple.[1] After entering He cast out those that sold doves. He did not cast out those who bought, for those who buy also own what they have bought. Jesus cast out of the temple of His Father those who sell and relinquish what they possess, after the example of that prodigal son who received from his father his portion and squandered everything in drunkenness. So whoever sells is cast out, especially if it was doves he sold. Why was there no mention of other birds, only of doves? This creature is simple and beautiful. Even in ourselves I fear faults of this kind may be discovered. For if I sell for money what is revealed to me by the Holy Spirit, and committed to me that I may impart it to the multitude, and if I do not teach without payment,[2] what am I doing but selling doves, that is, the Holy Spirit? But when I sell the Spirit, I am cast out of the temple of God.

---

[1] Luke xix. 45.

[2] The Rabbis taught without payment from their pupils, though they might accept other services. See Geikie, *Life and Words of Christ*, i. 77 *sqq*. Hausrath *N.T. Zeitgeschichte*, i. 100. Cynic and Stoic philosophers discouraged fees and even endowments. See Capes, *University Life in Ancient Athens*, 39. At the date of the *Didache* the Christian teacher was regarded as worthy of his hire, but was warned not to be covetous. xiii, xv. Origen was possibly still helped by Ambrosius and being now a presbyter may have taken his share of the Church's ordinary funds. There was a monthly distribution. See Bingham, *Antiquities*, Bk. V, ch. iv. For the position of the Christian teacher, see Harnack, *Mission* i. 354 *sqq*. E.T. When Augustine taught rhetoric at Rome, pupils cheated him of his fees, *Conf.* v. 12.

Therefore let us ask God that we may all buy and not sell. If we do not sell, we know and understand our salvation. Otherwise enemies will surround our city. If once the armies of our enemies surround us, we shall not deserve the tears of God. Let us rise then early and implore the Lord that at least we may be allowed to eat the crumbs which fall from His table.[1]

Scripture marvels at the queen of Sheba coming from the ends of the earth to hear the wisdom of Solomon.[2] When she saw his fare, and his ornaments, and the service of his house, speech failed her and she was full of wonder. If we do not gladly welcome the wonderful wealth of the Lord, the rich ornaments of the Word, the plentiful supply of His teaching, if we do not eat the bread of life, if we do not feed on the flesh of Christ and drink His blood, if we despise the banquet of our Saviour—then must we be aware that God has both goodness and severity. Of these we should pray the rather for His goodness in Christ Jesus our Lord. To Whom be glory and dominion for ever and ever. Amen.

LXVII

Prophets are like physicians and are treated with similar ingratitude. Jeremiah was not helped by His hearers, as a teacher may be. Nor, to take a variant reading, was He their creditor, as a true teacher should be. He especially of all the prophets was born a man of strife and contention. The account of him should often be interpreted as referring to Jesus Christ.—(In Jerem. Hom. xiv. 1–5 ; Lomm. xv. 256–62 ; B. iii. 106–11. From the Greek.)

On the passage, Woe is me, my mother, *down to,* Therefore thus saith the Lord, If thou return, then will I

---

[1] Matt. xv. 27 [2] 1 Kings x. 1 *sqq.*

bring thee again.[1] Physicians of the body spend their time with the sick and constantly devote themselves to the cure of their patients. According to the purpose of their profession they view the parts affected and handle repulsive cases. In the sufferings of other people they reap their own troubles, and their life is constantly at the mercy of circumstances. They never live with healthy persons but are continually with the disabled, with those who have spreading sores, with people full of discharges, fevers, various diseases. And if a man decides to follow the physician's calling, he will not grumble, nor neglect the purpose of the profession he has undertaken, when he finds himself in the situation we have described.

This introduction I have made, because in a sense the prophets are physicians of souls and ever spend their time among those who require treatment. For, They that are whole have no need of a physician, but they that are sick.[2] What physicians undergo for the sake of patients who have no restraint, prophets and teachers also suffer at the hands of those who decline to be cured. They are disliked because their directions conflict with the preferences of their patients' desires, because they forbid delicacies and indulgences to people who even in illness crave to have what is unsuitable for their state of illness. So patients who are without self-control avoid physicians, frequently even abusing and vilifying them, treating them exactly as one enemy would treat another. These people forget that physicians come to them as friends; they look to the troublesome character of their regimen, to the pain caused by the incision of the surgeon's knife, not to the result that follows such pain.

[1] Jer. xv. 10-19.   [2] Luc. v. 31.

They detest them simply as the authors of suffering, not as of suffering which brings the patient to good health.

Now the ancient people was fallen sick. Various diseases existed in the people that was called the people of God. And God sent them prophets as physicians. Jeremiah was one of these physicians. He reproved sinners, endeavouring to convert those who did evil. When they should have listened to his words, they accused the prophet and accused him before judges like unto themselves. The prophet was continually on his trial before men who, as regards his prophecy, were under treatment, but through their own disobedience remained uncured. At this he says in one place, And I said, I will not speak, nor will I name the name of the Lord. And it was as a burning fire, raging in my bones. I am altogether faint and unable to endure.[1] In another place, perceiving himself continually put on trial, vilified, accused, the victim of false witness, he says, Woe is me, my mother, how hast thou borne me a man—so run his words—who endures not causes contest, who endures not causes strife, with all the earth.[2] And since the sick did not listen to his wise professional advice, I have availed nothing, he says. He offered to lend them spiritual money, but they would not listen to his words, that they might be gainers by what they heard. Neither, says he, was any man indebted to me, nor was I myself in debt.

This I have said by way of anticipation, before explaining the words, I was not in debt, neither was any man indebted to me.[3] The text has two readings. In

---

[1] Jer. xx. 9. [2] *Ibid.*, xv. 10.
[3] *Ibid.*

most copies it runs, I was of no help,[1] nor did any man help me. But in the most correct, which agree with the Hebrew text, it stands, I was not in debt,[2] neither was any man indebted to me. We must then both explain the text that is current and usually commented on in the churches, and also not leave unexplained the text based upon the Hebrew. The prophet then preached the word; no one attended to what he said. It is like a physician squandering his drugs upon patients who are without self-control and just satisfy their desires. It is as if he too should say, I was of no help, neither did any man help me. A reciprocity perhaps there is through the good will of the man who receives help towards his helper, so that the speaker too is in a position to receive advantage, for blessed is he that speaks to the ears of those that hear. In this way would a teacher receive his help from hearers who made advance and improvement. He would be helped by having fruit in them. Failing to receive this from the Jews, Jeremiah says, No man helped me. For if the speaker should have fruit in his hearers, but he who hears misunderstands and is beyond reach of what is said, the words, Nor did any man help me, would apply. For the speaker has not received that help which he would have received through the hearer being himself helped and becoming a source of advance and blessedness to the man who gave him help. Besides, every teacher by his very teaching is helped in his teaching and his studies through the intelligence of his pupil. Lecturers become more competent in the very instruction they impart, when their hearers are intelligent and do not accept their words

---

[1] ὠφέλησα.
[2] ὠφείλησα.

right off, but criticise them and ask questions and examine the meaning of the language used. I was of no help, neither did any man help me.

But a further interpretation also is necessary, because the most accurate copies read thus; I was not in debt, neither was any man indebted to me. Let us then interpret the passage in this form. He who pays to all their dues, fear to whom fear is due, tribute to whom tribute, custom to whom custom, honour to whom honour,[1] and who renders to all their rights, so that he does not owe their rights to any, honouring, let us say, his parents as parents, brothers as brothers, sons as sons, bishops as bishops, presbyters as presbyters, deacons as deacons, believers as believers, catechumens as catechumens, if he pays all claims, is not in debt. But if he was under obligation to meet a claim and has not met it, he cannot say, I was not in debt. For he owed but he did not pay. But how then am I to interpret, Neither was any man indebted to me? I indeed was ready to lend and willing to give spiritual wealth, but they turned away from my words, and did not show themselves receptive so as to be in my debt. Consequently, not a man was indebted to me. For who received what I said, so as through receiving it to become a debtor for what he heard and liable as a debtor to the claim for interest on my words? In this sense it is better for the hearer to receive rational money from the speaker and to be in debt, rather than by not receiving and not gaining to avoid indebtedness. For the phrase, No man was indebted to me, stands as a reproach.

The words follow, Woe is me, my mother, how hast

---

[1] Rom. xiii. 7.

thou borne me a man of strife and of contention to the whole earth. I do not think they can be so appropriately used of the other prophets as of Jeremiah. For most of the prophets, after time had gone by, after wickedness, after their sins, repented and began to prophesy. Whereas Jeremiah was a prophet from childhood. One might give an instance from the Scriptures. Isaiah did not hear the words, Before I formed thee in the belly, I knew thee, and before thou camest forth out of the womb, I sanctified thee. I have appointed thee a prophet unto the nations. Nor did he say, I cannot speak, for I am a child.[1] But when he beheld the vision recorded in his prophecy, he beheld it and said, Woe is me, for I am undone; because I am a man of unclean lips, and I dwell in the midst of a people of unclean lips, and I have seen with my eyes the King, the Lord of Hosts. And there was sent unto me, he says, one of the Seraphim, and he touched my lips and said, Lo, I have taken away thy iniquities and this shall cleanse thy sins.[2] Thus after the sins he had previously committed, later on, Isaiah became worthy of the Holy Spirit and was a prophet. The same you would find also in the case of any other. But not so Jeremiah. He from his cradle was endowed with the prophetic spirit; he was a prophet from childhood. Hence he says, to take first the common interpretation, Woe is me, my mother, how hast thou borne me a man of strife and of contention to the whole earth.

But one of the teachers before my time made a comment on the passage and said that the prophet used these words not to the mother of his body but to the

---

[1] Jer. i. 5-6.
[2] Isa. vi. 5-7.

mother who bears prophets. But who is it bears prophets but the Wisdom of God? So what he said was, Woe is me, my mother, how hast thou borne me, O Wisdom. There is a reference also in the Gospel to the children of Wisdom;[1] And Wisdom sendeth forth her children. The words are then, Woe is me, my mother Wisdom, how hast thou borne me a man of strife. Who am I that I should have been born for this, to be a man of strife, a man of contest, through my rebukes, through my attacks, through my teaching, unto all who are on the earth? If it is Jeremiah that says, How hast thou borne me a man of strife and of contention to the whole earth, I cannot interpret the words, To the whole earth. Jeremiah had no contest with the whole earth. Or are we to force ourselves to say that, The whole earth stands for, The whole of Judaea? For his prophecy, at the time he was a prophet, did not extend to the whole earth. But possibly, just as in a hundred other places we have shown that Jeremiah stands for our Lord Jesus Christ, so too shall we say of this passage. Originally I put a mark against the words, See, I have set thee over the nations and kingdoms, to pluck up and to break down, to destroy and to build and to plant. Jeremiah did not do this. But Jesus Christ plucked up the kingdoms of the land of sin, and broke down the edifices of wickedness, and in place of these kingdoms made righteousness and truth to have kingly power in our souls. Just as then it was more appropriate to refer the earlier passage to Christ than to Jeremiah, so I think must we deal with many other passages and with these words.

---

[1] Matt. xi. 19; Luc. vii. 35.

LXVIII

Between the disciples and the multitudes we must recognize a distinction.[1]—(*Comm. in Matt.* xi. 4; Lomm. iii. 74–6. From the Greek.)

And straightway He constrained the disciples to enter into the boat and to go before Him unto the other side, till He should send the multitudes away.[2] We should observe how often in the same passage the term 'multitudes' is used and another term, 'disciples'. By such observation and by the collection of relevant passages we shall learn that it was the purpose of the evangelists to display by means of the Gospel narrative the distinctions among those who come to Jesus. Some of them are the multitudes and are not called disciples: others are the disciples and superior to the multitudes. For the moment it will be sufficient for us to quote a few passages, so that a reader may be induced by these to make similar observation throughout the Gospels. Thus it is written, when the multitudes were below, but the disciples were able to come unto Jesus who had gone up to the mountain where the multitudes could not come, that, Seeing the multitudes, He went up into the mountain: and when He had sat down, His disciples came unto Him: and He opened His mouth and taught them saying, Blessed are the poor in spirit, and so on.[3] Again, in another place, when the multitudes needed healing, it is said, Great multitudes followed him and

---

[1] This a characteristic passage. Origen has abundant place and recognition for simple uninstructed believers, but his sympathies are always in reality with the educated, the intelligent, the mentally alert. He belongs to the disciples, not to the multitude. The same was true of Clement. Cp. the interesting chapter on Les Simpliciores in De Faye's *Clément d'Alexandrie*, pp. 137 *sqq.*

[2] Matt. xiv. 22.   [3] *Ibid.*, v. 1–3.

he healed them.[1] But we do not find any healing mentioned in connection with the disciples, since if a man is already a disciple of Jesus, he is in sound health, and being well he has need of Jesus not as a physician but in his other offices.[2]

Again in another place, as He was speaking to the multitudes, His mother and His brethren stood without, seeking to speak with Him. This was told to Him and He answered the man, stretching forth His hand not to the multitudes but to the disciples, and said; Behold my mother and my brethren.[3] He bore testimony to His disciples that they did the will of His Father in heaven; He is my brother and sister and mother. And again in another place it is written that, All the multitude stood upon the beach, and He spake to them many things in parables.[4] Then, after the parable of the Sower, there come to Him not the multitudes but the disciples, and said unto Him, not, Why dost thou speak to us in parables? but Why speakest thou unto them in parables? Then He answered and said not to the multitudes but to the disciples; Unto you it is given to know the mysteries of the kingdom of heaven, but to the others in parables.[5]

Thus among those who come to the name of Jesus, they who know the mysteries of the kingdom of heaven would be called disciples, those to whom such knowledge was not given would be called multitudes, who would be accounted less than disciples. Observe carefully that it was to the disciples He said, Unto you it is given to know the mysteries of the kingdom of heaven, but in

---

[1] Matt. xii. 15. R.V. has only, Many followed him. This accords with the balance of MS. authority. Origen here, for his own purposes, quotes the Western text.
[2] Cp. § xviii.
[3] Matt. xii. 46-9.
[4] *Ibid.*, xiii. 2-3.
[5] *Ibid.*, 10-11.

regard to the multitudes, To them it is not given.[1] And in another place He sends away the multitudes and enters into an house. He does not send away the disciples. And in the house there come to Him not the multitudes but the disciples, saying, Explain unto us the parable of the tares of the field.[2] Also, in another place, when, after hearing about John, Jesus withdrew in a ship into a desert place privately, the multitudes followed Him. Then He came forth and saw a great multitude and had compassion on them and healed their sick—the sick of the multitudes, not of the disciples. And when it was late there come to Him not the multitudes but the disciples as distinct from the multitudes, saying, Send the multitudes away, that they may go into the villages and buy themselves food. Also, when He took the five loaves and the two fishes and looking up into heaven blessed and brake the loaves, He gave them not to the multitudes but to the disciples, that they might give them to the multitudes,[3] who were incapable of receiving them from Him and even had difficulty in receiving the loaves Jesus blessed by the hands of the disciples. Even all these they did not eat, for the multitudes being satisfied left the remainder, enough to fill twelve baskets.

LXIX

Ezekiel's reproof of cushions and kerchiefs may be applied to the seductive rhetoric which is so great a danger within the church. (*In Ezech.* Hom. iii. 3; Lomm. xiv. 43-6; B. viii. 350–52. From the Latin.)

Woe, he saith, to those who sew cushions upon every elbow, or on one of them.[4] Those who find their interest

---

[1] Matt. xiii. 11.   [2] *Ibid.*, 36.
[3] *Ibid.*, xiv. 13 *sqq*.   [4] Ezek. xiii. 18.

THE TEACHER'S TASK 175

in the life of the body and do not, even in a dream, behold those delights of the spirit, which the divine Word wishes us to possess when it says, Delight thyself in the Lord and He shall give thee the desires of thine heart[1]—those who have no knowledge of the pleasure of the blessed, of which it is written, Thou shalt make them drink of the river of Thy pleasure,[2] being lovers of comfort, not lovers of God, desire ever to enjoy the delights of the body. Now the cushion sewed under the elbow[3] seems to me to be an emblem of the pleasure of the flesh. For since, at the time of reclining to enjoy the good things of the body, we make open use upon the elbows of certain embroidered and patchwork pads, perhaps the divine Word is by this figure and token laying blame on those masters who by their empty rhetoric and repeated promises of bliss encourage the crowd of their hearers in licence, vice and pleasure. For the word of God and the man of God should utter what makes for his hearer's salvation, what encourages him to self-control, to a life of sound conduct, to everything for which a man intent upon labour not upon lust should exert himself, that he may succeed in obtaining what God has promised. When therefore any one, well in sympathy with the morals of the crowd, in order to charm the people who have itching ears, makes the speeches they gladly welcome, speeches that are on the borders of licence, a master of this kind is sewing cushions upon every elbow.

The next step for him who has this fault is to make

---

[1] Ps. xxxvii. 4.
[2] *Ibid*, xxxvi. 8.
[3] Ezekiel seems to have spoken of fillets or amulets used by the prophetesses in the process of divination. The original sense is lost in Origen's interpretation.

also kerchiefs for covering the head of whatever age. Let us also consider carefully of what the veil is an emblem. The man who has confidence and is truly a man wears no veil upon his head, but prays to God with head uncovered, prophesies with head uncovered, implicitly manifesting his spiritual disposition by the token of his bodily attire. Just as he has no veil over his head in the flesh, so has he no veil over the dominant principle in his heart. But whoever does the deeds of confusion and of sin, he, so to say, wears the woman's veil upon his head. Thus when a man teaches the things which soothe the ears of the crowd and arouses the applause rather of his hearers than their sighs, if, like a seductive enemy, he has soothed rather than cut out the wound, a man of this kind weaves kerchiefs for the head. And when the speaker's oration spends itself in exuberant rhetoric, when it comes at a bound to worldy licentiousness, he is weaving a veil over the head of every age, not alone of lads and young men, but even of the old. Just as the false Christ and the false prophet will work signs and wonders to deceive, if it be possible, even the elect, so also these men, who discharge their elaborated incitements, and are ever seeking for the things which charm their hearers rather than convert them from their faults, are making veils over the heads not of lads and young men only, but even, if it be possible, of old men and fathers. At last they deceive even those who through their soul's effort have advanced in the years and seniority of the spirit.

The prophet might have said, Upon the sons of thy people who prophesy. But, as though all who weave veils and sew cushions under every elbow are women, and none of them deserves the name of man, the prophet says, Upon the daughters of thy people who prophesy out of their own heart,¹ and act as is then described. Effeminate indeed are the souls and intentions of those masters who are ever putting together resonant and melodious speeches. Nay, that I may assert the truth, there is nothing manly, nothing strong, nothing worthy of God, in the men who preach according to the pleasures and wishes of their hearers. Therefore it is daughters rather than sons that he describes as sewing cushions. And note the appropriateness of his term. Sewing, he says, not, Weaving. Know you not that the robe of your Lord Jesus had nothing in it sewn, but was woven throughout?[2] It is these women who with craft and cunning patch word to word, sewing rather than weaving. They make cushions for the repose not of the head but of the elbow, so that, you see, the hand may not be at work or grow weary in labour, but be at rest, be at ease, be occupied in the things which minister to our pleasures.

LXX

The Law forbade the Israelites to eat yesterday's meat. So too should stale teaching be avoided in the Church. (In Levit. Hom. v. 8; Lomm. ix. 258–60; B. vi. 348–50. From the Latin.)

This point is not without significance, that the divine Word does not allow us to feed on yesterday's meat, but always on what is fresh and new.[3] This applies specially to those who offer the sacrifice of the Passover or the

---

[1] Ezek. xiii. 17. For Origen woman is always the weaker vessel. Cp. *In Matt. Com. Ser.* 49. Those who in each tribe are '*corporaliores et mundialiores*' are called women. *In Lev.* Hom. viii. 2; *In Josuam* Hom. ix. 9; Lomm. iv. 310; ix. 314–16; xi. 96–9; B. vi. 394–96; vii. 354–56.
[2] John xix. 23.   [3] Lev. vii. 15; xix. 7.

sacrifice of praise to God. Fresh meat, newly killed that very day, he bids them eat; yesterday's he forbids. I recollect that the prophet Ezekiel also says something of the kind, when the Lord bade him bake bread for himself in man's dung. He answered the Lord and said, Ah, Lord, my soul hath not been polluted; that which dieth of itself or is unclean hath not come into my mouth. Neither hath yesterday's meat come into my mouth.[1] On this point I have often wondered at the nature of the prophet's satisfaction; in God's presence he brings it out as some great matter and asserts, I have never eaten yesterday's meat. However, as I see from the teaching of this passage and the mystical significance it suggests, what the prophet said to the Lord was this, I am not such a worthless and degraded priest as to eat yesterday's, that is, stale meat. Hearken to this, all ye priests[2] of the Lord; give ye careful attention to what is said. This flesh, which is allotted to the priests from the sacrifices, is the word of God, which they teach in the church. Thus they are warned in this passage, by forms which have mystic meaning, not to bring out yesterday's fare, when they set about to address the people; not to set forth stale doctrines according to the letter, but by God's grace ever to bring forth new truth, ever to discover the spiritual lessons. If you produce to-day in the church what you learned yesterday from the Jews, this is just eating yesterday's flesh in the sacrifice. If you remember, the Lawgiver also uses the same language in regard to the offering of firstfruits; they must, he says, be fresh and

---

[1] Ezek. iv. 14 'Abominable flesh'. The term was used of the sacrificial flesh kept till the third day, but Origen makes the statement more definite.

[2] 'Sacerdotes', in the Latin. Note the use of the term in connection with teaching. 'The priest's lips should keep knowledge.'

new. Everywhere, you see, what belongs to the praise of God—for this is what the sacrifice of praise means—must be new and fresh, so that there be no risk of your lips speaking but your mind being fruitless, while you produce old teaching in the church.

But hear what saith the Apostle ; If, he says, I speak with tongues, my spirit prayeth but my understanding is unfruitful. What is it then ? I will pray, he says, with the spirit and I will pray with the understanding also. I will sing with the spirit and I will sing with the understanding also.[1] For you too then in like manner, if you fail to produce by spiritual learning and by the instruction of God's grace fresh and living discourse in the praise of God, your lips indeed offer the sacrifice of praise but your mind by its barrenness is proved guilty of yesterday's meat. The Lord too, when He gave bread to his disciples, saying to them, Take and eat,[2] did not make delay or order it to be kept for the morrow. Perhaps this is the secret meaning contained in the order that no bread be carried on a journey : always you are to bring forth the fresh loaves of the word of God which you carry within you. Those Gibeonites, to take another case, were condemned and became hewers of wood and drawers of water for this reason, that they had brought old bread to the Israelites, to whom the spiritual law gave command that they should ever use fresh and new.[3]

Of course there is a different figurative meaning in the command that what is left may be eaten on the following day ; whereas nothing is to be reserved until the third day. Into this we must look in its proper place. Another point also must not escape us ; that there is a time when to eat old food is a blessing. For it is said of the seventh

---

[1] 1 Cor. xiv. 14–15.   [2] Matt. xxvi. 26.   [3] Josh. ix.

year, which is called the year of remission or the Sabbatical year, Ye shall eat, it says, what is old and exceeding old.[1] Then, in the secret meaning of the seventh year, it is a blessing, as we said, to eat old food; but now it is forbidden. But it would be a long digression to linger here over details, and to go further afield at the suggestion of the records, when for the moment it is the explanation of the sacrifices that we have in hand.

LXXI

Different physical natures need different kinds of food. So do our minds find the diversities of fare appropriate to them in the word of God. Even the journeyings of Israel in the book of Numbers have their value. (In Num. Hom. xxvii. 1; Lomm. x. 332–35; B. vii. 255–58. From the Latin.)

When God made the world, He created countless varieties of foods to correspond, I suppose, to the diversity in the appetites of men and in the natures of the animals. Thus not only does a man, when he sees the food of animals, know that it was not created for him but for the animals, but even the animals themselves recognize their own proper fare. The lion, for example, feeds on one kind of food; the stag, the ox, the bird, on different kinds. And even among men there are certain differences of appetite; one man, who is healthy and in sound condition, needs robust fare, confident and assured that he can eat anything. Such are the strongest athletes. But any one who knows that he is ailing and delicate, enjoys vegetables, and declines robust fare on account of

---

[1] Lev. xxv. 22.

the infirmity of his body. And a little child, even though unable to express itself by speech, as a matter of fact needs no other nourishment than milk. Thus each one according to his age or vigour or health of body seeks the nourishment that is fit for himself and proportionate to his powers.

If you have sufficiently examined the parallel case of the body, let us now leave that and come to the study of the spiritual meaning. Every rational nature must be fed on food that is right and proper for it. Now the true food of a rational nature is the word of God. But just as we have shown a moment ago that there are many distinctions in the diet of the body, so too is it with our rational nature, which feeds as we have said upon the reason or word of God; every nature is not sustained by one and the same word. Thus, keeping up the comparison of the parallel of the body, some find in the word of God the food of milk. This is that plainer and simpler teaching, usual on moral subjects, which is normally supplied for those who are at the beginning of their divine studies and receive the early elements of rational instruction.[1] Such persons, when there is read to them some passage from the divine books which is clearly free from obscurity, gladly receive it; for example, the book of Esther or of Judith, or even the story of Tobias, or the admonitions of Wisdom.[2] But if the book of Leviticus is read to such a man, at once his mind is repelled, and he rejects it as not his proper fare. When a man has come

---

[1] How far the Catechumenate was developed in Origen's time is not entirely clear. See the references in Redepenning.

[2] Harnack, *Bible Reading in the Early Church*, pp. 72 *sqq*. E. T. quotes this passage at length and adds: ' Here we are told in plain words what we otherwise could only conjecture, that the Old Testament Apocrypha formed the first stage in Bible reading, the Psalms, Gospels and Epistles the second, while the remaining books of the Bible took their place in order as further stages.'

in order to learn how to honour God, and how to receive His commandments of righteousness and piety, and he hears orders given about sacrifices and instruction on the ritual of offerings, naturally he ceases at once to listen and rejects fare that is not convenient for him. Some one else, when the Gospels or the Apostle or a passage of the Psalms is read, receives it gladly and gives it cordial welcome and has the joy of deriving from it a cure for his weakness. If the book of Numbers is read to him, more particularly these passages we are now dealing with,[1] he will regard it as quite unprofitable for any good purpose, either for the cure of his weakness or for the salvation of his soul. He will at once refuse and reject it, like heavy and oppressive food, beyond the powers of sick and ailing souls.

Yet, if we may revert again to the parallel of the body, if you could, shall we say? give intelligence to a lion, he will not because he feeds on raw flesh therefore find fault with the quantity of grass that exists, nor say that it has been needlessly supplied by the Creator, because he does not feed on it himself. Nor again should a man, because he eats bread and other food that suits him, blame God because He has made serpents, which he sees God gives to the stags for food.[2] Nor must, say, the sheep or the ox find fault because other animals are allowed to feed on flesh, while for themselves grass alone is a sufficient fare. So is the case with rational food—I mean the holy volumes. A man must not straightway criticize or reject a scripture because it seems to be difficult or not clear in meaning, or to contain things of which a beginner or a child or one weak in understanding could make no use,

---

[1] Num. xxxiii.
[2] This curious idea occurs also in Com. *In Cant. Cantic.* iii. (Lomm. xv. 46 *sqq*; B. viii. 206.)

or because he thinks he can derive nothing advantageous or salutary from it. You must bear in mind that just as a serpent, a sheep, an ox, a man, a bundle of hay, are all creatures of God, and this variety contributes to the praise and glory of the Creator, because these things afford or receive the nourishment that is appropriate and in season for each of those for whom they were made ; in like manner all these things, which are words of God, containing diversity of food according to the capacity of souls, are appropriated by each individual according as he feels himself possessed of health and capacity. And yet, if we make careful examination, say, in a passage of the Gospel, or in some apostolic teaching, wherein you take evident delight and in which you find the food that is most fit and pleasant for you, how much there is that you fail to see, if you examine and investigate the commands of the Lord. If we are to reject and avoid right off whatever seems abstruse or difficult, you will find, even in passages where you are specially confident, so much that is abstruse and difficult that, if you keep to this principle you will have to abandon even these. And yet there are many things in these passages expressed with sufficient openness and simplicity to instruct a hearer even of little intelligence.

So much we have said by way of preface, to arouse your attention, since the passage we have to deal with seems likely to appear difficult of understanding and unnecessary to read. But we cannot say of the words of the Holy Spirit that anything in them is useless or unnecessary, even though some find it obscure. This rather ought we to do, to turn the eyes of our mind to Him who ordered these things to be written and to ask of Him their meaning, that if there be weakness in our soul, He who healeth all infirmities may heal us ; or if we be of little understanding, the Lord who protecteth little ones may be with us and nourish us and bring us to manhood's full estate. Each is in our power: we may come from weakness to strength, from childhood to the full grown man. Therefore it is in our power to ask these things of God. It is God's part to give to those who seek and to open to those who knock. But this introduction will be long enough.

LXXII

The little that is rightly gained is better than great riches acquired by wrong. So is the little faith of a Christian better than the abundant wisdom of the world. Yet the Scriptures also have their abundant wealth of knowledge. (Selecta in Psalmos. Hom. iii. 6; Lomm. xii. 187-91. From the Latin.)

Better is a little that the righteous hath than the great riches of the wicked.[1] In its literal sense this is clearly a profitable counsel, even for the uninstructed. On this something must first be said, although the passage has also a deeper meaning, which he who can receive it may receive. Let us see then what the literal sense teaches us. In this world both the righteous and the unrighteous share the same troublesome task of acquiring the means of subsistence necessary for life. But the righteous are not so much concerned with the trouble of the means of life as they are keenly anxious for righteousness, so that even if they are compelled to acquire the necessities of life, at least these are acquired without wrong. The very getting of these things, which is a necessity of daily life, is conducted in all righteousness. But the

---

[1] Ps. xxxvii. 16.

unrighteous care nothing for righteousness, but spend all their interest on getting. All their effort is to lay hands on profit, by any means and of any kind. They do not ask whether they get it honestly and justly. They take no pains that at the judgment of Christ their possessions may be found to have been righteously acquired. How could they do so?—people who add field to field,[1] and annex house to house, so as to plunder their neighbour. As then one of two things must happen, great gain with unrighteousness, or small gain with righteousness, The little, it says, that the righteous hath is better than the great riches of the wicked. In truth great riches, as by a sort of peculiar property, are accounted wrong. That I think is why our Lord and Saviour spoke of the Mammon of unrighteousness as indeed a god and lord, when He said, Make to yourselves friends out of the unrighteous mammon.[2]

So far for the literal sense. Let us now see whether the saying has also some inner meaning. Literary pursuits [3] are in this world many and various. You find large numbers commence with literature and learn by heart the verses of the poets, the plays of comedy, the imaginary and terrifying stories of tragedy, the long and varied books of history. Then they go over to rhetoric and acquire all the vapours of public speaking. After

---

[1] Isa. v. 8.
[2] Luc. xvi. 9. But throughout our Lord's teaching on riches it is not the *amount* of a man's possessions but the use he makes of them that matters.
[3] Cp. *infra* xcvi. Yet his attitude on the point is not very consistent. 'Eruditio saecularis' (v. 1 scholaris) has some value. *In Josuam*. vi. 1; Lomm. xi. 57; B. vii. 323. See also the *Address* of Gregory Thaumaturgus, xiii. and Koetschau's introduction to the *C. Celsum*. B. I. xxxvi. Denis, pp. 12-26 and Redepenning I. 324 *sqq.* should be consulted in regard to Origen's relation to philosophy.

this they come to philosophy, study logic, investigate the steps of the syllogism, poke into geometrical mensuration, examine the laws of the heavenly bodies and the courses of the stars, and do not even leave out music. Men of learning, after this multifarious and varied training—wherein they have not come to any knowledge of the will of God—they have indeed gathered great riches but it is the great riches of sinners. Whereas you may find some man of the church, untrained indeed in speech and learning but filled with faith and the fear of God, who by reason of his fear of God does not dare to offend in any matter, but fears even so much as to open his mouth, lest some bad word should chance to issue from it, and restrains himself from even the least offence, a restraint of which he who is rich in the wisdom of this world is not capable. Putting these two side by side, the divine Word says, Better is the little the righteous hath than the great riches of the wicked. Whatever be the great riches of the wicked and the wisdom of this world, whereby they are rich and overflowing in their powers of speech, yet they gain thereby no power to keep themselves from sin. But the little thing belongs to the righteous man, who has faith like a grain of mustard seed, small indeed but living and keen, whereby he fortifies and restrains himself from sin. This little measure then of faith is a better thing for the righteous man than the great riches that the wicked possess in the eloquence and wisdom of this world, which is perishing.

Yet if a man have the power both to have riches and not to have the riches of the wicked, but to collect something from the treasures of the Lawgiver Moses, to make some gain from the property of the Prophets, Isaiah, Jeremiah, Ezekiel, to investigate the hidden meaning of Daniel, and to make his way to the dark and secret treasures of the other prophets—such a man is not on the same level with the wise men of this world, so as to be called better than they. Rather must he be classed with those who said, Ye were enriched in all utterance and in all knowledge.[1] These men destroyed the wisdom of this world and became conquerors over it, and declare themselves ready to take captive every thought that lifts up and erects itself against the knowledge of Christ.[2] Though the man we described above be untrained and without education, yet faithful and godfearing, that little measure of faith is a better thing for this righteous man than the great riches the wicked have acquired together with this world's wisdom. But better than both of these is he who is rich in the word of God and in the knowledge of the truth, who, that is, in Paul's words, Is rich in all utterance and in all knowledge, and who not the less is rich in good works. If you desire to know what it is to be rich in all utterance, I will teach you in a word. Begin your enquiry with the first book of Genesis. Then take the book of Exodus; then the books of Leviticus, Numbers, Deuteronomy. Take the wealth of Joshua, son of Nun; the wealth of all the Judges in one book. And so on through all the sequence of the particular books of the divine Scripture, till you arrive at the riches of the Gospels and of the Apostolic books. For, to take an example, if any one gives attention to the single book of the Psalms, and sings the whole Psalter through at will, he is rich, yet not rich, In all utterance and in all knowledge, but rich only in the book of Psalms. Or if any one spends his time on reading the Gospels, or the Apostolic writings, and trains himself in the commandments of the New Testament, he too is

---

[1] 1 Cor. i. 5.   [2] 2 Cor. x. 5.

rich, yet not rich, in all utterance, only in the Gospels and the Apostolic books. But if he has power to learn by heart with equal diligence the New Testament and the Old, and to be so instructed by all their learning that he is ready to explain particular points in the Scriptures, and to regulate his life according to the word of truth contained in the Scriptures—he indeed is rich in all utterance and in every good work. I believe it is of these riches that it is said, The ransom of a man's life is his riches.[1] Better then the little thing the righteous hath than the great riches of the wicked.

LXXIII

Moses did not decline to receive advice from Jethro. The incident shows that Christians should be willing to learn from others : also that Gentiles can contribute something to the law. (In Exod. Hom. xi. 6 ; Lomm. ix. 138–40 ; B. vi. 259–60. From the Latin.)

Indeed when I observe that Moses, a prophet filled with God, to whom God spoke face to face, received advice from Jethro, a priest of Midian, my mind grows bewildered, so great is my surprise. For the Scripture says, So Moses hearkened to the voice of his father-in-law and did all that he said unto him.[2] He did not say, To me God speaks ; what I am to do is told me by a voice from heaven ; how shall I receive advice from a man, a man who is a Gentile, a stranger to the people of God? No, he listens to his voice, and does all he says, and gives ear not to the speaker but to his words. This shows that we also, if we chance any time to find something wisely said by the Gentiles, should not straightway

---

[1] Prov. xiii. 8.   [2] Ex. xviii. 24.

reject along with the status of the speaker also the things he has said; nor, because we have the law given by God, ought we to swell with pride and to reject the words of wise men, but rather to do as the Apostle says, Proving all things, holding fast that which is good.[1]

Yet among those who have authority among the people to-day, who is there—I do not say if he have already some revelation from God, but even if he have any slight pretension through his knowledge of the law—that will condescend to receive advice from a priest of clearly lower standing, let alone from a layman or a Gentile?[2] But Moses, who was meek above all men, receives advice from an inferior, so as to set an example of humility to the leaders of the peoples and present an emblem of a mystery of the future. He knew that at some future time the Gentiles would bring to Moses good advice, that they would apply good and spiritual interpretation to the law of God. He knew that law would hearken to them and do all as they say. For the law is not able to do as the Jews say, because the law is weak in the flesh, that is, in the letter, and can do nothing according to the letter; for the law brings nothing to perfection.[3] But according to the advice which we bring to the law, all things can be done in a spiritual sense.

---

[1] 1 Thess. v. 21.

[2] Pride and ambition seem to have been common failings among the clergy of Origen's day. Position was eagerly sought and responsibility lightly regarded. He pleads for greater humility and urges that mere position does not save. Funds were sometimes misappropriated and offices in the Church sometimes sold. Yet on the whole, admitting defects, he still contends that the standard among officials is higher in the Church than in the state. Passages to note are *In Matt.* xvi. 8, 22; *In Matt. Com. Series*, 12; *In Ep. ad Rom.* Com ii. 2, 11; *In Jer.* Hom. xi. 3; *C. Cels.* iii. 30; Lomm. iv. 20-27; 64-7; 202-5; vi. 72; 114-15; xv. 224-27; B. iii. 80-81.

[3] Rom. viii. 3; Heb. vii. 19.

Even the sacrifices can be offered in a spiritual sense, which are now impossible according to the flesh. The law of leprosy too can be observed in the spirit, which is impossible according to the letter. Thus then according to our interpretation, according to our view and the advice that we give, the law accomplishes all things; according to the letter not all, but very few.[1]

LXXIV

Abimelech was sometimes at variance with Isaac, sometimes at peace with him. Similar are the relations between Philosophy and Christianity. (*In Gen.* Hom. xiv. 3; Lomm. viii. 254-56; B. vi. 123-25. From the Latin.)

Abimelech also, he who previously had paid respect to Abraham, comes now from Gerar to Isaac with his friends. And Isaac says unto them, Wherefore are ye come unto me, seeing ye hate me and have sent me away from you? To this they reply, We saw plainly that the Lord was with thee, and we said, Let there now be an oath betwixt us and thee, and let us make a covenant with thee, that thou wilt do us no hurt,[2] and so on. This Abimelech, as I observe, is not always at peace with Isaac, but sometimes is at variance and sometimes seeks for peace. If you recollect how we previously remarked about Abimelech that he represents the learned and the wise men of the world, who through the study of philosophy have learned also much of the truth, you can under-

---

[1] To some extent his estimate of the value of the letter varies with his immediate purpose in writing. e.g. '*Nos vero, qui ex utroque genere Israelitae sumus, et literam et spiritum in scripturis sanctis defendimus.*' *In Lev.* Hom. xiv. 2; Lomm. ix. 414; B. vi. 480. See p. xxii. *sqq., supra.*

[2] Gen. xxvi. 27-9.

stand how it is that he can neither be always at variance nor always at peace with Isaac, who represents the word of God which is in the law. For philosophy is neither in all points contradictory to, nor in all points in accordance with, the law of God. For many of the philosophers say in their writings that there is one God who created all things. In this they agree with the law of God. Some even make this addition, that God has made and orders all things by his word, and that it is by the word of God that all things are regulated.[1] In this they write what is in agreement not only with the law but also with the Gospels. Also moral and natural philosophy, as it is termed, holds almost all the views that are ours. But it is at variance with us in asserting that matter is co-eternal with God.[2] It is at variance in denying that God is concerned with the affairs of men, maintaining that the limits of His providence are above the altitude of the orb of the moon.[3] They are at variance with us in making our lives depend, at the time we are born, on the movements of the stars. They are at variance when they assert that this world is eternal and to be terminated by no limit. Also there are many other points in which they are either at variance or in agreement with us. On this account Abimelech, to follow out the comparison, is stated at one time to be at peace with Isaac, at another to be at variance.

[1] Cp. Harnack, *Hist. Dogma*, E.T. i. 328 ; ii. 10. 'The Logos had long been regarded by cultured men as the beginning and principle of creation.' 'The Logos doctrine is Greek philosophy *in nuce.*'
[2] Cp. *De Prin.* II. i. 4-5 ; *C. Cels.* iv. 60. Philo probably believed in the eternity of matter. Drummond, *Philo Judæus* i. 297 *sqq.* So did the Gnostics. Harnack *Hist. Dogma*, i. 256. Cp. Tert. *Adv. Hermog.* 8. The Christian view is more decided in Origen than in Clement. Photius, *Bib. Cod.* 109.
[3] Cp. Clem. Al. *Protrep.* v.

There is a further point which I do not suppose the Holy Spirit, who wrote this, was at pains to include without good reason, namely, that two other men come with Abimelech, that is Ahuzzath, his son-in-law, and Phicol, the chief captain of his army. Ahuzzath means ' Holding ', and Phicol, ' The mouth of all ', while Abimelech himself is ' My father, the king.' These three, as I believe, are a picture of complete philosophy, which among its adherents is divided into three sections, logic, physics, ethics, that is, rational, natural and moral philosophy. Rational philosophy is that which acknowledges God, the Father of all, like Abimelech. Natural philosophy is that which is fixed and holds all things, relying on the forces of nature itself. This Ahuzzath, who is called ' Holding ', represents. Moral philosophy is that which is in the mouth of all men, belongs to all men, and by the general agreement of its principles is in the mouth of all men. For this stands that Phicol, who is by interpretation, The mouth of all. Thus these all, men trained in studies of this kind, come unto the law of God and say, We saw plainly that the Lord was with thee, and we said, Let there now be an oath betwixt us and thee, and let us make a covenant with thee, that thou wilt do us no hurt, but just as we have not cursed thee, so art thou the blessed of the Lord.[1]

It may be that those three men, who seek peace from the Word of God, and desire to secure his friendship by a covenant, represent the Magi, who come from the east, being taught by their ancestral books and by the instruction of their elders, and say, We saw plainly that a king was born ; we saw that God is with him and we are come to adore him.[2] Also, they stand for any man who has

---

[1] Gen. xxvi. 28-9. [2] Matt. ii. 2

been trained in learning of this kind, who sees that God is in Christ, reconciling the world to Himself, who admires the greatness of His works, and who says, We saw plainly that God was with thee, and we said, Let there be an oath betwixt us. For as he approaches the law of God he is impelled to say, I have sworn and am determined to keep thy commandments.[1]

[1] Ps. cxix. 106.

PART VII

SPECULATIONS AND ENQUIRIES

LXXV

Many questions may be asked about the soul. We should understand our own nature ; failure so to do is spiritually dangerous. (In Cant. Cantic., Lib. ii. Lomm. xiv. 404–6. From the Latin.)

It is then the chief function of knowledge to know the Trinity, and in the second place to know what the Trinity has created. Such was the teaching of him who said, For Himself gave me an unerring knowledge of the things that are, the constitution of the world and the operation of the elements, the beginning and end and middle of times,[1] and so on. This will include for the soul a certain understanding of itself, whereby it should know the nature of its constitution, whether corporeal or incorporeal, whether single or composed of two, three or more elements. Also, to meet questions some have raised, whether it be made or altogether unmade by any ; and, if made, by what process it is made ; whether, as some believe, its substance is contained in the semen of the body and its germ is passed on together with the germ of the body ; or whether it comes in a completed state from outside and clothes itself in the body already formed in the organs of the woman. And, if the latter, whether it comes recently created, made for the first time when the body appears to have been already formed, so

---

[1] Wisd. vii. 17–18.

that the cause for the making of the soul may be thought to lie in the need for providing life for a body; or whether, having been made some time previously, it may be held to come to take a body for some other reason; and if it is believed to be brought down to this body for some other reason, it is the work of knowledge to discover what this reason is.[1]

There is also a further question, whether the soul clothes itself in a body only once and after laying it aside seeks for its body no more; or whether, after once laying aside the body it has worn; it again takes on this body a second time; and, if it does so, whether it retains what it has taken on, or after a time once more rejects it. Now if, according to the statement of the Scriptures, the consummation of the world is close at hand, and this state of corruption is to pass into one of incorruption, it does not seem that there can be any question of the soul coming a second or a third time into a body under the conditions of life as it now is. For if that were accepted, it would be a necessary consequence that, as one succession followed another, the world would know no end. Also the soul may seek this further degree of self-knowledge; whether there be a sort of scale, whether some spirits be of the same substance as itself, others not of the same but different from it; that is, whether

---

[1] He has mentioned three possibilities, Traducianism, Creationism, Pre-existence. It is with the last named his own convictions lie. Cp. *De Prin.* 1. vii. 4. The question was one the Church had left open. (*Ibid.* Praefat. 5.) Yet Origen was attacked for his belief in pre-existence. *In Gen.* Hom. xii. 4; Lomm. viii. 237; B. vi. 110. There is a further reference to the question in *Com. in Joann.* vi. 14. Lomm. l. 198-99; Br. i. 128-29; B. iv. 122-24. Cp. Denis 217 *sqq.* who quotes both that passage and the one translated here, adding '*Il est évident que l'imagination seule peut répondre à de pareilles, questions, et qu'en s'occupant sans cesse de l'âme, Origène n'a pas soupconné ce que la science de l'ame pouvait être*' (p. 236). Cp. § xxvi.

other spirits too exist which have reason, as the soul has, and others which are devoid of reason; whether its constitution be the same as that of the angels, since it is held that there is no difference between one reasonable being and another. Or, if it be not the same by constitution, still it will be the same, if it deserves, by grace; or whether it be altogether incapable of becoming like unto the angels, unless some property or likeness in its own nature has made this possible. For it will seem possible for what has been lost to be restored, but not for something which the Creator did not originally bestow to be imparted.

This too for fuller self-knowledge the soul may ask; Whether the excellence of a soul can come and go. Is such excellence unchanging? Once acquired does it never ebb away? What need is there for me to prolong my account of the reasons for the soul's self-knowledge? The danger is that, if the soul be careless about full knowledge of itself, it may be bidden to go forth by the footsteps of the flock and to feed the kids, not beside its own tent but beside the tent of the shepherds.[1] It is an easy matter for any one who will to follow out this train, and to derive from what we have said above abundant opportunity for practising himself in the word of wisdom according to his ability. Our remarks must be regarded as addressed by the Word of God to the soul which is in a state of progress, but has not yet climbed to the height of perfection. By virtue of its progress it is described as beautiful, but to secure its arrival at perfection there is need that warning be addressed to it. For unless it acquire self-knowledge in the way we have detailed above, and carefully practise itself in the word of God

---

[1] Cant. Cantic. i. 8.

and the divine law, its fate will be to gather on these points the views of various teachers, and to follow after men whose words have no excellence, no prompting of the Holy Spirit. That is the meaning of going forth by the footsteps of the flock and following the teaching of those who have ever remained sinners themselves and never had power to afford to those who sin any cure. He who follows them will just seem to be feeding kids, who are a type of sinners, going from one shepherd's tent to another, that is, to the various schools of philosophy. Give full regard then to the terrible fate foreshadowed in this figurative phrase, Go thy way forth, so it runs, by the footsteps of the flock. It is as if he speaks to the soul already within, already in its place among the mysteries. Yet because it is careless about self-knowledge, about enquiring what it is, what it should do and how, and what leave undone, to this soul it is said, Go thy way forth, like one sent forth by the master for this fault of sloth. So great a danger is it for the soul to neglect the knowledge and understanding of itself.

LXXVI

On the causes of disasters in nature and in human society. (*In Matt. Comm. Series*, 36; Lomm. iv. 261-63. From the Latin.)

For nation shall rise against nation and kingdom against kingdom: and there shall be famines and pestilences and earthquakes in divers places. All these things are the beginning of travail.[1] Mark says the same, but adds, And troubles.[2] Luke gives the passage in the

---

[1] Matt. xxiv. 7-8.
[2] Mark xiii. 8. The balance of MS. authority is against the added words.

same form, but adds, And fearful sights shall there be from heaven and great signs and storms.[1] Let us give the passage first its simple and outward significance. Just as the bodies of persons, who are suffering from no violence externally inflicted, fall sick before their death; and even as in all men a way is made through weakness for the separation of the soul from the body; even so this vast and wonderful creation of the world, when once, as having a beginning and an end, it has begun to decay—since, The things which are seen are temporal,[2] and because, Heaven and earth shall pass away[3]—must of necessity before it decays grow feeble. Hence the earth will more often be shaken by earthquakes, and the atmosphere generating a contagious malignity will become pestilential. In addition, the vital force of the earth would decline rapidly and check the growth of crops; it would be so with all kinds of trees through the failure of the very force that made them grow. When this occurs the result follows that motive energy, being by nature an integral factor in the whole universe, becomes involved in all the change which all nature undergoes. Failing no doubt to receive its customary supply of nourishment, it falls into decline and is brought to naught. For, The heavens shall perish; they shall wax old like a garment.[4] That which is becoming old and waxeth aged is nigh unto vanishing away.[5]

The result is that owing to shortage of food men are roused to predatory wars upon those who are not affected by shortage in the same degree. Through contrast with

---

[1] Luke xxi. 11. Here too MSS. differ.
[2] 2 Cor. iv. 18.
[3] Luke xxi. 33.
[4] Ps. cii. 26.
[5] Heb. viii. 13.

others who are well supplied with the necessities of life risings occur of class against class; nation fights against nation, kingdom against kingdom. It is quite possible that along with the lack of other supplies there will also be a deficiency of right-minded men. Hence in many cases a life of quiet and peace will be undiscoverable, but uprisings will occur and contentions and disturbances, sometimes through greed, sometimes through the passion for supremacy, sometimes through the mad desire of vain glory, and at times by reason of the desire for vain glory in sovereigns who are not satisfied with their own kingdoms, but desire to extend their empire and to subjugate many nations to their rule.

LXXVII

Our blessings come from God, our curses from ourselves. On the nature of the eternal and invisible fire. (*In Matt. Comm. Series*, 72. Lomm. iv. 383-84. From the Latin.)

One should note however that it is said of the saints not alone that they are 'blessed', but blessed with the added name of One who holds no ordinary rank, of none other indeed than God the Father Himself.[1] On the other hand those who are called cursed are not called 'cursed of my Father.'[2] For of blessing the Father is the giver; of cursing every man is unto himself the cause, by doing deeds that deserve a curse. Those who fall away from Jesus fall into eternal fire, which is fire of a different kind from that we ordinarily use. With men no fire is eternal;

---

[1] Matt. xxv. 34.   [2] *Ibid.*, 41.

it does not last long and is quickly quenched. The eternal fire is that of which Isaiah says at the end of his prophecy, Their worm dieth not and their fire is not quenched.[1] Possibly it is of such a nature that, itself invisible, it consumes invisible things, for, The things which are seen are temporal, the things which are not seen are eternal.[2] So, if the things which are seen are temporal, while the things which are not seen are eternal, inevitably, if that fire can be seen, it must be temporal also. Whereas, if the fire in which those who fall away from the Saviour are punished is eternal, it is invisible also. It is something of this kind that Job says, The fire that is not kindled shall consume him.[3]

And be not surprised at hearing that there is an invisible fire and one that punishes, seeing that among men there is a burning heat that attacks the body, causing no little pain, especially to those who are most violently attacked by it. Note too that he speaks of the kingdom as prepared from the foundation of the world for none others except the righteous,[4] and therefore Christ, their king, shall award it to them. Whereas he makes it clear that the eternal fire is not prepared,—as the kingdom is prepared for the righteous,—for those to whom it is said, Depart from me ye cursed, but for the devil and his angels.[5] God for His part did not create men for ruin but for life and joy. But when men sin they associate themselves with the devil. As those who are saved are made equal with the holy angels and become sons of the resurrection and sons of God and angels; so those who perish are made equal with the devil's angels and become his sons.

---

[1] Isa. lxvi. 24.
[2] 2 Cor. iv. 18.
[3] Job xx. 26, LXX.
[4] Matt. xxv. 34.
[5] *Ibid.*, 41.

LXXVIII

Pharaoh's host 'sank as lead in the mighty waters'. So there is a leaden element in all human nature. The purifying office of fire is to consume this and leave the gold pure. (*In Exod.* Hom. vi. 4; Lomm. ix. 62-4; B. vi. 195-96. From the Latin.)

They went down into the depths like a stone.[1] Why did they go down into the depths like a stone? Because they were not stones of the kind from which sons can be raised up to Abraham,[2] but such stones as love the deep, and delight in the watery element, who enjoy, that is, the bitter and fluctuating pleasure of this present world. Wherefore it is also said of them, They sank as lead in the mighty waters.[3] Sinners are heavy. For instance wickedness is described as sitting upon a talent of lead; as Zachariah the prophet says, I saw, the words are, a woman sitting upon a talent of lead and I said, who is this? And he answered, This is Wickedness.[4] Thus it comes that the wicked were drowned in the depths, like lead in the mighty waters. The saints however are not drowned but walk upon the waters, because they are light and not borne down by the weight of sin. For instance, our Lord and Saviour walked upon the waters. He it is who verily knows not sin. Peter, too, His disciple walked, though he felt some fear, for he was not of the build or quality to be altogether free from any admixture of the leaden element in his nature. Some he had, though little. For this reason the Lord

---

[1] Ex. xv. 5. [2] Matt. iii. 9.
[3] Ex. xv. 10. [4] Zach. v. 7-8. The quotation is not exact.

says to him, O thou of little faith, wherefore didst thou doubt?[1]

Consequently whoever is saved is saved by fire, so that the fire may melt and dissolve any admixture the man has of the leaden element, so that all may become good gold, for it is said that the gold of that land which the saints shall possess is good. As the furnace tests the gold, so trial tests righteous men. All then must come to the fire, all must come to the furnace. For the Lord sits and refines and purifies the sons of Judah.[2] And when we come there, if a man bring many good works and some small mixture of wickedness, this small item is dissolved and purged away like lead by the fire, and all that is left is pure gold. The more a man brings there of lead, the more he suffers burning, that the lead may be fully melted, so that even if there be little gold it may still be left in purity. But if a man comes there all of lead, in his case there occurs what is written, He is drowned in the depths, like lead in the mighty waters. But it is a long matter to attempt detailed exposition. These few remarks are sufficient.[3]

---

[1] Matt. xiv. 31. For Peter, see § liv.
[2] Mal. iii. 3.
[3] On the doctrine of fire as we find it in the Alexandrine fathers, where it is partly Christian and partly Stoic, the reader may compare the note in Hort and Mayor's edition of Clement of Alexandria, *Strom.* vii. pp. 250-51. Fire is usually regarded as remedial and purifying, rarely, if ever, as merely retributory and punitive. It is a spiritual agency, $\pi\hat{v}\rho$ $\nu o\eta\tau \acute{o}\nu$, consuming what is better consumed, testing human deeds and characters. By our sins we kindle such fire for ourselves, yet it illuminates as well as burns, and is throughout one of God's many agencies for good. Other passages worth notice, in addition to those here translated, are Clem. Al. *Eclog, Proph.* 25; Origen, *De Prin.* II. x. 4; *C. Cels.* iv. 13; v. 14-16; *In Ex.* Hom. xiii. 4; *Sel. in Pss.* Hom. iii. 1; *In Ezech.* Hom. i. 13; *In Jer.* Hom. xx. 8-9; Lomm. ix. 157-58; xii. 181-82; xiv. 27-8; xv. 381-85; B. iii. 190-93; vi. 275-76; viii. 337-38.

LXXIX

The stars are not the causes of events, though they may be the signs of them. No configuration of the heavenly bodies can be the cause of events anterior to it.—(*Comm. in Gen.* iii. 9. *Philocal.* xxiii; 14–15; Lomm. viii. 27–31; xxv. 217–20; *Philocal.* Ed. Robinson, 202–4. From the Greek.)

Come then let us maintain our point that the stars are in no sense the causes of human affairs but only the signs of them.[1] Now it is evident that if a particular configuration of the stars should be regarded as the cause of certain events which occurred to some man in question—we will take it that this is the point we are now seeking to deal with—the configuration which holds with regard to a particular man, say, for to-day could not be thought to have caused previous events in the life of another man or even of several others. For every cause is anterior to its effect. As for the calculations of the professed astrologers, they usually declare events in human life which are anterior to the configuration. It is their professional method to ascertain in a particular way [2] the birth-time of some person, and then to discover in what relation each planet stood to the perpendicular, what was the situation of some

---

[1] Astrology in Origen's day was an important influence. The Emperor Septimius Severus had been a noted believer in it. Many Christians accepted its teaching; Bardaisan of Edessa, for example, was a Christian astrologer. Cp. Origen's own words, '*Si quis vestrum mathematicorum deliramenta sectatur, in terra Chaldæorum est*'. *In Jer.* Hom. xx. 4; also in *Gen.* iii. 1; Lomm. viii. 7–8; xv. 400. He was himself opposed to it, though he defends the visit of the Magi against Celsus' criticisms. *C. Cels.* i. 58–60.

[2] Reading τρόπον, which gives better sense, though the variant τόπον has good MS. evidence.

portion of the zodiac or of the lesser stars within it, which star in the zodiac was in proximity to the eastern horizon, which star to the western, which star was on the meridian, which on the antimeridian. And when they have arranged the stars, the positions of which they believe they have discovered, as standing in a particular configuration at the season of the man's birth, the moment that is when the person they are considering was born, they not only investigate coming events, but even past occurrences, things which took place before the birth or the begetting of the man in question. The man's father, where did he come from? Was he rich or poor? Sound in body or maimed? Good or bad in character? Without means or wealthy? A man who lived in this way or in that? They make the same enquiry also about his mother, and about his elder brothers, if there are any.

For the present let us allow that they do ascertain the truth of the matter—latter on we shall show that even this is not the case—and let us accordingly ask those who suppose that the affairs of men are under the compulsion of the stars, In what way can to-day's particular configuration have been the cause of previous events? For if this is impossible, then to whatever extent their claim in regard to earlier events [1] proves upon enquiry true, still it is clear that a particular movement of the stars in the heavens has not been the cause of earlier events which occurred before the stars were in that position. That being so, he who maintains that the stars do tell truth, laying stress upon their utterances with regard to the future, will say that they are true not in the sense of being causes but only as signs. But

---

[1] I.e. allowing that the stars do reveal (not cause) past occurrences.

if some one asserts that the stars are not the causes of past events, but that other configurations have been the causes of their occurrence,[1] and that the present configuration has only the nature of a sign, but that future events are revealed by the configuration which exists at the time of a man's birth—let him explain to us the distinction between being able to prove that one thing must be held true because the stars cause it and another thing because they only declare it. Being unable to make the distinction good they will come round to agreement with us that nothing in the life of man is caused by the stars, though, as we said, possibly something is revealed by them. For even if one did not learn the past and the future from the stars, that might be done from the mind of God through some word of prophecy.

We have already demonstrated that God's knowledge of what each man will do is no infringement of the principle of our freedom.[2] Neither, likewise, do the signs which God has ordained to be tokens hinder our free action. Like a book which contains future events in the form of prophecy, the whole heaven, as a book of God, may contain the future. So, in the prayer for Joseph, we may in this sense understand the words of Jacob, I read in the tablets of the heavens what shall happen to you and to your sons.[3] Perhaps too the text, The heavens shall be folded up like a book,[4] is a declaration that the words contained in it, significant of future events, shall be accomplished and, so to say, fulfilled, just as prophecies are said to be fulfilled by

---

[1] Reading γενέσεως, with Robinson. Lomm. has γνώσεως.
[2] See § vi.
[3] Cp. *Test.* xii. *Patr.* Levi. v. 4 ; Asher vii. 5, where the reading is uncertain.
[4] Isa. xxxiv. 4.

taking place. In this sense the stars will have been made for signs, as the words say, Let them be for signs.[1] And Jeremiah, bidding us look to ourselves and ridding us of the fear of those things which are held to be declared, and perhaps are even supposed to be caused from this source, says, Fear ye not the signs of the heavens.[2]

LXXX

On Lunacy. Not natural causes but evil spirits produce it. Our state is determined by our previous acts of will and not by the heavenly bodies. (Comm. in Matt. xiii. 6. Lomm. iii. 220–22. From the Greek.)

And now let us look at the language carefully and enquire first how it comes that a person overshadowed and cast down by an unclean spirit, deaf and dumb, is said to be 'lunatic', and why lunacy derives its name from the great light in heaven, second after the sun, which God made to rule the night.[3] As for the doctors, we must let them explain the facts by natural causes; they do not think that in this passage[4] any unclean spirit existed, only a certain condition of the body. So let them say in their naturalistic account that the humid elements in the head are stirred through some affinity with the light of the moon, which has a humid character. We however, who believe the Gospel that this disease is evidently the result of the action in those who suffer from it of an unclean spirit, deaf and dumb; we who recognize that, like the enchanters of the Egyptians, those who are in the habit of undertaking the cure of such cases seem sometimes to succeed therein; we shall say that perhaps the unclean spirit, in order to discredit

---

[1] Gen. i 14.   [2] Jer. x. 2.
[3] Gen. i. 16.   [4] Matt. xvii. 14 *sqq*.

the creation of God—That their iniquity may be spoken unto the height and they may set their mouth against the heavens [1]—observes certain phases of the moon and so operates that, from its being noticed that men are affected at a certain phase of the moon, the responsibility for this great evil may not seem to fall on the deaf and dumb demons but on the great light in heaven, which is set to rule the night and has no sort of rule over this kind of disease among men.

And those who say that the cause of all things on earth, whether things in general or particular events, lies with the configuration of the stars, do speak their iniquity unto the height. Such people indeed set their mouth against the heavens, asserting that some of the stars cause evil and others good, whereas no star was made by the God of the universe to cause evil. So Jeremiah held, for it is written in Lamentations, Out of the mouth of the Lord shall come forth what is excellent and good.[2] And it is probable that, just as this evil spirit, which causes what we term lunacy, observes the phases of the moon, so as to operate in any one who is given over to him for certain reasons and has not made himself deserving of an angel guard;[3] so do other spirits and demons with regard to certain collocations of the other stars, so that not the moon alone but the other stars as well may receive abuse from those who utter their inquity unto the heights. At any rate we may hear the casters of nativities assign the cause of every sort of madness and insanity to the phases of the moon. It is well known that those who suffer from lunacy, as we call

---

[1] Pss. lxxiii. 8-9 ; LXX.
[2] Lam. iii. 38. R.V. ' Out of the mouth of the Most High cometh there not evil and good ? ' LXX has τὰ κακὰ καὶ τὸ ἀγαθόν. There is no MS. authority for Origen's τὰ καλὰ καὶ ἀγαθόν.
[3] A common idea in Origen : Cp. § lviii.

it, sometimes fall into water and into fire also, which is less frequent but still does happen; also that the cure of this disease is very difficult. Hence those who have a popular repute for curing cases of possession sometimes decline to attempt this phase of it and sometimes succeed after fastings and prayers and considerable trouble.

Also you may ask whether such cases occur among spirits as well as among men, so that some of them speak and some are dumb, some hear and some are deaf. Just as the cause of their being unclean lies in themselves, so will it be found that their freedom of choice has occasioned their condemnation to be dumb or deaf. Even among men some will suffer this condemnation, if we are to regard as uttered by the Holy Spirit the prayer of the prophet in which it is said of certain sinners, Let the lying lips be dumb.[1] So perhaps people who have made bad use of their powers of hearing and have listened to foolish talk, will be made deaf by Him who said, Who made the deaf and the dull of hearing?[2] that they may no longer listen to foolish talk.[3]

LXXXI

The Law prescribes purification for a woman after childbirth. There is a connection between sin and birth. Hence good men do not celebrate their birthdays and the Church baptizes infants for the remission of original sin. (In Levit. Hom. viii. 3; Lomm. ix. 316–18; B. vi. 396–98. From the Latin.)

And now let us ascertain another point. What is the reason that a woman, by the discharge of whose natural functions men in this world are born, is said to be unclean

---

[1] Ps. xxxi. 18.　　[2] Exod. iv. 11.
[3] That is, through misuse of our faculties we come under the power of evil spirits. The explanation is supplementary, not alternative to what has been previously said.

not only when she conceives seed but also when she has borne a child? On this account she is commanded to offer for her purification young pigeons, or turtle doves for sin, at the door of the tabernacle of witness, that the priest may make atonement for her, as though she have need of atonement and purification from sin because she has assisted in the birth of a man into the world. For this is what is written; The priest shall make atonement for her and she shall be clean.[1]

On such subjects I am not bold enough to make assertions, yet I feel sure that some secret meaning is contained in the words, and that there is some hidden mystery on account of which both the woman who conceives seed and the woman who has borne a child is called unclean and ordered, like a guilty person, to offer a sacrifice for her sin and so to be made clean. Besides, even in regard to the child who is born, boy or girl, Scripture says that, He is not clean from sin, though his life be one day long.[2] And to show you that there is some great significance in this, something which none of the saints has ever regarded with satisfaction, not one of all the saints can be found to have held festivities or any great entertainment on the day of his birth; not one can be found to have had rejoicing on the birthday of his son or daughter. It is only sinners who have joy over this kind of birth. For we find that in the Old Testament Pharaoh[3] king of Egypt kept his birthday with festivity, and Herod[4] the same in the New. Yet each of them stained the festal character of his very birthday by shedding human blood. The one put to death the chief of the bakers, the other the holy prophet John in prison.

But the saints not only do not hold festivity on their

---

[1] Lev. xii. 8.
[2] Job xiv. 4; LXX.
[3] Gen. xl. 20.
[4] Mark vi. 21.

birthdays, but even in the fulness of the Holy Spirit curse the day of birth. A prophet of eminence and mark—Jeremiah, I mean, who was sanctified in the womb of his mother and consecrated a prophet among the nations—would not have buried some mere piece of foolishness in books destined to remain for ever, unless there had been a secret meaning in it, a content of mighty mysteries. The passage is where he says, Cursed be the day wherein I was born and the night in which they said, A man child is conceived. Cursed be the man who brought tidings to my father saying, A man child is born unto thee. Let that man's joy be as the joy of the cities which the Lord overthrew in His wrath and repented not.[1] Think you the prophet could have called down these grievous and mighty curses, unless he had known that there was something in the nature of bodily birth which plainly deserved imprecations of this kind; something on account of which the Lawgiver brought so many charges of uncleanness, for which he was bound in consistency to impose the appropriate purifications? It would be a long task, for which we need another opportunity, to explain the passage we have taken from the prophet, for our present purpose is to discuss a lesson not from Jeremiah but from Leviticus. Yet Job too, speaking not without the Holy Spirit, cursed the day of his birth. He says, Cursed be the day wherein I was born and the night in which they said, There is a man child conceived. Let that night be darkness, and let not the Lord again regard it, nor let it come into the days of the year nor be numbered among the days of the month.[2] If you do not consider that Job said this through the prophetic and divine Spirit, then regard the matter in

---

[1] Jer. xx. 14-16.   [2] Job iii. 2-6.

the light of what follows, for he adds, Let him curse it who hath cursed that day on which he shall slay the great leviathan.[1] You see how in the Holy Spirit he prophesied of that great leviathan, which the Lord was to slay, whereof Jonah's whale was the type. Hence the Lord too, who was to slay that leviathan, the devil, says, As Jonah was three days and three nights in the belly of the whale, so must the Son of Man be three days and three nights in the heart of the earth.[2] And if you like to hear what other saints also have felt in regard to physical birth, listen to David when he says, I was conceived, so it runs, in iniquity and in sin my mother hath borne me,[3] proving that every soul which is born in the flesh is tainted with the stain of iniquity and sin. This is the reason for that saying which we have already quoted above, No man is clean from sin, not even if his life be one day long.[4] To these, as a further point, may be added an enquiry into the reason for which, while the church's baptism is given for the remission of sin, it is the custom of the church that baptism be administered even to infants.[5] Certainly, if there were nothing in infants that required remission and called for lenient treatment, the grace of baptism would seem unnecessary.[6]

---

[1] Job iii. 8. Probably the original reference is to magicians, who were supposed to have the power of causing an eclipse by bringing a cloud—this is leviathan, as Hamlet's cloud was 'very like a whale'—across the sun.

[2] Matt. xii. 40.

[3] Ps. li. 5.

[4] Job xiv. 4.

[5] Cp. *In Luc.* Hom. xiv ; Lomm. v. 135–37 ; Warren, *Liturgy of the Ante-Nicene Church*, 62 *sqq*. Origen's views on infant baptism are discussed in Prof. N. P. Williams' Bampton Lectures, *The Ideas of the Fall and of Original Sin*, pp. 208–31.

[6] This passage is more ascetic and pessimistic than is usual with Origen. Clement also (*Strom.* iii. 16) quotes the passages from Jeremiah and from Job, but has more to say on the other side of the question. See Harnack, *Texte und Untersuchungen*, xlii. 3, p. 60 *sqq*.

LXXXII

Was Elijah reincarnate as John the Baptist? The arguments for and against. (Comm. in Joann. vi. 10–13; Lomm. i. 191–96; Br. i. 122–27; B. iv. 119–22. From the Greek.)

And they asked him, What then? Art thou Elijah? And he saith, I am not.[1] Who of those that hear Jesus say about John, If ye are willing to receive it, this is Elijah which is to come,[2] would not ask how it is that to those who ask him, Art thou Elijah? John says, I am not? And how too are we to understand that John was the very Elijah who was to come according to the statement of Malachi, which runs, And behold, I send unto you Elijah the Tishbite before the great and notable day of the Lord comes, who shall restore the heart of the father unto his son and the heart of a man unto his neighbour, lest I come and smite the earth utterly?[3] Also the saying to Zacharias of the angel of the Lord, which appeared unto Zacharias standing on the right of the altar of incense, has a significance somewhat similar to the words of Malachi. It runs, And thy wife Elizabeth shall bear thee a son and thou shalt call his name John.[4] Then, a little later on, He shall go before His face in the spirit and power of Elijah, to turn the hearts of the fathers to the children and the disobedient to walk in the wisdom of the just; to make ready for the Lord a people prepared for Him.[5]

Now to the first question one man will reply that John was Elijah but did not know it. Probably that is the line they will take who adhere on the grounds afforded by this

---

[1] John i. 21.
[2] Matt. xi. 14.
[3] Mal. iv. 5–6.
[4] Luke i. 13.
[5] Luke i. 17.

passage to the theory of metensomatosis, holding that the soul puts on body after body without any memory of its former lives. The same people will also say that it was owing to their agreement with this theory that certain of the Jews said of the Saviour that He was one of the ancient prophets,[1] arisen not from the tombs but from birth. For how could they suppose, seeing that Mary was clearly His mother and Joseph the carpenter was supposed to be His father, that He was one of the prophets risen from the dead ? And these same people, making use of the text in Genesis, I will wipe out all resurrection,[2] will draw into controversy any one who has spent thought upon the solution of the deceitful sophistries which are derived from the Scriptures, if he opposes their opinion.

But some one else who is a churchman and who rejects as false the theory of metensomatosis, not admitting that the soul of John was ever Elijah, will appeal to the saying of the angel already quoted, for it was not the soul of Elijah that the angel mentioned in connection with the birth of John, but the spirit and power. The words are, And he shall go before His face in the spirit and power of Elijah, to turn the hearts of the fathers to the children.[3] He will be able to prove by a thousand passages that the spirit is different from the soul,[4] and that what is termed power is different from the spirit and from the soul. On these matters it is not now opportune to make many

---

[1] Luke ix. 19.
[2] Gen. vii. 4. Origen's words, $\pi\hat{\alpha}\sigma\alpha\nu\ \tau\dot{\eta}\nu\ \dot{\epsilon}\xi\alpha\nu\dot{\alpha}\sigma\tau\alpha\sigma\iota\nu$, are suggested by LXX, $\pi\hat{\alpha}\nu\ \tau\dot{o}\ \dot{\alpha}\nu\dot{\alpha}\sigma\tau\eta\mu\alpha$. R.V. has 'every living thing.'
[3] Luke i. 17.
[4] Cp. 1 Thess. v. 23. For Origen the soul was 'quasi medium quiddam inter carnem infirmam et spiritum promptum'. *De Prin.* II. viii. 4. Cp. Inge, *Plotinus* ii. 90–91, and § lxxv. *supra*.

remarks, lest we should have a complete diversion of our argument. For the present, with regard to the distinction of power from spirit, it will suffice to quote, The Holy Spirit shall come upon thee, and the power of the Most High shall overshadow thee.[1] To show that the spirits in the prophets are spoken of as if they were their possessions, as bestowed upon them by God, there is the text, The spirits of the prophets are subject to the prophets;[2] and again, The spirit of Elijah doth rest on Elisha.[3] For in this way there will be nothing strange, according to our speaker, in John, who in the spirit and power of Elijah turns the hearts of the fathers to the children, being termed by virtue of this spirit Elijah which was to come. For confirmation of this he will also employ the argument: If the God of the whole world, through His association with the saints, becomes their God, being named in this way, God of Abraham, and, God of Isaac, and, God of Jacob, how much more possible will it be for the Holy Spirit through His association with the prophets to be called their spirit, so that the Spirit may in this way be named the spirit of Elijah, or the spirit of Isaiah. And this same churchman will say that those who supposed that Jesus was one of the prophets risen from the dead may have been in error, both in regard to the theory we have mentioned,[4] and in supposing Him to be one of the prophets; and that possibly, in addition to their thinking Him to be one of the prophets, they were also mistaken and led astray by their ignorance of His so-called father and actual mother, and supposed He had arisen from the tombs. To the passage in Genesis about resurrection the churchman will make answer by quoting, The Lord raised up for me another seed instead of Abel,

---

[1] Luke i. 35. [2] 1 Cor. xiv. 32. [3] 2 Kings ii. 15.
[4] I.e. that of metensomatosis or reincarnation.

whom Cain slew,[1] the term, Raising up, being used also of birth. The churchman will have a different answer to the original question from the believer in metensomatosis ; he will say, on the grounds which we have just given, that in a sense John was Elijah which was to come, but that he replied, I am not,[2] to the priests and Levites because he divined the intention of their question. For the mission of enquiry from the priests and Levites to John, mentioned above,[3] did not aim at learning whether the same spirit was in both, but whether John was the very Elijah who was taken up, now appearing, according to the Jews' expectation, without natural birth, for possibly those who were sent from Jerusalem were in ignorance about his birth. To this enquiry he naturally replies, I am not, for the Elijah who was taken up had not changed his body and come under the name of John.

But the first speaker, whose view we have presented as holding that metensomatosis is proved by the passage, still pursuing his investigation into the text, will say to the second that it is improbable that the son of a priest so well known as Zacharias, born contrary to all human expectation in the old age of both his parents, should have been unknown to leading Jews in Jerusalem and to the Levites and the priests who were sent by them, in ignorance, as it is said, of the circumstances of his birth. This has special force in view of Luke's testimony ; And fear came on all that dwelt round about them—that is, round about Zacharias and Elizabeth—and all these sayings were noised abroad throughout all the hill country of Judaea.[4] But if the birth of John from Zacharias was not unknown, and yet the Jews in Jerusalem sent to ask through the Levites and priests, Art thou

---

[1] Gen. iv. 25.
[2] John i. 21.
[3] Keeping Brooke's text.
[4] Luke i. 65.

Elijah? it is clear that they said this in the conviction that the theory of metensomatosis was true, as being a doctrine derived from their fathers and not in conflict with their secret teaching. Therefore John says, I am not Elijah, because he is unaware of his own former life.

But though these arguments have a force that must not be underrated, the churchman will press on the first speaker the further question, Whether it accords with the character of the prophet who was enlightened by the Spirit, and prophesied by Isaiah, and whose birth was foretold by a mighty angel before it occurred, who had received of Christ's fulness,[1] who partook of special grace, who understood that the truth came through Jesus Christ, who made such remarkable statements regarding God and the only begotten Son who was in the bosom of the Father, that he, I say, should be deceived and, though ignorant of what he was, should not even keep silence.[2] It was his duty in regard to matters obscure to confess that he could say nothing and to give neither assent nor denial to the question proposed. And how natural it would have been, if many did hold this theory, for John to hesitate about himself, wondering whether his soul was once in Elijah.

Also the churchman will challenge the first speaker in regard to the facts, and bid him enquire of those who profess to know the secret teaching current among the Hebrews, whether any such view is held among them. For if there is no evidence that this is the case, clearly the first speaker's argument goes to the winds. However, all the same, the churchman will make use of the explanation that has already been given, claiming further to give his own interpretation of the purpose of the

---

[1] John i. 16. [2] Again following Brooke's text.

enquiries. For if, as he maintained, those who sent the mission were aware of John's birth from Zacharias and Elizabeth, while those who were sent knew it even better still, being men of the priestly tribe who must have heard of the unexpected happiness of their well known fellow tribesman Zacharias, then what is in their minds when they ask, Art thou Elijah? Now it is the question of men who have read of Elijah being taken up to heaven and who are expecting his advent. Probably then, as at the end of the world they expect Elijah before Christ and Christ after him, we may suppose that they ask the question in a figurative sense, 'Art thou he who proclaims the message that was to be given before Christ at the end of the world? And to this he answers with full understanding, I am not.[1]

LXXXIII

It was really Samuel who was brought up from Hades by the witch of Endor at Saul's request. (In Lib. 1 Sam. Hom. 4–6; Lomm. xi. 321-24; B. iii. 286-88. From the Greek.)

The woman saw Samuel.[2] The words and the assertion are part of the narrative. And the woman cried with a loud voice and said to Saul, Why hast thou deceived me, for thou art Saul? And the king said unto her, What is it? Be not afraid. What has thou seen? And the woman

---

[1] The subject of this section is again discussed in the *Comm. in Matt.* xiii. 1-2; Lomm. iii. 205-16. There, as here, but more decisively, Origen rejects $\mu\epsilon\tau\epsilon\nu\sigma\omega\mu\acute{a}\tau\omega\sigma\iota\varsigma$, laying stress upon the arguments that it has no support in Scripture, and that, if occurring at all, the process would be an unending one. There is no considerable change in Origen's view on the subject though about twenty years separate *In Joann.* from *In Matt.*

[2] The passage under discussion is 1 Sam. xxviii. 12-19.

said unto Saul, I saw gods ascending out of the earth. And he said unto her, What was their appearance? And she said unto him, An old man cometh up and is clad in a folding ephod. She says she saw it, and also the priestly garment. I am aware that our opponent may say, ' No wonder. For Satan himself is transformed into an angel of light. It is no great matter then if his ministers too are transformed into ministers of righteousness.[1] But what was it the woman saw? It was Samuel. And why did it not say, The woman saw a demon, which pretended to be Samuel? No; it is written that Saul perceived that it was Samuel. If it had not been Samuel, the Scripture should have said, And Saul supposed that he was Samuel. As it is, we have the words, Saul perceived. No one perceives what is not. Saul then perceived that it was Samuel, and he bowed with his face to the ground and did obeisance. Then once more Scripture is represented as saying, And Samuel said to Saul, Why hast thou disquieted me to bring me up? Samuel said—Scripture speaks; we must believe it—Samuel said, Why hast thou disquieted me to bring me up?

Then to this Saul replies, The Philistines make violent war against me, and God is departed from me and answereth me no more. By the power of the prophets and in dreams I have called thee that thou mayest make known unto me what I shall do. And again the Scripture tells us that no one else is speaking, but Samuel himself says, And wherefore didst thou ask of me? And, The Lord is departed from thee.—Is this statement true or false?—The Lord is departed from thee and is become thine adversary. He hath chosen Him another, as He spake by my hand. And He shall rend the kingdom out of thine

---

[1] That is, those who did not believe that Samuel really appeared would explain the event as a dæmonic apparition.

hand. Does a demon prophesy concerning the kingdom of Israel? What does the argument of our opponent mean? See what controversy arises in the word of God. It demands hearers who have capacity to understand even sacred and mighty words, words of mystery that concern our departure hence, the earlier still unexplained and even the later not plain. The word is still under enquiry.

Now I maintain that both the narrative and enquiry into the narrative are essential, that we may see what awaits us after our departure hence. He hath spoken by my hand, and the Lord shall rend the kingdom from thy hand and shall give it to thy neighbour, even to David. But a demon cannot know about David's kingdom, to which he was appointed by the Lord. Because thou obeyedst not the voice of the Lord; thou didst not execute his fierce wrath upon Amalek. Are not these the words of God? Are they not true? For of a truth Saul did not execute the will of God, but he preserved the king of Amalek alive,[1] for which both before his falling asleep and after his departure hence Samuel reproached Saul. Therefore hath the Lord done this thing unto thee this day. And the Lord will also deliver Israel into the hands of the Philistines. Has a demon power to prophesy concerning the whole people of God, that the Lord will deliver up Israel? And the Lord shall deliver the host of Israel into the hands of the Philistines. Make haste, Saul. To-morrow both thou and thy sons shall be with me. Can a demon know this, concerning a king appointed by the prophet's anointing, that to-morrow Saul would pass out from life and his sons with him? To-morrow thou and thy sons shall be with me.

All this makes it evident that the statements are not

[1] 1 Sam. xv.

false, and that he who came up was Samuel. What then has the witch to do here? What concern has a witch with bringing up the soul of a righteous man? Our opponent who raised the first objection has been routed. His assertion was—that we may spare him fighting his case on the many other points for enquiry in the passage—It is not Samuel; it is the demon who tells lies, since Scripture cannot lie. But the words are the words of Scripture. It is not the demon speaking, but Scripture speaking, in the words, And the woman saw Samuel. Saul spoke. . .[1] These things were said by Samuel. What explanation then can be found of the witch's part in the passage? I put an enquiry to the speaker who previously said, What Samuel in Hades? and so on—Let him give answer to my question, Which is the greater, Samuel or Jesus Christ[2]?

LXXXIV

'*Whither I go ye cannot come.*' *At his death did Jesus go to Hades or to Paradise? Solutions of this difficulty.* (*Comm. in Joann.* xxxii. 32; Lomm. ii. 480–84; Br. ii. 209–10; B. iv. 479–80. From the Greek.)

If the words, As I said unto the Jews,[3] had not been placed before the saying, Whither I go ye cannot come, we might have supposed the phrase to have a simpler

---

[1] The text is defective here.
[2] Origen then proceeds to argue that, as Christ is admitted to have been in Hades, no difficulty need be found in statements which imply that Samuel was there. There is no further discussion in the fragment of the part played by the witch. The whole homily is of much interest. It is reprinted together with the adverse criticism of Eustathius, Bishop of Antioch (*c*. A.D. 324-31), in *Texte und Untersuchungen* ii. 4. Origen's conviction in regard to the witch of Endor may be contrasted with his belief that divination, augury and oracles were the work of demons. *C. Cels.* iv. 89 *sqq*; vii. 3, 4.
[3] John xiii. 33.

meaning and to refer to the departure of the soul of Jesus from life. As it is however both the Jews were to die and Jesus was to go when dead to Hades. Can it be said they were unable to go where Jesus was leading the way? But some one will say that as He was about to be in the Paradise of God, where they who would die in their sins would not come, while the disciples of Jesus were unable to come there then but would come later; consequently to the Jews, who would die in their sins, the words were said, Whither I go ye cannot come; but to the disciples, Whither I go ye cannot come now. For the continuation of the passage runs thus, As I said unto the Jews, so say I unto you, Whither I go ye cannot come now. In this way the place gives rise to not a little discussion in view of the saying, The Son of man shall spend three days and three nights in the heart of the earth.[1] For how is any one to spend three days and three nights in the heart of the earth who, immediately on his departure, was to be in the Paradise of God,[2] according to the words, To-day shalt thou be with me in the Paradise of God?

The passage so distresses some people by its discrepancy that they make bold to suppose that the words, To-day shalt thou be with me in the Paradise of God, were an addition to the Gospel made by some unscrupulous hand. Our interpretation is, in a simpler sense, that perhaps, before He went to the so termed heart of the earth, He brought to his place in the Paradise of God the man who said to him, Remember me when thou comest in Thy kingdom.[3] But, in a deeper sense, the term 'to-day' frequently in Scripture covers the whole of this present age. For instance, in the passage, This saying

---

[1] Matt. xii. 40. [2] Luke xxiii. 43. [3] Luke xxiii. 42.

was spread abroad among the Jews and continueth until this day.[1] Again, He is the father of the Moabites unto this day.[2] Again, To-day, if ye will hear his voice[3] and not forsake the Lord. In the word 'to-day' the promise is given him, after he had asked Jesus to remember him in the Kingdom of God, that in this present age, before the world to come, He would cause him to be with Him in the Kingdom of God. This however must be a passing remark, made by way of additional comment on the passage.

But to the disciples who desire to follow Jesus, not as the simpler sort would suppose in a physical sense, but in the meaning of, Whosoever doth not take up his cross and follow Me, is not worthy to be My disciple,[4] the Lord says, Whither I go ye cannot follow me now.[5] For if they did wish to follow the Word and confess Him, finding no cause of stumbling in Him, still they had not yet the power to do this. As yet there was no Spirit, for Jesus was not yet glorified.[6] And, no man can say that Jesus is Lord but in the Holy Spirit.[7] But the Word goes on His own way and he who follows the Word goes after Him. But he cannot go after Him who is not well equipped to tread firmly in His steps. The Word guides to His Father those who make every effort to be able to follow Him, and to go after Him, until they say unto the Christ, My soul followeth hard after Thee.[8] This thirty-second book of our Commentary on the Gospel according to John being now of sufficient length, we will close the discussion at this point.

[1] Matt. xxviii. 15.   [2] Gen. xix. 37.
[3] Ps. xcv. 7.   [4] Matt. x. 38.
[5] John xiii. 33. Origen misplaces the word 'now'. But cp. xiii. 7.
[6] John vii. 39.
[7] 1 Cor. xii. 3.
[8] Ps. lxiii. 8.

LXXXV

The Baptist gave directions to the publicans. Possibly there are spiritual publicans, customs officers who examine us and claim their dues as we leave the world. For the Baptist's words were addressed even to angels and unseen powers. These are present in the assemblies of men and the Christian preacher addresses a twofold audience, one visible, one invisible. (In Lucam. Hom. xxiii ; Lomm. v. 175–78. From the Latin.)

And there came also publicans to be baptized of Him.[1] The passage, even in its simple meaning, teaches that the publicans were not to demand more than was authorized in the law. For they who exact more break, not the commandment of John, but that of the Holy Spirit who spoke in John. And I am not sure whether, on the higher method of interpretation,[2] the text has not a more wonderful meaning, and whether in such an audience we ought to reveal matters of so mystical a character, especially among persons who do not see into the marrow of the Scriptures, but only derive a superficial pleasure from them.[3] There is risk, I know. Still in short and summary fashion the subject should be mentioned.

When we have left the world, and this our life has undergone change, there will be beings seated at the world's boundaries who will make most careful enquiry, like customs officers on duty, to see if they can discover in us anything they can claim. The Prince of this world seems to me to be a sort of customs officer. Hence it is written of him, The prince of this world cometh ; and he

---

[1] Luke iii. 12.
[2] Secundum $\dot{a}\nu a\gamma\omega\gamma\acute{\eta}\nu$.
[3] On the lack of intelligence and interest in his congregations, Origen was often quite outspoken. Cp. § liii.

hath nothing in Me.[1] In a spiritual sense too we must understand the passage we have in the Apostle's writings, Render to all their dues; tribute to whom tribute is due; custom to whom custom; honour to whom honour. Owe no man anything, save to love one another.[2] Let us therefore be on our watch lest perchance, when we have nothing that we can pay over as our custom due, we should be ourselves arrested for our debt. So it often happens with those who are liable for the taxes of this world; a man for the discharge of his liability is detained for the service of the state. Many of us will be liable to arrest by customs officers of that order. The holy man Jacob had no great dread of them, nor was he afraid that any of the custom dues payable to the collectors would be found in his possession. Thus he boldly addressed the collector Laban, Discern thou what is thine with me.[3] Scripture gives evidence on the point, saying, And Laban did not discern anything with Jacob.

Now our Saviour, and the Holy Spirit who speaks in the prophets, teach not men alone but also angels and invisible powers. Why should I mention the Saviour? The very prophets and apostles address all their utterances not only to men but also to angels. You may see how true this is. Give ear, it says, and I will speak.[4] Again, In the sight of the angels I will sing praises unto Thee.[5] Again, Praise the Lord, ye heaven of heavens and ye waters that be above the heavens; let them praise the Name of the Lord.[6] Again, Let the angels

---

[1] John xiv. 30. [2] Rom. xiii. 7-8.
[3] Gen. xxxi. 32-5. The illustration is not quite happily chosen, as Rachel had stolen Laban's teraphim and they were in the tent, though Laban did not discover them.
[4] Deut. xxxii. 1
[5] Ps. cxxxviii. 1; LXX. R. V. Before the gods.
[6] Ps. cxlviii. 4-5.

praise Him.¹ Again, In all places of His dominion bless the Lord, O my soul.² In many passages and especially in the Psalms you will find words addressed to the angels, for power to speak to the angels is given to men, at least to him who has the Holy Spirit. Of these passages I will quote one instance to show us that even the angels are instructed by the words of men. In the Apocalypse of John it is written, To the angel of the church of the Ephesians write; I have somewhat against thee. And again, To the angel of the church of Pergamum write; I have something against thee.³ Clearly it is a man who is writing to the angels and giving directions. I have no doubt that the angels are present in our gathering, not only with the whole church in general but even with individual worshippers. Of these the Saviour says, Their angels do always behold the face of my Father which is in heaven.⁴ A twofold church is with us here, a church of men, a church of angels. Whatever we say that is in accord with reason and with the mind of the Scriptures gives the angels joy, and they join their prayers with ours. The presence of the angels in the church, at least in the church that is worthy and belongs to Christ, is the reason of the order given to women at prayer, that they must wear a veil over their heads, because of the angels,⁵ those, evidently, which accompany the saints and find delight in the church. We, because our eyes have on them the unclean film of sin, do not behold them. But the apostles of Jesus see them, and to them He says, Verily, verily, I say unto you, ye shall see the heavens open and the angels of God ascending and descending upon the Son of man.⁶

---

[1] Ps. cxlviii. 2.
[2] *Ibid.*, ciii. 22.
[3] Rev. ii. 1, 12.
[4] Matt. xviii. 10.
[5] 1 Cor. xi. 5 *sqq.*
[6] John i. 51.

LXXXVI

The second Advent of the Lord will not be limited to one particular place. How at His fuller manifestation the good and the bad shall be separated.—(In Matt. Comm. Series, 70; Lomm. iv. 376–78. From the Latin.)

When the Son of God shall come in His glory, He will not appear in one particular place and not appear in another. His advent will be as He deliberately described it when He compared it with a flash of lightning. If, He said, they shall say unto you, Behold he is in the wilderness, go not forth. Behold he is in the house, believe it not. For as the lightning cometh forth from the east and is seen even unto the west, so shall be the coming of the Son of man.[1] As then the lightning, starting from the east, because it fills all things, shines even unto the west, so when Christ comes in His glory, because He will be everywhere, both He will be in the sight of all men everywhere and everywhere all men will be in His sight. So will they be placed before the seat of His glory, that is before His royalty and the power of His authority. And His 'throne' is clearly the name given either to certain of the more perfect among the saints, of whom it is written, There are set thrones for judgment;[2] or else to certain angelic powers of whom it is said, Whether they be thrones or dominions.[3] And so God the Word, king of the ages, who was also made in the form of a man, shall in this way sit upon the throne of His glory, and unto Him shall be gathered all the nations, no longer scattered among the many false doctrines concerning Him. They will be before Him in such a manner that we must not under-

---

[1] Matt. xxiv. 26–7.   [2] Ps. cxxii. 5.
[3] Col. i. 16.

stand all nations to come before Him in any particular place, just as it is not in a particular place that we must understand the righteous to utter what they have to say.

Now so long as the wicked are in confusion, not knowing themselves nor Christ but held in the darkness of error, and so long as the righteous see as in a mirror and in a riddle [1] and know themselves in part and not as they really are; so long the good are not separate from the bad. But when by the manifestation of the Son of God all come to know Him, then the Saviour shall separate the good from the bad. Those who are saved are called sheep in virtue of the gentleness they have learned from Him who says, Learn of me for I am meek and lowly in heart,[2] and in virtue of their readiness to go even unto death in the imitation of Christ, who was lead as a sheep to the slaughter and was dumb as a lamb before His shearers,[3] not dumb merely, but dumb before His shearers, that is before one who robs and despoils Him of His own. The bad are called the goats, because they wickedly climb up the rough hard rocks and advance over the steep place. By the holy on the right hand I would have you understand those who do right works and turn fully unto righteousness, which is ever on God's right hand. Therefore according to the merit of their right deeds they stand upon His right hand and receive the reward of their right conduct, even the king's right hand, where is peace and glory. But those who by their evil and left hand actions have separated themselves from His right hand unto perversity of life, take the lower place on the left, and are, that is, condemned to the misery of punishment, on account of which they stand upon His left.

---

[1] 1 Cor. xiii. 12. [2] Matt. xi. 29. [3] Isa. liii. 7.

LXXXVII

The Resurrection of the body.—(*Super Isaiam.* Frag. Pamphili *Apologia* vii; Lomm. xiii. 236–38; xxiv. 385–87. From the Latin.)

It is better then to say that we shall all rise again. Even the wicked will come to that place where is weeping and gnashing of teeth and where the righteous shall, each in his order, receive reward according to the merit of his good deeds. Then the body of their humiliation shall be transformed so as to become like to the glory of the body of Christ. For it is sown in corruption, but it will rise in incorruption; it is sown in dishonour, it will rise in glory; it is sown in weakness, it will rise in power, at the time of resurrection; it is sown a natural body, but it will rise a spiritual body.[1] But though all will rise again, and each will rise in his own order, it is still right, in view of the saying which John has in his Apocalypse, Blessed is he that hath part in the first resurrection; over him the second death hath no power,[2] to enquire whether perhaps the whole scheme of the resurrection ought not to be divided into two portions; one, that is, of those who are to be saved, the righteous; the other, of those who are to be punished, the sinners. One, called the first, will be the resurrection of the good; the other, the resurrection of the unhappy, we must call the second. The one is in all respects pure, joyous, full of all gladness. The other is altogether wretched, altogether full of sadness, appropriate to the deeds and life of men who in this present existence have despised God's commandments and, putting aside all fear of His judgment, have given themselves over to the working of all uncleanness and covetousness. They have never

---

[1] 1 Cor. xv. 42–4.   [2] Rev. xx. 6.

made an effort of preparation, so as to be able to resist the adversary in the contest against powers that are adverse and hostile to the race of men. The graves of the dead in this passage, as in many others, must be understood, according to the special significance of Scripture, as not only places expressly built, or cut in rock, or dug in the earth, as receptacles for human bodies; but as every place in which either an entire human body or any part of one is laid. For though it may happen that one body is dispersed in several places, still it will not be incongruous that all the places in which any part of the body lies should be called the graves of that body. If we decline to believe that in this manner there do rise from their graves, by divine power, the dead who have never been properly buried or laid in graves, but who have somewhere or other perished by shipwreck or in the deserts, so that they could not be properly buried; how can we regard them as included among those who are spoken of as being raised from their graves? If not, the absurdity is plain.

A little later on.—When then Paul writes that, As star differeth from star in glory, so shall be the resurrection of the dead; and when he says, It is sown in corruption, it will rise in incorruption,[1] and other things of the same kind, clearly he writes this of the body alone. For the soul is not sown in corruption, or in weakness, or in dishonour. Lastly, in plain terms, he concludes by saying, It is sown a natural body, so that no one can suppose that it is the soul which is sown in corruption or in dishonour or in weakness.[2]

---

[1] 1 Cor. xv. 41 *sqq*.
[2] For Origen's doctrine of the resurrection see *De Prin.* II. x; *C. Cels.* V. xiv-xxiii; VII. xxxii-iv; Pamphilus, *Apologia* vii; Lomm. xxiv. 379 *sqq.*; Bigg, *Platonists*, 225-26. There is a

LXXXVIII

On the Resurrection. The literalists are in error. It is not this actual body that shall be raised. Form shall remain, not material substance. This mortal body shall be spiritualised.—(*Selecta in Psalmos.* Lomm. xi. 384–91. From the Greek.)

Therefore the wicked shall not rise up in judgment,[1] etc. Prompted by this passage the simpler sort of believers hold that the wicked will have no share in the resurrection, though they by no means make it clear what they understand by the resurrection, or what sort of idea they have of the judgment. For even if they appear to offer explanations on these points, examination will prove them at fault, for they cannot maintain consistency in further discussion. Thus if we ask them of what part of them it is that a resurrection takes place, they answer that it is of the bodies wherewith at present we are clothed. Then, on our further asking whether it is of the whole of their substance or not, they say without consideration, Yes, of the whole. But if, accommodating ourselves to their simplicity, we put the further question, Whether blood that has been lost through incision of the veins, or the flesh or hairs that previously existed, shall rise again, or only those we had at the

---

very full consideration of Origen's doctrine of the resurrection in Denis, pp. 297 *sqq.*, where its relation to other elements in his system is reviewed. See also the two following passages, Redepenning, ii. 118 *sqq.* and Huet, *Origeniana*, ii. 9. It is not easy to bring into consistency his various statements. There are differences between the teaching of this section and that of the two following. In reality he is divided between the church's doctrine and the Platonic theory of immortality. His position was much and often unfairly criticised in later times.

[1] Ps. i. 5 ; LXX. has $ἀναστήσονται$, but there is no idea of resurrection in the Hebrew. R. V. is 'stand'.

time of death, being pressed in argument[1] they take refuge in saying that we must allow God to do as He wills. The better sort of them, to avoid being driven by their theory to reassemble the very blood which has happened on various occasions to be lost from our bodies, say it is our body in its last state that will rise again.

But we put the further difficulty, arising from the changing nature of the body and like substances; that just as food is digested in our own body and alters its affinities, so our bodies undergo change and become in carnivorous birds and beasts parts of their bodies. These in turn being eaten by men, or by other animals, undergo further change and become the bodies of men and of other animals. As this process continues, necessarily the same body will frequently be a part of several men. Whose body then shall it be in the resurrection? And so the result is that we shall go headlong into the depths of nonsense and have not a word to say. After such straits they take refuge in all things being possible to God. And they bring forward passages of the Scriptures which can by superficial interpretation give support to their views. Such is the passage in Ezekiel, And the hand of the Lord was upon me, etc. (*The Vision of the dry bones, ch. xxxvii. 1-6, is then quoted.*)

Of this passage they make use as very convincing. Other passages they cite from the Gospels, such as, There shall be weeping and gnashing of teeth;[2] also, Fear him which is able to destroy both soul and body in hell;[3] and the passage from Paul, He shall quicken your mortal bodies through His Spirit that dwelleth in you.[4] Every lover of truth should give independent consideration to these passages and endeavour in regard to the

[1] Reading $\theta\lambda\iota\beta\acute{o}\mu\epsilon\nu o\iota$.
[2] Matt. viii. 12.
[3] *Ibid.*, x. 28.
[4] Rom. viii. 11.

resurrection both to maintain the tradition of the ancients and to avoid falling into the absurdity of beggarly ideas, which are both impossible and unworthy of God. One principle in this subject must be recognized ; that every body which is held together by a nature which assimilates to it certain elements from without by way of nourishment, and gets rid of others in place of what is taken in—such are the bodies of plants and animals— never retains its material substance the same. Hence it is not a bad name for the body to call it a river. Possibly, to be exact, the existing substance does not remain the same in our body for even two days. And yet Paul, let us say, or Peter, is always the same, and this not only in his soul, the substance of which is not with us in a state of flux nor ever has fresh elements introduced ; he is the same, however fluid may be the nature of the body, because the form which distinguishes the body is the same. Thus the features remains unaltered, and they determine the bodily characteristics of Peter or of Paul. Among such characteristics scars remain on the body from childhood, and certain other peculiarities such as moles.

And further though the bodily form, which at the resurrection is again thrown around the soul, has some resemblance to the form by which Peter or Paul are recognized, yet it changes for the better and it is certainly not this original substance that is still imposed upon it. Up to its limit form is form, even though features appear to admit of considerable modification. So we must conceive for our present subject that the body that is to be will have the same form, though there will be the greatest possible change for the better. For the soul, while it exists in bodily regions, must make use of bodies corresponding to those regions. Just as, if we had become aquatic creatures and obliged to live in the sea, we should inevitably have had all the other constitution of fishes ; so, as we must one day inherit the Kingdom of Heaven and dwell in the regions of bliss, we shall necessarily make use of spiritual bodies, yet the form of the earlier body will not be lost, even though a change to a more glorious condition takes place in it. It was so with the form of Jesus, of Moses and Elijah ; it did not become in the Transfiguration wholly different from what it was. Do not then take it amiss if any one say that the original substance will not one day remain the same, since consideration shows to those capable of forming an opinion that even now the original substance cannot continue for a couple of days. The statement deserves notice that, It is sown of one kind, it is raised of another. It is sown a natural body, it is raised a spiritual body.[1] And the Apostle adds at the close, practically making it clear to us that we shall one day put off earthly characteristics, though the form in the resurrection will be retained, This I say, brethren, that flesh and blood cannot inherit the Kingdom of God, neither can corruption inherit incorruption.[2] Possibly the insistence of the saints is a little unnecessary, since God will one day claim the flesh.[3] But it will be flesh no more, though the features which once existed in the flesh will remain the same features in the spiritual body.

As for the words of Scripture which our brethren quote, this is what may be said. First as to the passage from Ezekiel. According to the sense in which our simpler friends wish to understand the words, there will not be a resurrection of the flesh at all, but only of bones, skin,

---

[1] 1 Cor. xv. 44.   [2] 1 Cor. xv. 50.
[3] Possibly Origen means to suggest that the simpler Christians were needlessly anxious about the body. Whatever happens to it, God will claim His own work. But the text is uncertain. '*Hic locus corruptus est*' is the Benedictine editor's comment.

sinews. And at the same time we may suggest to them that they have been carried away through not understanding the words of Scripture. Because bones are mentioned, it does not follow that these bones are intended. That is not so in the words, All my bones are out of joint;[1] or in, Heal me, for my bones are vexed.[2] It is evident that bones are not there mentioned in their ordinary meaning. Can it be implied by the saying, Surely, they say, our bones are dried up, that these very persons say, Our bones are dried up, because they wish them to be collected and raised up? But that is impossible. They mean, Our bones are dried up, because we have been in captivity and lost all the moisture of life. They add at any rate, Our hope is cut off; we have perished. Thus the resurrection of the people that is promised is a resurrection from their fallen state, from the sort of deadness they have suffered in being handed over to their enemies through their sins. Sinners too are said by the Saviour to be tombs, full of bones and of all uncleanness.[3] It is God's part to open the grave of each of us and to bring us out of our graves, restored to life, as the Saviour brought forth Lazarus.

The words, There shall be weeping and gnashing of teeth,[4] may be quoted against them, since, as the Creator in this life has made every member for a definite use, He has accordingly made the teeth for masticating solid food. What then is the good of teeth to those in torment? Our friends will not say that people will eat when they are in hell. We must show them that one is not to take every word literally as it stands. Thou hast broken the teeth of the wicked,[5] and, The Lord hath broken the great teeth of the lions.[6] Who is so foolish as to suppose that

---

[1] Ps. xxii. 14. [2] *Ibid.*, vi. 2. [3] Matt. xxiii. 27.
[4] *Ibid.*, viii. 12. [5] Ps. iii. 7. [6] *Ibid.*, lviii. 6.

God preserves the bodies of sinners and breaks only their teeth? As any one who maintained this would be driven through stress of argument to allegory, we must investigate in this sense the gnashing of teeth of those in torment. The soul has a power of mastication. At the time of reproof for sin, setting its teeth together as it comes to realize, it shall gnash its teeth. The words, Fear him which is able to destroy both soul and body in hell,[1] possibly mean that the soul is incorporeal, or possibly declare that the soul will not receive punishment apart from a body. It was in investigating this subject that we discussed the question of the form and of the original substance. The words in the Apostle, He shall quicken your mortal bodies,[2] since the body is mortal and has no share in the true life, may assert that the bodily form, of which we have spoken, a thing by nature mortal, When Christ who is our life shall be manifested,[3] itself undergoes change from being a body of death and is endowed with life, because by the Spirit it has become life-giving spirit. And the words, But one will say, How are the dead raised up and with what manner of body do they come?[4] are a naked assertion that our original substance will not be raised up. For if we have rightly understood the comparison, it may be said that the seminal word or reason in the grain of corn lays hold of the surrounding substance, entirely permeates it, takes possession of its form, and implants all its own powers in what once was earth, water, air, fire; it overpowers their qualities and transforms them into that quality of which it is itself the creator. Thus is the ear of corn perfected, excelling beyond comparison the original grain in size and form and variety.

[1] Matt. x. 28.
[2] Rom. viii. 11.
[3] Col. iii. 4.
[4] 1 Cor. xv. 35.

LXXXIX

In their denial of the Resurrection the Sadducees intended to deny entirely the survival of the soul after death. But even supposing the resurrection of the body were not true, the soul might still survive. The teaching of Paul is not opposed to this opinion.—(*Comm. in Matt.* xvii. 29; Lomm. iv. 144–47. From the Greek.)

Now the Sadducees in denying the resurrection not only rejected what simpler people, in common usage, describe as resurrection of the flesh, but even wholly did away with, not the immortality alone, but even the survival of the soul. They held the view that the after-life of the soul was nowhere indicated in the writings of Moses. And unto this day the Samaritans hold a doctrine about the human soul identical with that of the Sadducees.[1] They claim to have received from them a knowledge of the law, and they contend even unto death for the law of Moses and for circumcision. This view of the resurrection, I mean that held by Sadducees and Samaritans who reject the after-life of the soul, was also maintained by certain Corinthians in the time of the Apostle, who asserted that there was no resurrection. Of them he writes, If Christ is preached that He hath been raised from the dead, how say some among you that there is no resurrection of the dead?[2] That the people in Corinth who said that there was no resurrection of the dead rejected the resurrection in the Sadducees' significance of the term, meaning the survival of the soul, he makes evident by the words, If in this life only we have hoped in Christ, we are of all men most pitiable.[3]

---

[1] The Samaritans were hostile to Christianity. At a later date they were severely punished by Justinian for murdering Christians and destroying churches.
[2] 1 Cor. xv. 12.
[3] *Ibid.*, 19.

Carefully examine the words and you will see that a man who rejects the resurrection of the dead as it is believed in the church, even though he be mistaken in rejecting it, does not necessarily hope in Christ in this life only. For suppose, for the sake of argument, that the resurrection in the sense in which the many have believed in it, is not true, the man who rejected that was not hoping in Christ in this life only, provided the soul lives on, not receiving back its former body but putting on an etherial and a better one.[1] ' Neither are we of all men most pitiable, if we say that the soul lives on and is in being, though this present body be not its garment nor do we assert that the soul receives it back. And for further proof that what the Apostle in the First Epistle to the Corinthians specially opposes is the view we have described, we will quote the words, If the dead are not raised at all, why are we then baptized for them? Why do we stand in jeopardy every hour?[2] Also the words, If after the manner of men I fought with beasts at Ephesus, what doth it profit me if the dead are not raised? Let us eat and drink for to-morrow we die.[3] For suppose that what is regarded among the many as true, be not true—the resurrection, I mean, of the dead—how is it a consequence of this that we have run vain risks in striving for the salvation of our souls? How does it not profit a man to have fought with beasts for Christ, if his soul lives on, receiving every care that it deserves, even though it does not get back its former body? How is it a consequence of there being no resurrection of the flesh that we must eat and drink for to-morrow we die? In saying this we do not cast any doubt upon the passage in Isaiah which runs, All flesh shall see the salvation of

---

[1] 2 Cor. v. 1, *sqq.*   [2] 1 Cor. xv. 29-30.   [3] *Ibid.*, 32.

God,[1] nor on the words spoken by Job, Everlasting is he who shall redeem me upon earth and raise up my skin that hath endured so much.[2] Nor do we cast any doubt upon the utterance of the Apostle which says, He shall quicken your mortal bodies through His Spirit that dwelleth in you.[3] Only to the best of our power we are cleansing the significance of the term resurrection[4] in the passage of the Gospel which lies before us. That is why we also quoted the words from the First Epistle to the Corinthians.

XC

Some hold that since in a future state, being free, we may fall again, Christ must suffer a second time for our salvation. This is not so. His one death suffices for the past and for the future. Besides, we shall be saved from future fall by the power of love. (Comm. in Ep. ad Rom. v. 10; Lomm. vi. 407–11. From the Latin.)

Hence I am astonished that some persons, in spite of this clearly expressed opinion of Paul,[5] insist on maintaining that it will be necessary for Christ in the ages to come to undergo a second time the same or similar sufferings, in order to set at liberty those whom in this present life His remedial treatment had not been able to cure. They say, Is it possible that in the future there should be any age in which nothing good and nothing

---

[1] Luke iii. 6. Cp. Isa. lii. 10. All the ends of the earth shall see, etc.
[2] Job xix. 25–6. From LXX, which differs from the Hebrew considerably.
[3] Rom. viii. 11.
[4] Shewing, that is, that the resurrection of the body is one thing, while the survival and immortality of the soul, with or without the body, are another.
[5] *Sc.* Rom. vi. 9. ' Death no more hath dominion over him.'

bad is done, but the world stands inactive and all things remain silent as the deep. This they maintain is clearly absurd. So we will agree; some activity there is. And, say they, when anything is done, necessarily one act is right, another less right, and in the very action some advance and become better, others worse.[1] Freedom of choice will belong for ever to the rational nature. It was possible even for him who because of the brightness of his glory was Lucifer,[2] who by reason of the light of knowledge rose as the morning star, to be changed from his high estate and because of the wickedness he entertained to become darkness. He who from his birth was without spot, and dwelt with the Cherubim,[3] and had his place amid the stones of fire, and was arrayed in every adornment of virtue, nor was there any tree of virtue in the Paradise of God fit to be compared with him, even he after all this had iniquity found in him and was thrown down from heaven to earth.

In like manner it may come about that, in whatsoever state the soul shall be, and in whatsoever perfection of virtue, still, since virtue is liable to change, the soul will be capable of a fall; as it moved from vice to virtue, so may it move from virtue to vice. If this be so, it seems to follow that when sickness comes the soul needs a physician, for according to the Saviour's own saying, They that are sick have need of a physician.[4] By these

---

[1] For the thought of the rise and fall of the soul in a future life cp. *De. Prin.* III. i. 23; vi. 6. It is interesting to note that Origen's views on this point had not greatly changed. Westcott (*D.C.B.*) thinks the *De Principiis* was written when Origen was about thirty years of age. Koetschau dates it rather later, '*nicht viel nach* 220'; B. v. xi. He wrote the *Com. in Ep. ad Rom.* when over sixty (so Redepenning, ii. 70; 189).
[2] Isa. xiv. 12.
[3] Ezek. xxviii. 14.
[4] Matt. ix. 12.

and similar arguments they come to the view that in the ages to be the work of salvation must be re-enacted identically by Christ. To this contention, as briefly as possible, we will reply. That free will belongs always to a rational nature we do not deny. But we maintain that the power of the cross of Christ, and of this death which in the end of the ages He has undergone, is so great that it avails for the healing and the restoration not only of the present age and of the future, but even of the ages that are past; not alone for this human order of ours but even for the powers and orders of heaven. For, according to the opinion of the Apostle Paul himself, Christ made peace through the blood of His cross not only for the things on earth but even for the things in heaven.[1]

And what it is that in the future ages restrains the freedom of the will from falling once again into sin, the Apostle tells us in a short sentence, saying, Love never faileth. It is on this account love is said to be greater than both faith and hope,[2] because it is love alone that saves from the possibility of another fall. For if the soul has risen to such a state of perfection as to love God with all the heart and with all the soul and with all the strength and a neighbour as one's self,[3] what place will there be for sin? For this reason both in the law this is said to be the first commandment and in the Gospels the command about love comes before all the rest.[4] When authority for feeding the sheep was entrusted to Peter, and the church was founded upon him as upon the ground, acknowledgment of no other virtue save of love is asked of him.[5] John, among his many sayings about love, has

---

[1] Col. i. 20.
[2] 1 Cor. xiii. 13.
[3] Matt. xxii. 37, 39.
[4] *Ibid.*, 38.
[5] John xxi. 15–17; Matt. xvi. 18.

also this, He that abideth in love abideth in God.¹ Therefore by right it is love, greater alone than all else, which shall preserve every creature from falling. Then God shall be all in all.²

To this stage of perfection had the Apostle Paul risen; standing herein he said with confidence, Who shall separate us from the love of God which is in Christ Jesus? shall tribulation, or anguish, or persecution, or famine, or nakedness, or peril, or sword?³ And again, I am persuaded that neither life, nor death, nor things present, nor things to come, nor angels, nor powers, nor height, nor depth, nor any other creature, shall be able to separate us from the love of God which is in Christ Jesus our Lord.⁴ In all this there is clear proof that if all these things which the Apostle recounts are unable to separate us from the love of God, when a man has risen to that summit of perfection, much more shall it be impossible for the freedom of the will to separate us from His love.

XCI

In Canaan each tribe had its own territory. So in Heaven there will be different portions for different souls.—(In Num. Hom. xxviii. 2; Lomm. x. 366–68; B. vii. 281–83. From the Latin.)

According to the view of Paul, which led him to describe earthly things as the shadow and pattern of the heavenly, there will probably be considerable distinctions

---

[1] 1 John iv. 16.
[2] Few particular texts had greater influence with Origen than this. 'These words were never out of Origen's mind. He looks upon the hope that they enshrine as the golden key to every doubt.' Bigg, *Platonists*, 299. Cp. *De Prin.* III. vi. 3.
[3] Rom. viii. 35.
[4] *Ibid.*, 38–9.

of locality even in the heavenly regions. You observe the names and designations by which they are marked off, and whence these are derived, and how names are assigned not only to the districts of the heavens but also to all the stars and heavenly bodies. He that made the multitude of the stars, as says the prophet, giveth them all their names.[1] In regard to these names many secret and cryptic statements are to be found in the books which bear the name of Enoch, but since these books do not appear to have recognized authority with the Hebrews, we will for the present forbear to cite the evidence to be found in them, and rather pursue our enquiry after the truth on the evidence of the passage with which we are dealing, as to which no question can arise.[2]

In the divine law, then, the boundaries of the land of Judaea are given in the words of God, and we are told these must be regarded as the pattern of things in heaven. And in heaven it is expressly stated by the Apostle that there is a city Jerusalem and a mount Sion. It follows that just as round about the earthly Jerusalem there lie also other cities and villages and various districts, so too that heavenly Jerusalem, conformably to the pattern of things on earth, has also round about it other cities and villages and various districts, in which the people of God and the true Israel must one day be settled through the true Jesus, of whom that Jesus or Joshua, the son of Nun, was a type. By the assignation of the lot, that is by the examination of merits, Israel will receive its inheritance. So here in this passage the Lord says that in the distribution of the land the boundaries of this tribe, say, are these, but of another

---

[1] Ps. cxlvii. 4.   [2] Cp. *Book of Enoch*, lxix-lxxxii.

they are different. Probably it is because the merits of those who are to obtain the inheritance of the Kingdom of Heaven will be various, that this distinction of boundaries is ordered to be carefully marked even in regard to the tribes of Israel, so that we may realize that these diversities of merit will be taken into account in every case.

For example, there will be the man who has led indeed a careless life, yet still deserves on the ground of his faith to be reckoned among the sons of Israel. Still because of the carlessness of his life and the laxity of his conduct he must be held to belong to the tribe of Reuben or of Gad or to the half tribe of Manasseh, and not to receive the lot of his inheritance on this side Jordan but beyond it. Whereas there will be another who by the improvement of his life and the principle of his conduct has reached such a condition as to deserve, for those reasons which God only knows, to have his place in the tribe of Judah or even in the very tribe of Benjamin, in which Jerusalem itself and the temple of God and the altar stand. One will be in this tribe, another in that. In this manner these statements here recorded in the book of Numbers may be a sort of shadow of the future lot in heaven of those who, through Jesus our Lord and Saviour, will as we have said receive their inheritance in the kingdom of heaven.

There, I suppose, will also be carefully maintained those privileges of the priests foreshadowed here, for whom localities near to the cities, adjoining the very walls, are ordered to be separated off from the sons of Israel. There too, I suppose, will be those cities, the pattern of which is here described, which the writer calls Cities of Refuge, to which not every manslayer but those who have committed homicide unawares may flee. For there are, it may be, certain sins which, if we commit them deliberately and on purpose, render us manslayers. And there are others for which, if we commit them unawares, there is, I suppose, a certain place appointed for us and made ready by God's direction, wherein for a certain period any of us who have committed involuntary sins must dwell; provided, that is, we are found clear and free from the sins of deliberate commission. For this end certain cities are separated as a refuge. There are some who think that even the situation and grouping of particular stars may be termed and accounted a city in the heavens. On this I dare not speak definitely.[1] For I see that all creation is made subject in hope by reason of Him who subjected it, and yet is waiting for its liberty in the unquestioned redemption of the sons of God,[2] and that some grander and more wonderful event is hidden from our eyes.

XCII

The family relationships of this present life will not be carried over into the world to come. Yet under the altered conditions their spiritual equivalents may exist. (Comm. in Matt. xvii. 33; Lomm. iv. 159–63. From the Greek.)

Come then let us examine after this another passage of the Gospel beginning with the words, Now there were with us seven brethren, and the first married and deceased,[3] and so on. Isaiah in his prophecy says, Seven

---

[1] This is his habitual tone in all matters of speculation. See the note in Bigg, *Platonists*, 193 : ' *discutiens et pertractans potius quam affirmans* ', is the description in Pamphilus *Apologia*, cap. i ; Lomm. xxiv. 312 ; *supra*, pp. xliii–xliv.
[2] Rom. viii. 23.
[3] Matt. xxii. 25.

women shall take hold of one man, saying, We will eat our own bread, and wear our own apparel; only let us be called by thy name; take thou away our reproach.[1] But the Sadducees who came to the Saviour speak of a case, the opposite of that in the prophecy, of seven men marrying one wife. I think their problem was an imaginary one; by this imaginary case they intended to invalidate the theory of a resurrection. For they supposed it was a consequence of the resurrection that each of those who rise shall retain the same relationship to those who belonged to him in this life, so that a husband in obtaining resurrection would also get back his wife, and a father remain in his relationship to his son, and a brother to his brother. Evidently they were unaware that the Creator, doing all things for a useful purpose, has of necessity arranged these relationships where there is birth and decay, so that one man may be a husband, ministering through his wife to the birth of children, while those who are born, being brothers, have an affinity through their birth from the same parents. Father and son, mother and daughter, are the product of birth.

If then, in a state of bliss, those who have merited reward by means of this present world in which they have lived well, are to have share in the other life, while none of those who have not striven here is accounted worthy of the resurrection from the dead, it is evident that what exists in this world for the purposes of birth, will not exist in the other world. For God creates nothing superfluous, neither is anything made by Him in vain. The Sadducees should have seen the consequences of their supposition that each man would receive back his wife.

---

[1] Isa. iv. 1.

There would again in the other world be procreation of children and child-birth and death. And if so, disease as well. If birth, also infancy, and advance from infancy to fully articulate speech, and then to reasoned language, and in the attainment of language to vice, and possibly again to virtue, so rarely found in the few who seek it. What could be more futile than this? It would be better that there were no resurrection than that there should be such a resurrection as the Sadducees supposed, imagining it to be a consequence of the resurrection that each would receive back his own wife. From that each of the results I have named would follow. If then it is for a new world that we hope, as Isaiah termed it, A new heaven and a new earth,[1] or, as is written in the Gospel, The cup of the new covenant,[2] made I suppose, from the new vine, then all things in the new life must be greatly different and in reality blessed.

And just as it follows, as our discussion made clear, from there being wife and husband that there will be children of fathers and brothers of brethren and mothers of children, so perhaps may it not follow from there being no wife or husband that there will no longer be father or mother or any brothers one of another, possibly not only as regards new relationships but even as regards those of the past? No memory will remain in the other world of our family according to the flesh among those who have the blessedness to hear, Remember ye not the former things, neither consider the things of old. Behold I make all things new.[3] Accordingly in the world to come Haran will not be called Abraham's father, nor Abraham the father of Ishmael or of Keturah's children, nor perhaps even of Isaac. For the old things are passed

---

[1] Isa. lxvi. 22.   [2] Luke xxii. 20.   [3] Isa. xliii. 18 19.

away.¹ Then shall it be said, Behold, all things are made new.

But whether there be a brother in a sense distinct from the brother after the flesh, or a father and son in a sense different from the facts of birth, and all this no longer through a wife nor by means of the unseemly parts of the body, but in a sense corresponding to that in which the Saviour is the Son of God, is matter for him to consider who is able to make due enquiry into such topics because he has received the Spirit that searcheth all things, yea, the deep things of God.² For my part it is not only in regard to these that I accept a different relationship, as it were under the same name, in regard I mean to brother and father and son and even in regard to wife and husband. For in the resurrection of the dead the saying is also true that, They neither marry nor are given in marriage, but are as the angels in heaven.³

True also is the saying in a parable concerning a marriage different from marriages on earth. The kingdom of heaven is likened unto a certain king which made a marriage for his son,⁴ and so on. Again, Then shall the kingdom of heaven be likened unto ten virgins, which took their lamps,⁵ and so forth. Thus the king's son in the resurrection of the dead will wed in a marriage which is beyond every marriage which eye has seen or ear heard or has entered into the heart of man.⁶ That holy and divine and spiritual marriage is among the words which it is not lawful for a man to utter.⁷ But one may ask whether, in similarity to the marriage of the Bridegroom in the resurrection of the dead, there are other marriages

---

¹ 2 Cor. v. 17. ² 1 Cor. ii. 10.
³ Matt. xxii. 30. ⁴ *Ibid.*, 2.
⁵ *Ibid.*, xxv. 1. ⁶ 1 Cor. ii. 9 ; Isa. lxiv. 4.
⁷ 2 Cor. xii. 4.

as well, or whether in the resurrection of the dead only the Bridegroom, after doing away with all marriages, is to have a marriage, not one in which twain shall be one flesh, but one in which it is more right to say that the Bridegroom and the Bride shall be one spirit. But take care in hearing such expressions that you do not slip into acceptance of the mythical theory of aeons, male and female, following those who fashion their Syzygies,[1] which have no sort of evidence in Holy Scripture.

[1] The συζυγίαι were the pairs of aeons or personified abstractions, as arranged in the system of the gnostic Valentinus. Cp. Tert. *De Præscript. Haeret* 49: Valentinus... '*introducit pleroma et aeones triginta ; exponit autem has per syzygias, id est conjugationes quasdam*'. Cp. Gwatkin, *Early Church History*, ii. 37 *sqq*.

PART VIII

THE CHRISTIAN LIFE

XCIII

The various elements in a perfect faith.—(Comm. in Joann. xxxii. 16; Lomm. ii. 425-29; Br. ii. 177-79; B. iv. 450-53. From the Greek.)

If we wish to understand who it is that holds the faith complete, let us make for illustration a summary of those items in belief which save the believer. Let us suppose they are in number a hundred. Let us say that he who accepts without any doubt the hundred items in question, and believes steadfastly in each, holds the faith complete. He who falls short, whether it be in any number of the saving items in belief, or in steadfastness in regard to what he believes, falls short of holding the complete faith in exact proportion to the items missing in his belief, or to his want of steadfastness in regard to the things he believes, all or some of them. For our argument it must be granted that in some things a man may believe steadfastly, while in others he believes but not steadfastly. Certainly it would be granted by general agreement that it is impossible to show that he who in a single item is imperfect, cannot have steadfastness in regard to any. For not every one of those who, to use the language of Scripture, are of little faith[1] and have not yet acquired steadfastness in regard to what they believe, stands removed from such steadfastness by exactly the same distance.

[1] Matt. vi. 30, etc.

It is clear, as a next step, from the words, According to thy faith be it done unto thee,[1] and, Thy faith hath saved thee,[2] that, according to the award made in the righteous judgment of God, a salvation awaits each of us that is proportionate to the extent and quality of our faith. I suppose here too there is some difference among those who are saved, so that the saying, With what measure ye mete, it shall be measured to you again,[3] applies both to the measure of faith and to the measure of the award of salvation that comes from God. He who recognizes the principle in these matters, will see with what good reason it is said, as unto men who have not power to judge, Judge not, that ye be not judged,[4] and, Judge nothing before the time, until the Lord come.[5] Further, since I said for illustration that there were a hundred saving elements in belief, and that a man who had steadfast belief in the hundred holds the faith complete, while he who fell short in his faith in any of the hundred items or in steadfastness in regard to what he believed, failed in various degrees to have complete faith, we will for clearness sake make the following declaration.

Believe first of all that there is one God, who created all things and set them in order and brought everything from non-existence into existence.[6] We must also believe that Jesus Christ is Lord, and in all the truth about Him regarding His divinity and His humanity. And we should believe in the Holy Spirit; and that by virtue of our freedom we are punished for our sins and rewarded for our good deeds. Suppose now, for the sake of argument, that a man who, as it seems, believes in Jesus, does not believe that the God of the Law and of the

---

[1] Matt. ix. 29.
[2] *Ibid.*, 22.
[3] Luke vi. 38.
[4] Matt. vii. 1.
[5] 1 Cor. iv. 5.
[6] Wisdom i. 14.

Gospel is one,[1] Whose glory the heavens, as made by Him, declare and the firmament sheweth His handiwork,[2] being the product of His hands; this man would fall short in the most important particular of the faith. Again if a man believed that He who was crucified under Pontius Pilate visited the world as a holy being of saving power, but that He derived His birth not from Mary and the Holy Spirit but from Joseph and Mary, he too would lack the elements most essential for holding the faith complete. Again if a man should accept His divinity, but, finding difficulty in His humanity, should believe that His life had no human element, and that He never became a person; he too would fall short of the complete faith by no inconsiderable measure. Or if, on the other hand, he should allow the human elements, but reject the personal existence of the Only Begotten and Firstborn of all creation,[3] this man also could not say that he held the faith complete. So I pray you consider the matter, item by item, that we may see how great a thing it is to hold the complete faith, steadfastly and without defect. Such power has faith when it exists complete in a man's soul that it can remove mountains,[4] whatever the mountains may be. All men have the power to remove the mountain pointed out by Jesus,[5] and the things pointed out to him,[6] but whatever is lacking for complete faith is lacking also for the power to remove mountains.

For our purpose I will also make use of another illustration. So many men having so much power are sufficient to launch the ship into the sea. If the whole team fell short by even one member, or one man's power

---

[1] The common Gnostic view. [2] Ps. xix. 1.
[3] Col. i. 15. [4] 1 Cor. xiii. 2.
[5] 'This mountain,' Matt. xxi. 21; Mark xi. 23.
[6] If the text is correct the reference is possibly to the withering of the fig-tree. Cp. the passage in Mark referred to.

failed, the ship would not be launched. So the complete faith resembles many men removing mountains. Deficiency of power to remove the mountains is proportionate to the deficiency in the faith of the man who is still imperfect in respect of it. Consider if all this enquiry have not been profitable to the disciples whose feet Jesus washed, to whom He said, regarding them as not yet believers—so a man who has not examined the passage would imagine—From henceforth I tell you before it come to pass, that when it is come to pass ye may believe that I am he.[1] And then, when the discourse is investigated, it shows what virtue there is in the complete faith and that it is rarely found, and that each of us falls far short of having complete faith so as to remove mountains.[2] It is no inconsiderable aid to faith in connection with our present subject that the prophets foretold the events of Jesus' life, and according to their word the events foretold did occur to the Saviour.[3]

XCIV

Paul criticized the zeal of the Jews as being ' not according to knowledge.' So may our fear of God, our love, our faith, our care for the poor, be ' not according to knowledge.' Indeed knowledge should qualify all our virtues.—(Comm. in Ep. ad Rom. viii. 1 ; Lomm. vii. 192-96. From the Latin.)

For I bear them witness, he says, that they have a zeal for God but not according to knowledge.[4] Although, he says, they are entangled in the great and numerous evils of their own sin, still they have an inexpressible zeal and jealousy for God. And this reason prompts me to

---

[1] John xiii. 19.
[2] 1 Cor. xiii. 2.
[3] § lxi may be compared with this.
[4] Rom. x. 2.

entreat God on their behalf, that some day, even at last, they may attain to salvation. For they have a zeal for God, but not according to knowledge. And he makes clear in what sense the zeal they have is not according to knowledge; Being ignorant, he says, of God's righteousness they observe a righteousness of their own. So it is not of much advantage to have a zeal for God and not to have knowledge in this zeal. The Jews, for example, believing themselves to act from a zeal for God, were guilty of impiety towards the Son of God, because the zeal they had was not according to knowledge. It was not like the zeal of Phineas, the son of Eleazar, who with zeal according to knowledge slew with one stroke the Midianitish woman and the Israelite who was committing fornication with her;[1] or the zeal of Elijah, who said, I have been very jealous for the Lord Almighty, because the children of Israel have forsaken Thee, have slain Thy prophets, and have thrown down Thine altars;[2] or the zeal of Matthias, of whom it is written in the first book of the Maccabees that, He was zealous in the law of God and his reins trembled and his wrath rose up according to judgment.[3] The zeal and jealousy of all these men was according to knowledge. But the zeal of the Jews was not according to knowledge, because being ignorant of the righteousness of God they tried to establish one of their own; tried, that is, to fulfil what seemed righteousness to men, when their duty was to obey rather the righteousness of God, which is Christ.

But now consider whether it be not to them alone that this saying, They have a zeal for God but not according to knowledge,[4] would appear to be directed. For of others also the Apostle may say in like fashion, I bear

---

[1] Num. xxv. 7-8.
[2] 1 Kings xix. 10.
[3] 1 Macc. ii. 24.
[4] Rom. x. 2.

them witness that they have a fear of God, but not according to knowledge; or of others that they have a love of God, but not according to knowledge. For suppose a man has an affection for God, but is unaware that love must be long-suffering, kind, envying not, not rash in action, not puffed up, not scheming for advantage, not seeking its own [1]—if he lacks these or similar qualities in his love and loves God merely in feeling, to him too it will be appropriately said, that he has a love of God but not according to knowledge. In the same way it may be said of another that he has a faith in God, but not according to knowledge, if he is unaware that faith apart from works is dead,[2] and that faith in God does not lie in words alone, which are sometimes learned off after they have been put together or written by another, but in a spiritual experience like that of the woman who said within herself, If I touch the hem of his garment, I shall be whole.[3] Thus if a man does not have faith so as to make it manifest by his good deeds in whom he believes, to him too may it be said that he has faith in God but not according to knowledge. Of another it may be said that he has chastity before God, but not according to knowledge. Another has a care for the poor, but not according to knowledge; all he desires is to have the praise of men. Another may be called temperate, but not according to knowledge, if he only fasts to be seen of men.[4]

So one by one with all our actions, unless we act according to knowledge and understanding, it may be said that we have the zeal for a good work, but not according to knowledge. On this account must we give special care to knowledge, lest we should find ourselves

---

[1] 1 Cor. xiii. 4–5.
[2] James ii. 20.
[3] Matt. ix. 21.
[4] *Ibid.*, vi. 16.

in the sorry situation of having our place in faith and yet being baulked of faith; of having a zeal for good things and yet falling away from goodness. Would you be assured that a man, if he has not knowledge, may grow weak in faith? Hear Paul himself as he says to some, Except ye believed in vain.[1] It is the case then that those who give no care to knowledge, so as to receive in their faith an understanding of the truth as well, have believed in vain. The Apostles for instance, perceiving there was this distinction between faith merely handed on and faith according to knowledge, said to the Saviour, Increase our faith.[2] Having already, they mean, the faith which is not according to knowledge, may we have also the faith which is according to knowledge. So Paul bears the Jews witness that they are jealous for God but not according to knowledge. Still, because they have in some sense a jealousy for God, they give the Apostle ground for making entreaty to God in their behalf. For it is better to have a zeal for God, albeit not according to knowledge, than not to have any at all. He that hath—so it is written—to him shall be given,[3] even at the last hour, when all Israel shall be saved.[4] But he that hath not, from him shall be taken away even that which he hath.

XCV

The degrees and consequences of sin.—(Comm. in Joann. xix. 14; Lomm. ii. 165–68; Br. ii. 18–20; B. iv. 313–14. From the Greek.)

Also, with the words, Ye shall die in your sin,[5] one will compare the passage from Ezekiel which runs, The soul that sinneth, it shall die.[6] For sin is the death of

---

[1] 1 Cor. xv. 2.   [2] Luke xvii. 5.   [3] Matt. xiii. 12.
[4] Rom. xi. 26.   [5] John viii. 21.   [6] Ezek. xviii. 20.

the soul, not, I take it, every sin, but the sin which John says is unto death.[1] And then one may draw the distinction that one sin is the death of the soul and another is its infirmity. Perhaps there is even a third, the kind of sin which is the soul's loss. That this is sin is evident from the words, What shall a man be profited if he shall gain the whole world and destroy, or suffer loss of, his soul?[2] and also from the text, If any man's work shall be burned, he shall suffer loss.[3] It is to those then who shall die in their sins that He says, I go away, and ye shall seek me, and shall die in your sin: whither I go, ye cannot come.[4] But to Peter he says, Whither I go, thou canst not follow me now; but thou shalt follow me afterwards.[5] For, in the discipleship of Jesus, a man may not be prepared to follow Him at once as He goes away to His Father, yet afterwards, by treading carefully in His steps, he may follow the Master and go close after the Word of God.

It is probable that, because of the view which we have suggested in regard to the final state, a reader will dwell upon the words, Whither I go, ye cannot come,[6] and say in reply that possibly a man cannot now but that he can later. And if there is a present world[7] and another world to come, they to whom it was said, Ye cannot come, during this present world—and long is the time still to run for its fulfilment—cannot come where Jesus is, that is, where truth and wisdom and reason are, for that is where Jesus is. Some I know who not only in this present world but also in the world to come are under the mastery of their own sin, like those of whom the Word says, If he blaspheme against

---

[1] 1 John v. 16.   [2] Matt. xvi. 26. R.V. marg. 'soul'; text, 'life'.
[3] 1 Cor. iii. 15.   [4] John viii. 21.   [5] John xiii. 36.
[6] John viii. 21.   [7] Gal. i. 4.

the Holy Spirit, he hath no remission, neither in this world, nor in the world to come,[1] though even if he have it not in the world to come, it does not follow that he shall not have it in the worlds that follow after that.[2]

As for Heracleon,[3] in setting out the passage about the Treasury, he makes no comment upon it. But in regard to the words, Whither I go ye cannot come,[4] he remarks, Being in ignorance and unbelief and sins how can they come into a state of incorruption? Even in this point he fails to understand his own opinions. For if those who are in ignorance and unbelief and sins cannot come into incorruption, how did the Apostles, who were once in ignorance and unbelief and sins, come into a state of incorruption? This shows that those who are in ignorance and unbelief and sins can come to a state of incorruption, if they change, and that such change is possible for them.

XCVI

We make to ourselves other gods. Such are not idols alone but money, pleasure, honour, when we give them the first place in our affections.—(In Lib. Jud. Hom. ii. 3; Lomm. xi. 230–32; B. vii. 475–77. From the Latin.)

We are not then to suppose that, because it is evident we do not worship images, therefore these

---

[1] Matt. xii. 32; Mark iii. 29; Luke xii. 10. The quotation agrees mainly with Mark, partly with Matthew.
[2] Eph. ii. 7. Cp. *De Prin.* III. v. 3. *Quibus testimoniis (he has quoted.* Ecc. i. 9–10) *utrumque simul probatur, quod et ante fuerint sæcula et futura sint postmodum.* Also Bigg, *Platonists,* 227. 'Origen speaks of a vast stretch of cycles reaching onwards in almost illimitable extension to the Consummation of All'. Throughout, the rise and fall of the soul is possible. § xc.
[3] Cp. § xxxiv. [4] John viii. 21.

words[1] have no application to any of us. What each man honours before all else, what before all things he admires and loves, this for him is God. In a word what before all things and above all things God demands of man by His commandment, is this; Thou shalt love, it says, the Lord thy God with all thine heart, and with all thy soul, and with all thy might.[2] God desires in some way to secure for Himself these affections in the mind of man, and He knows that what a man loves with all his heart and with all his soul and with all his might, this for him is God. Let each one of us now examine himself and silently in his own heart decide, which is the flame of love that chiefly and above all else is afire within him; which is the passion that he finds he cherishes more keenly than all others. You must yourselves pass judgment on the point and weigh these things in the scales of your conscience; whatever it is that weighs heaviest in the balance of your affection, that for you is God. But I fear that with very many the love of gold will turn the scale, that down will come the weight of covetousness lying heavy in the balance. To such a man it is certainly said, Thou canst not serve God and Mammon,[3] that is covetousness. I fear that in others the love of licence and pleasure will weigh so heavy as to sink right down to earth; that in others the passion for worldly honour, or the craving for prominence among men, will outweigh all else.

Few indeed I think there are who, on inwardly measuring their affections and testing them in unbiassed scales, will find that the weight of their love for God outbalances all other things that have human interest.

---

[1] i.e. Judges ii. 11-12, 'The children of Israel . . . served the Baalim; and they forsook the Lord, the God of their fathers.'
[2] Deut. vi. 5.   [3] Matt. vi. 24.

Of one man I know who held the balance in his own case with the closest scrutiny and who, on finding that all his inward affections tended in the direction of the love of God, declared with full conviction that, Neither death nor life nor angels nor powers nor things present nor things to come nor height nor depth nor any other creature shall be able to separate us from the love of God which is in Christ Jesus our Lord.[1] But it is Paul who could thus assert that neither things present nor things to come nor any other creature can separate him from the love of God. As for ourselves, how I would that we could even say that neither gold nor silver, neither the pleasures of the flesh nor the glory of the world, nor its shortlived transitory honour, no physical allurement, no delight of children or of wife, shall be able to separate us from the love of God. One thing at least would we wish to assert with confidence, that neither the love of worldly literature,[2] nor the sophistries of philosophers, nor the tricks of astrologers and the courses of the stars as they invent them, nor the occult science that passes current through the subtle trickery of the demons, nor any craving for clairvoyance secured by unlawful means, shall be able to separate us from the love of God which is in Christ Jesus our Lord.

Does not the error of the whole heathen world start from this point, that they seek to make gods of the things that men desire greatly and give the divine name to human vices and passions? Greedy for money and aflame with the lust of covetousness they call Mammon, the Syrian divinity, the god of this passion. As lovers of licence and pleasure they term Venus the goddess of this turbulent vice. Likewise in their other sins they

---

[1] Rom. viii. 38-9. [2] Cp. § lxxii, *supra*.

make the very passion by which they are driven their god. Thus it is the Apostle says the same thing. Covetousness, he says, which is idolatry.[1] So you see not the mere worship of an idol but the devotion to money is accounted idolatry and bondage. So with ourselves; when we are so given over to any vices as to love them with all our heart, with all our soul, and with all our might, we are said to be worshippers of idols and to have gone after strange gods.

XCVII

The sun, moon and stars correspond to Christ, the Church and the Saints. These illuminate us, not all equally but each in proportion to his capacity to receive illumination. (*In Gen.* Hom. i. 7; Lomm. viii. 113–15; B. vi. 8–10. From the Latin.)

As the sun and the moon are said to be the great lights in the firmament of the heaven,[2] so also in us are Christ and the Church. And as God set the stars also in the firmament, let us see too what stars there are in us, that is in the heaven of our heart. Moses is a star within us, which lightens and illuminates us by its influence. So are Abraham, Isaac and Jacob, and Isaiah and Jeremiah and Ezekiel and David and Daniel; so all of whom Holy Scripture has testified that they pleased God. For just as star differeth from star in glory,[3] so does each of the saints shed his light on us in proportion to his greatness. And just as the sun and moon shed light on our bodies, so too are our minds enlightened by Christ and by the Church. It is a condition of our being enlightened that we be not spiritually blind. . The sun and the moon may

---

[1] Col. iii. 5.   [2] Gen. i. 16.   [3] 1 Cor. xv. 41.

pour their light on those whose bodily eyes are blind, but these have no power to receive their light. In like manner Christ bestows His light upon our minds, yet will He only give us real illumination if there is no sort of spiritual blindness to prevent this. And even if this should happen, still the first duty of the blind is to follow Christ, addressing Him and crying out, Son of David, have mercy upon us.[1] So from Him may they receive their sight and be able afterwards to be illuminated by the glory of His light.

Yet are not all who have sight illuminated by Christ in equal measure; each has illumination in proportion as he has capacity to receive the power of the light. The eyes of our body do not receive the light of the sun in equal measure, but the higher the levels to which one climbs, the more lofty the view point from which one watches the vista of the sunrise, the larger is one's sense of the power of the sun's light and heat. So it is also with our spirit; the higher and the further it goes in its approach to Christ, the more nearly it exposes itself to the glory of His light, the more finely and splendidly is it illuminated by His radiance. So He himself says by the prophet, Draw near unto me and I will draw near unto you, saith the Lord.[2] Again He says, I am a God at hand and not a God afar off.[3] Yet we do not all come near to Him in like degree, but each in proportion to his own attainment. Either we come to Him with the multitudes,[4] and he restores us through His parables, simply in order that we may not faint through long fasting on the road. Or else we sit ever at His feet,[5] with a purpose we never relax, our one interest being to hear

---

[1] Matt. ix. 27.
[2] Zech. i. 3; Jas. iv. 8.
[3] Jer. xxiii. 23. LXX.
[4] Cp. § lxviii.
[5] Luke x. 39.

His word, never troubled over much serving but choosing the good part which shall not be taken from us. Certainly they who so draw near to Him secure a far larger share of His light. But if, like the Apostles, we never leave Him at all, but remain always by His side in all His afflictions, then does He in secret explain to us and open up what He had said to the multitudes, and sheds on us His light in greater radiance. And if a man be even so advanced as to be able to go up with Him to the mount, as Peter and James and John, he shall have the illumination not only of the light of Christ but even of the very Father's voice.

XCVIII

The raising of Lazarus. Lazarus is with us still. The stages of spiritual restoration.—(Comm. in Joann. xxviii. 7; Lomm. ii. 321–24; Br. ii. 116–18; B. iv. 397–98. From the Greek.)

And when He had thus spoken, He cried with a loud voice, Lazarus, come forth. He that was dead came forth, bound hand and foot with grave clothes, and his face was bound about with a napkin. Jesus saith unto them, Loose him and let him go.[1] Jesus raised His eyes upward and was heard before He prayed, and in place of a prayer gave thanks, perceiving that the soul of Lazarus had entered into his body and needed the strength that would come to him from the command of Jesus, in order to come forth from the tomb. Therefore, after the thanksgiving to His Father, He spoke with a loud voice, which gave Lazarus power. Lazarus required the voice to be loud, for his hearing was not yet quick to catch the

---

[1] John xi. 43 *sqq.*

cry that summoned him from the tomb. And this we must regard as an action characteristic of Jesus, that He not only prayed that the dead might live, but also cried aloud to him, and summoned the man within the cave or tomb to come forth.

We must recognize that there are some Lazaruses to-day, people who after intimacy with Jesus have lost strength and become dead and remained in the tomb or place of the dead, dead amongst the dead. Afterwards they have been restored to life by the prayer of Jesus, and are summoned by Jesus with a loud voice from the tomb to the outer world. He who obeys Him comes forth, with the bands that betoken death and result from past sin bound about him, his eyes still bandaged, with neither sight nor power to walk or to act, by reason of the bands of death, until Jesus gives order to those that can loose him and let him go. And let every one who can say, Do ye seek a proof of Christ that speaketh in me?[1] endeavour to deserve that Christ should speak to him with a loud voice, as He cries aloud to the man who after death can move, but not quickly, and therefore needs the loud cry of Jesus, Lazarus, come forth.[2]

Consider as in Hades with the shades and the dead, as in the place of the dead or in the grave, any one who after receiving knowledge of the truth and being enlightened, after tasting the heavenly gift and being partaker of the Holy Spirit, after tasting the good word of God and the powers of the age to come,[3] becomes a renegade from Christ and reverts to his heathen life. When Jesus in such a case comes to the man's grave and stands outside and prays and is heard in His request that there may be power in His voice and words, He cries

---

[1] 2 Cor. xiii. 3. [2] John xi. 43. [3] Heb. vi. 4-5.

with a loud voice, summoning forth from the life of heathen ways, from the grave and cavern of such ways, one He now loves as a friend. Then may a follower of Jesus observe how such a man comes forth indeed at the voice of Jesus but is still bound and hampered by the wrappings of his sins. Because of his repentance, because he has heard Jesus' voice, he is alive. But because he has not yet been loosed from the bands of sin and is not yet able to step with feet at liberty or even to accomplish without restraint the things that are excellent, he is bound foot and hand in the bands that are the grave clothes of dead bodies. A man in such a state, by reason of the deadness in him, in addition to bands on his hands and feet, has his sight also veiled and wrapped in ignorance. Then the man—since Jesus wishes him not merely to live and remain in the grave—comes to the exit of the grave, still, as was said, in the bands that restrain his life. Because so long as he is in bands he cannot come forth from the grave, Jesus says to those who can assist him, Loose him and let him go.[1] I suppose such a man comes from the grave without any sort of assent to the doctrine of conversion after sin, and still too feeble to live by himself, because his soul's capacities of movement and action and vision are stifled. He is still bound feet and hands with grave clothes, and his vision is still bandaged with a napkin. But when Jesus says to those who can loose him, giving command as Christ the Master, Loose him and let him go, and he is loosed feet and hands, and the veil placed upon his eyes is removed and taken away,[2] then he goes upon his road in such a fashion that he will come at last to be himself one of those who sit at meat with Jesus.[3]

---

[1] John xi. 44.   [2] 2 Cor. iii. 14–16.   [3] John xii. 2.

XCIX

Christian Fasting, in the spirit and also in the letter.—(*In Levit.* Hom. x. 2 ; Lomm. ix. 371-72 ; B. vi. 444-45. From the Latin.)

So too the Apostle Paul, in his wish to withdraw us from these visible things of earth and to raise our minds and thoughts to heavenly things, calls to us and says, If then ye were raised together with Christ, seek the things that are above, not the things that are upon the earth.[1] Is he not clearly telling you, Seek not the earthly Jerusalem, nor the practices of the law, nor the fast of the Jews, but the fast of Christ. For you must approach Christ, your High Priest, in a state of fasting, and He is not to be sought on earth but in heaven, and through Him you must offer sacrifice to God. Shall I now show you what kind of fast you should observe ? Fast from all sin ; take no food of wickedness; decline the banquet of pleasure ; forego the heating wine of luxury. Fast from bad deeds; abstain from evil speech; restrain yourself from wicked thoughts. Do not touch the stolen bread of perverted teaching. Crave not after philosophy's deceptive fare, which will lead you astray from truth. A fast of this kind is pleasing to God. But to abstain from food which God has created for the faithful to partake of with thanksgiving, and to do this in company with men who have crucified Christ, cannot be a thing acceptable with God. The Pharisees once angrily asked the Lord why His disciples did not fast. And He answered them that the children of the Bridegroom cannot fast so long as the Bridegroom is with them.[2] They then may fast who

---

[1] Col. iii. 1-2.   [2] Matt. ix. 15.

have lost the Bridegroom; we, having the Bridegroom with us, cannot fast.

And yet we do not say this for the purpose of slackening the reins of Christian abstinence. We have our days of Lent dedicated to fasting. We have the fourth and sixth days of the week,[1] on which we keep a regular fast. The Christian has full liberty to fast at any time, not from some punctilious rule but by the virtue of self-control. How are they to preserve a chastity undefiled, unless it rest upon the strict foundation of restraint? How shall they pay attention to Scripture? How shall they be zealous for knowledge and for wisdom? Must not these things come through control of the belly and of the appetites? How is a man to make himself an eunuch for the sake of the kingdom of heaven save by cutting off excess of food and by the practice of helpful temperance? This for Christians is the true way of fasting. And there is a second also, sanctioned by religion, whose praise is told in the letter of certain Apostles. In a certain book we find this apostolic saying; Blessed is he that fasteth in order to feed to poor.[2] This man's fasting is truly acceptable with God, and indeed deservedly so. For he copies Him who laid down His life for his brethren. Why do we mix new garments with the old rags? Why pour the new wine into the old wineskins?[3] Old things are passed away; behold, all things are made new,[4] through Christ our Lord, to whom be glory and dominion for ever and ever. Amen.

---

[1] For the already recognized observance of Wednesday and Friday see Clem. Al. *Strom*. vii. 75 and Hort and Mayor's note.
[2] Cp. *Shepherd of Hermas*. Sim. v. iii. 7–8.
[3] Matt. ix. 16–17.
[4] 2 Cor. v. 17.

C

Cultivate the field that is within.—(*Selecta in Psalmos.* Lomm. xii. 160–62. From the Latin.)

Do good; dwell in the land, and thou shalt feed upon its riches.[1] Be not like the parched grass, be not like the herb of the field, which soon wither, but hope in the Lord, and be doing good, and dwell in the land. What is the land He bids us dwell in, if we are doing good? Clearly, if he had meant this land in which we do dwell, both those who do good and those who do not are dwellers in that land. It seems an unnecessary command, if that land is to be understood. Let us see however if He be not perhaps speaking of that land or ground, of which it is written that, Some seed fell upon good ground, which brought forth fruit,[2] by which ground it appears the heart of the hearer is intended. It is in this we are bidden to dwell, not, that is, to go wandering away, nor to hurry here and there, but to dwell and to settle down within the boundaries of our own soul, to give careful attention to it, to become the husbandman of it as Noah was, to plant in it a vineyard, to cultivate the inward soil, to start again on the fallow land of our soul, and not to sow among the thorns. This is done when we rid our soul of vices, and train rough and boorish ways to the gentleness of the imitation of Christ. So we feed at last upon the riches of virtue. We cannot suppose it is earthly riches we are bidden to seek, for these we are ordered to despise and reject.

So he says, Dwell in the land. This means, Stay continually with your soul, ever abide there, and cultivate your own ground, so that when you start to have abundance

---

[1] Ps. xxxvii. 3 ; LXX.   [2] Matt. xiii. 8.

of the fruits of righteousness, you may feed upon its riches. What is the meaning of feeding upon its riches? It means, Whatsoever a man soweth, that shall he also reap. And, He that soweth in the flesh, shall of the flesh reap corruption. But He that soweth in the Spirit, shall of the Spirit reap eternal life.[1] Now if you dwell in your land and sow therein, in the spirit not in the flesh, you shall feed upon its riches, like those sheep which are said to feed in a green pasture, of which the divine Word says, He maketh me to lie down in a green pasture.[2] Thus it is clear that each of us prepares within himself a green pasture, where he is fed by the Lord, as he cultivates the fields of his soul. Sowing in the spirit, he continually brings them to the fertility of spiritual husbandry.[3]

---

[1] Gal. vi. 7-8.   [2] Ps. xxiii. 2.
[3] With this passage the reader may compare Marcus Aurelius' frequent reference to the inner ' field ' of seclusion and retirement. *Meditations* iv. 3; x. 23 with Rendall's introduction; also the well known closing words of Voltaire's *Candide*, ' *Mais il faut cultiver notre jardin.*'

INDEX

Abimelech, 190
Abstraction, 151
Acts of Paul, xvi
Advent, 33, 64, 226
Alexander, Bishop, xv, 162
Allegory, xxvi, 4, 72
Amanuenses, xiv, 163
Ambrosius, xiii, 161, 163
Angels, 61, 144, 200, 212, 218, 247
Anthropomorphism, xxv, 19
Antioch, xiii
Apelles, xxiv, 149
Apocrypha, 112, 181, 216
Apostles, 131
Aquila, xxxvi
Aristotle, 3
Asterisk, 110
Astrology, 203, 207
Augustine, xlv, 130, 164
Aurelius, Marcus, 268

Baptism, 211
Baptist, The, 69, 106, 212, 223
Bardaisan, 203
Basil, 26
Basilides, 104, 113, 149
Bethabara, xxxvi, xli
Bigg, C., xxxiii, 24, 33, 62, 125, 130, 149, 152, 229, 244, 257
Bingham, J., 164
Birth, Birthday, 209, 245
Bishops, 129, 141, 169
Body, 41, 247
Books, xiv, 160
Bread, 31, 179
Bright, W., 46
Britain, 45
Butler, Bishop, 95

Cæsarea, xv, xlvii
Canaan, 241

Canôn, xvi, 99, 114
Capernaum, 105
Capes, 164
Catechetical School, xi
Catechumens, 169, 181
Celsus, xvi, xxi, xxxii, xxxvii
Charles, 112
Cheyne, 9
Chronicles, 116
Church, The, 79, 123, 128-155, 189, 223, 260
Clement of Alexandria, xxvii, xxxi, 19, 41, 83, 125, 135, 145, 172, 191, 202, 211, 266
Clement of Rome, 125
Conscience, 55
Corban, 137
Cushions, 174

Daniel, 39, 159
Darkness, The, 114
Deacons, 130, 169
Decius, xv
Demetrius, xii, xv, 162
Demons, 206, 218
Denis, M. J., xxxiii, 2, 26, 41, 152, 185, 195, 230
Disasters, 197
Docetism, xxviii, 42, 150
Driver, 9, 159
Drummond, J., xxx, xxxi, xxxv 191

Ebionites, 150
Eclipse, 114, 211
Elijah, 212, 253
Endor, 217
Enoch, Book of, 242
Enquiry, 158
Epiphanius, x, xiv, 45
Epistles, 120
Eternal, Eternity, 125

Eucharist, 31
Eustathius, 220
Evil, 12, 199, 209
Ezekiel, 174, 178, 231
Ezra, 99

Faith, 145, 153, 249, 254
Fasting, 265
Faye, E. de, x, 77, 149, 172
Field, 267
Fire, 2, 199, 202
Firmilian, xv
Foods, 180
Foreknowledge, 12, 205, 219
Freedom, 153, 196, 238
Future Life, 238, 241, 244, 257

Geikie, 164
Generation, Eternal, 23, 24
Gibeonites, 179
Gnostics, Gnosticism, 10, 35, 78, 152, 251
God, gods, 1–24, 119, 257
Gospels, 48, 64, 104, 105, 114, 156
Gregory Thaumaturgus, xv, xlvii, 185
Gwatkin, H. M., 77, 149, 248

Hades, 133, 217, 220, 263
Harnack, A., xxxv, 114, 164, 181, 191, 211
Hausrath, A., 164
Heavens, The, 70
Hebrews, Epistle to, 26, 113, 124
Heraclas, xii
Heracleon, xviii, xlii, 77, 257
Heresy, Heretics, xvii, xxvii, xxxiv, 149, 153
Hexapla, xv, xxxvi, 110
Homilies, xiv
Huet, Bishop, xxxiii, 24, 38, 230
Hypythians, 113

Idiots, 61
Infants, 61
Inge, W. R., 67, 213

Irenæus, 39, 104
Isaiah, 139

Jebusites, 148
Jeremiah, 165, 210
Jerome, x, xiv, xv, xxxvi
Jethro, 188
Jews, The, xvi, xxiii, xxxiv, 33, 47, 66, 252
Job, 210
Jonah, 140, 211
Josephus, 53
Joshua, 51, 53
Judah, 33, 145, 147
Judas, 138
Justin, 112, 151

Kiss, 83
Knowledge, 252

Law, Laws, xx, xxiv, xxix, 53–67, 81, 85, 156, 177, 208
Lazarus, 262
Leonidas, x
Leviathan, 211
Light, 2, 23
Lightfoot, 56
Literature, xx, 160, 185
Liturgies, xxi, 83
Lucifer, 86, 239
Luke, St., 125
Lunacy, 206

Magi, 192, 203
Mammæa, Julia, xiii
Marcion, xviii, xxiv, xxxvi, 77, 149
Marriage, 244
Matter, 191
Maximin, xv, 146
Maximus of Tyre, xxxi
Metensomatosis, 212
Money, 137, 184, 257
Moon, 114, 191, 206, 260
Moses, 51, 53, 139, 188
Muratorian Fragment, 122
Multitudes, The, 172

INDEX

Names, xl
Nations, The, 9
Nature, xx, 55, 58, 94, 198
Number, xl, 98

Obelus, xxxvi, 110
Office, Responsibility of, 142

Pamphilus, xliii, 24, 149, 229
Pantænus, xi, xiv, xxxi
Paradise, 220, 241
Passover, 106
Patripassians, 151
Paul, St., xxxii, xl, 48, 72, 75, 120, 141, 229
Perfection, 122
Persecutions, xi, xv, 146, 160
Peter, St , 130, 201, 256
Pharaoh, 201
Philistines, 91
Philo, xxxi, 98, 191
Philosophy, 185, 190, 259
Phlegon, 116
Physicians, 165, 206
Pirates, 154
Plato, xx, 230
Plutarch, xii
Poverty, 135
Pre-existence, 194
Priests, 129, 178, 189
Prophets, 111, 165
Psalms, xi, 96–101, 187
Publicani, 223
Punishment, 142, 202
Pythagoreans, 98
Pythian Priestess, xxi

Quinta Essentia, 3

Redepenning, E. R., x, xxxiii, xxxvii, xxxix, 75, 181, 185, 230, 239
Reincarnation, 195, 212
Relationships, 244
Rendall, G. H., 268
Restoration, Final, 18

Resurrection, 152, 228, 230, 236, 245
Revelation, 75
Rhetoric, 175
Romans, Epistle to, 120
Rule of Faith, xxxv, 152, 249
Ruler, The Young, 107
Ryle, H. E., 99, 114

Sabellianism, 151
Sadducees, 236
Salmon, G., 130
Samaritans, 236
Samuel, 217
Scripture, xvi, 47–127, 157, 181, 184, 218
Septuagint, xxii, xxxvii, xxxviii, 110
Serpents, 182
Severus, Emperor, x, 203
Shadows, 84
Shepherd of Hermas, xvi, 266
Sin, 255
'Son of Man', 38
Song of Songs, 79
Soul, 57, 79, 94, 126, 152, 194, 213, 236, 255
Spirit, Spirits, xxi, 2, 26, 57, 63, 89, 95, 126, 154, 206, 214, 222
Stars, The, 191, 203, 260
Steward, The Unjust, 58
Stoics, xxxi, 4, 164, 202
Substance, 90
Swete, H. B., xxxvii, 26, 29
Symmachus, xxxvi
Syzygies, 248

Teacher, Teaching, xiii, xliv, 136, 156–193, 260
Temple, The, 161
Temptation, The, 119
Tertullian, 39, 73, 83, 122, 191, 248
Tethiani, 149
Testament, 72
Testaments of XII Patriarchs, 205
Text of Scripture, xxxvi, 62, 107, 117, 169, 221

Theodotion, xxxvi, 159
Theoctistus, xv, 162
'To-Day', 221
Transfiguration, The, 233, 262
Trench, R. C., 145
Trinity, The, 27, 72, 89, 151, 194
Tyre, xv

Valentinus, Valentinians, xiii, 45, 77, 149, 248
Veil, 176, 225
Virgins, 52, 130
Virgin Birth, The, 39, 45, 150, 251
Voltaire, 268
Warren, F. E., 83, 211
Waterland, Bishop, 33

Wedding Gifts, 80
Wells, 77, 87
Westcott, Bishop, x, xxxiii, 51, 63, 114, 125, 130, 146, 239
Williams, Prof. N. P., 211
Wisdom, 171, 185
Woman, 177
Word, The, xxi, 23, 25-46, 79, 89, 150, 162, 181, 187, 260
Worlds, Many, 238, 246, 257

Year, The Sabbatical, 98, 180

Zahn, O., xi
Zeal, 252
Zeiler, Ed., xxxi

www.ingramcontent.com/pod-product-compliance
Lightning Source LLC
Chambersburg PA
CBHW050334230426
43663CB00010B/1857